THE SECRET
SURRENDER

Other Works by Allen W. Dulles

The Boer War: A History (1902)

Can We Be Neutral? (1936)
(with Hamilton Fish Armstrong)

Germany's Underground (1947)

The United Nations (1947)

Challenge of a Soviet Power (1959)

The Craft of Intelligence (1963)

Great True Spy Stories (1968)

Great Spy Stories from Fiction (1969)

THE SECRET SURRENDER

THE CLASSIC INSIDER'S ACCOUNT OF THE SECRET PLOT TO SURRENDER NORTHERN ITALY DURING WWII

ALLEN W. DULLES

THE LYONS PRESS
Guilford, Connecticut
An imprint of The Globe Pequot Press

To Clover, a discreet observer of the Sunrise negotiations
and a major contributor to this story

The Lyons Press is an imprint of The Globe Pequot Press.

10 9 8 7 6 5 4 3 2 1

Printed in the United States of America

ISBN-13: 978-1-59228-368-2
ISBN-10: 1-59228-368-3

Library of Congress Cataloging-in-Publication Data

Dulles, Allen Welsh, 1839-1969.
    The secret surrender : the classic insider's account of the secret plot to surrender Northern Italy during WWII / Allen Dulles.
        p. cm.
    Originally published: New York : Harper & Row, 1966.
    Includes bibliographical references and index.
    ISBN 1-59228-368-3
    1. United States. Office of Strategic Services. 2. World War, 1939-1945-Secret service-United States. 3. World War, 1939-1945-Italy. I. Title.

D810.S7D8 2004
940.54'8673-dc22

2004048342

Contents

A group of illustrations will be found following page 88

THE SECRET SURRENDER

1

"Great Secrecy Was Necessary"

A few days before the end of World War II in Europe, on the evening of May 2, 1945, Winston Churchill made a surprise appearance in the House of Commons. The atmosphere was charged with expectation. Yet the Prime Minister did not immediately intervene in the debate which was then in progress. Whetting the appetites, as he was wont to call it, he let the suspense build up as he glanced through his notes before asking the Speaker's indulgence to make a brief statement. Then, without flourish or rhetoric, letting the bold facts speak for themselves, he quietly announced the first great German surrender to the Allies of World War II. Close to a million men had capitulated in Northern Italy. The war against Nazism and Fascism on that front was over. The war on all European fronts was approaching its end.

"Field Marshal Sir Harold Alexander," Mr. Churchill said, "has just announced that the land, sea and air forces commanded by General von Vietinghoff, the German Commander-in-Chief of the Southwest Command and Commander-in-Chief of Army Group C, have surrendered unconditionally. The instrument of surrender was signed on Sunday afternoon, April 29th, at the Allied Forces Headquarters at Caserta by two German plenipotentiaries and Lieutenant General W. D. Morgan, Chief of Staff at the Allied Forces Headquarters. The terms of surrender provided for the cessation of hostilities at twelve o'clock noon, Greenwich mean time, on May 2nd."

There was a murmur of surprise in the Commons. The Members of Parliament realized that the Prime Minister had been holding this important news secret since April 29th, the actual date, as he announced it, of signing the surrender. He had only released it at that moment, three days later. Sensing that he owed the Commons some word of explanation, Mr. Churchill added that until the last minute there had been many elements of uncertainty. "It was not until effective confirmation was obtained by the actual orders issued to the troops by the German High Command that Field Marshal Alexander issued the statement."

The Prime Minister then gave a brief review of the Italian campaign. In the long trek up the Italian peninsula, a motley army—Americans, Japanese-Americans, British and Dominion troops, French, Poles, Brazilians, Italians and other nationalities—had fought side by side over difficult terrain against a stubborn foe. To this army fell the honor of effecting the first great unconditional German surrender to the Allies.

The German and Fascist forces which capitulated, Churchill said, comprised the battered remnants of twenty-two German divisions and six Italian Fascist divisions. The territory opened to Allied arms included all North Italy to the Isonzo, the Austrian provinces of the Vorarlberg, Salzburg and the Tyrol and portions of Carinthia and Styria. The whole southern flank of the German position in the Alps was taken. If the Nazis had had any serious notion of holding out there, the key to that mountain fortress had been wrested from them.

After Churchill concluded his tribute to Field Marshal Alexander, to General Mark Clark and to the national units which made up the Allied forces in Italy, one of the members of the Commons inquired about the circumstances of the surrender and asked whether the German General had surrendered on his own responsibility. To this Churchill replied in the affirmative and then continued, "The discussions have been of a highly private nature for some time. At times they have appeared more hopeful than at others, but for the last two days I have known what was coming, yet one was not certain that it might not be snatched away at the last minute. Therefore, great secrecy was necessary."

Unknown to the outside world, since the end of February, 1945, emissaries and messages had been passing secretly between the OSS mission in Switzerland, of which I was in charge, and German generals in Italy. For two crucial months the commanders of contending armies locked in battle had maintained secret communications through my office in Bern seeking the means to end the fighting on the front in Italy, hoping that a Nazi surrender there would bring in its wake a general surrender in Europe. We had given the code name "Sunrise" to this operation to facilitate speed and secrecy in the handling of our messages. We did not know until later that Winston Churchill, who was closely following the proceedings, had already named the operation "Crossword."

What prevented our early success was the stubborn and insane policy of one man, Adolf Hitler. Despite the hopeless position of his armies, he would not countenance any surrender anywhere. His generals had good reason to fear that they would pay with their lives for any unauthorized attempt to stop the fighting. This meant there could be no parliamentarians crossing enemy lines with white flags, no public parleys, no formalized negotiations. Instead, a secret intelligence organization took over the unusual function of establishing the first contact and actively pursuing the negotiations with the enemy until the surrender was ready to be signed. We became, in agreement with Field Marshal Alexander, the channel through which communications between the Allied and the German High Commands were maintained.

The fact that the American Office of Strategic Services, better known by its initials OSS, was then in existence with clearly defined responsibilities and a nucleus of personnel ready to act in the surrender operation was due to the foresight and initiative of William J. Donovan, who was the creator and director of the OSS.

Donovan was a born leader of men. He had indefatigable energy and wide-ranging enthusiasm combined with great courage and resourcefulness. His persuasive personality made him an effective negotiator.

Donovan had performed distinguished military service in World War I in which he rose rapidly through the ranks to a colonelcy in the famous Fighting Irish 69th Division. For his valor in combat, he earned the Congressional Medal of Honor and the unshakable nickname of "Wild Bill." Between the two world wars he became prominent in New York City as a lawyer, and ran for governor on the Republican ticket in 1933 against Herbert Lehman, who said that Donovan's campaign was the cleanest he had ever seen. But 1933 was not a good year for Republican candidates and Donovan came out second, which was a loss to American politics but an incalculable gain for American intelligence.

Donovan's interests were not restricted to law and politics. In the years before the outbreak of World War II he was already at work studying military affairs and planning the type of intelligence organization

America would need as soon as we became a belligerent—which he felt was inevitable. He always liked to see things at first hand and wherever there was a fighting front he visited it if he could. Thus he had made a special trip to Ethiopia during the Italian-Ethiopian campaign in 1936, and to Spain during the Civil War in 1936–37.

When World War II broke out in September, 1939, he was one of the few Americans who had an insight into the changed nature of modern warfare. In the thirties he had anticipated the global character of the conflict that was to come so soon. He was convinced then that what we now call "unconventional" or psychological warfare would have a major place in the battles of the future.

In this he thoroughly shared the views of Winston Churchill with regard to the mistaken strategy followed during World War I. The "dull carnage of the policy of exhaustion," as Churchill phrased it, was evidenced in the Anglo-French offensives of 1915, 1916 and 1917, when France and Britain consumed, during these successive years, the flower of their national manhood. "Battles," Churchill wrote, "are won by slaughter and maneuver. The greater the general, the more he contributes in maneuver, the less he demands in slaughter." He added: "There are many kinds of maneuvers in war, some only of which take place upon the battlefield. There are maneuvers far to the flank or rear. There are maneuvers in time, in diplomacy, in mechanics, in psychology; all of which are removed from the battlefield, but react often decisively upon it, and the object of all is to find easier ways, other than sheer slaughter, of achieving the main purpose."*

Donovan similarly had rejected the idea of bloody trench warfare. The enemy, he thought, must be forced to fight where he was weak and we were strong; we must exploit his weaknesses and determine ourselves the field of battle. He felt that unconventional warfare and special operations would permit us to take advantage of the discontent within the enemy camp, evidenced by the turbulent undergrounds in all the Nazi and Fascist controlled countries.

Donovan threw himself into the task of arousing his countrymen to the dangers they faced as the Nazi colossus began to change the map of Europe. Fortunately, he had the trust and confidence of the President, Franklin Delano Roosevelt, and was particularly close to his Secretary of the Navy, Frank Knox. While he often tangled with members of the

* Winton S. Churchill, *Great Destiny* (New York: Putnam, 1962), p. 283.

Joint Chiefs of Staff about the role of intelligence and the conduct of unconventional operations, he held their respect and eventually gained their cooperation.

Shortly after the fall of France, on a hot August day in 1940, in the bleakest phase of the Battle of Britain, he came to Washington to testify on the military training bill then before the Congress. He was unexpectedly summoned to the White House. He found there in conference with President Roosevelt Secretary of State Cordell Hull, Secretary of War Henry L. Stimson and Secretary of the Navy Frank Knox. Colonel Donovan had no idea why he had been summoned. Secretary Knox was the first to speak. Would Donovan undertake a secret mission to Great Britain and report back to the President on the situation there, and specifically on these questions: Would England continue to fight on alone against Hitler, as Churchill had promised they would? And did they have the means to do so? If they did continue to fight, what aid could America give to help them most effectively? He was also to report on the Nazi Fifth Column activities in Europe, and this was, in part, cover for his main mission.

The fortunes of Britain were then at their lowest ebb. France had sued for peace and the armistice had been signed. Britain had survived Dunkirk and saved the major part of her limited military manpower, but as for munitions of war and the wherewithal to fight, she was in a desperate situation. The President of the United States had to decide, and quickly, whether to proceed with lend-lease, the transfer of overage destroyers to Britain and other plans for aiding her. What the President wanted of Donovan was his judgment—not whether the British would or could win the battle but whether, given the means to fight, they would carry on the battle.

After a series of talks with British leaders in London, Donovan returned to the United States. He told the President of his firm opinion that Britain would fight no matter how slim the odds of victory. He could not predict whether they would win, but the President could count on their determination. Donovan also proposed a series of measures to bolster Britain's ability to defend herself. Later, under the Lend-Lease Administration, these were largely put into effect.

While in Britain, he also made a study of the organization and techniques of British intelligence. He was convinced that America's military planning and its whole national strategy would depend on intelligence as never before and that the American intelligence setup should be completely revamped. From the British he also learned what was known to them about Nazi Fifth Column operations, which had played a large role in their conquest of Poland, Belgium, Holland and Norway. Donovan knew that we in the United States had no adequate defenses against the enemy Fifth Column and that we were not in the least organized to take the offensive in such operations. He felt strongly that we should equip ourselves to do this.

In collaboration with Edgar A. Mowrer, of the Chicago *Daily News*, he published a series of newspaper articles designed to wake America up to the danger of Fifth Column activities. These appeared with the blessing of Secretary Knox under the joint signatures of Donovan and Mowrer and were disseminated on a world-wide basis by the leading American news agencies.

His trip to Britain had also convinced Donovan that the Mediterranean would shortly become a theater of vital importance to the Allies, and that it was essential to keep open the Mediterranean lines of communication. He therefore became an eager participant in the project which, in the fall of 1942, led to the successful landings in French North Africa. This was just the technique he was advocating! Force the Nazis and the Fascists to fight the battle as far as possible from their own homelands and base of supplies, make them lengthen their lines of communication where they would be vulnerable to the growing naval and air strength of the Allies.

Donovan was not to stay long in the United States following his mission to Britain. He had convinced Roosevelt of the soundness of his views and that the Mediterranean was destined to become a crucial theater of battle. When on December 1, 1940, he was called down to Washington and asked by the President if he would go on a second mission to make a strategic appreciation—economic, political and military—of the Mediterranean area, he quickly accepted. On December 6, 1940, he left on a voyage that was to last almost three and a half months and cover twenty-two thousand miles, mostly by air, from one end of the Mediterranean to the other.

In a report to the President on his return in April, 1941, he laid great stress on implementing his ideas about our intelligence service and, particularly, psychological and political warfare, sabotage and guerrilla warfare. Donovan saw all these instruments as part of an integrated whole, and he presented a plan for an organization which would create and direct them. His report included a special section on what he had found out about the British commandos during his Mediterranean trip. He pointed out that the Imperial General Staff had made its first task after Dunkirk the creation of a special force of British guerrillas and, against this background, urged the President to apply like principles to the American position. It would take at least two years, he estimated, to raise, train and equip armies that would be necessary to defeat the Germans in a straight fight. Meanwhile, America must prepare to employ the techniques of unconventional warfare.

At this time, in an address in Philadelphia, Donovan said: "Our orientation has been wrong. We have been talking of aid to Britain as if Britain were a beggar at the gate, whereas, in point of fact, Britain has been our shield behind which we can pull up our socks, tie our shoelaces and get ready—and also our laboratory."

President Roosevelt appointed a special Cabinet committee consisting of Stimson and Knox, Secretaries of War and the Navy, and Robert Jackson, the Attorney General, to consider Donovan's ideas and to recommend a plan of action. The result was an Executive Order, signed on July 11, 1941, by President Roosevelt, acting both as President and as Commander-in-Chief of the Army and Navy of the United States, creating the Office of Coordinator of Information and designating Donovan as its chief. The duties of the Coordinator were "to collect and analyze all information and data which bear upon national security; to correlate such information and data and to make it available to the President, and to such departments and officials of the Government as the President may determine."

It will be noted that this order did not specifically deal with unconventional warfare, although the additional authority granted in the order to carry out "such supplementary activities as may facilitate the securing of information, important for national security," pointed in that direction. Undoubtedly, it was so interpreted by Donovan. At the time the order was signed, we were, of course, still nominally neutral. Pearl Harbor was still five months away.

After Pearl Harbor, a new order was issued changing the Office of the Coordinator of Information into the Office of Strategic Services, with Donovan at its head. That order, signed by the President on June 13, 1942, placed the OSS under the jurisdiction of the Joint Chiefs of Staff. The OSS was authorized, in addition to the collection and analysis functions of its predecessor, COI, "to plan and operate such special services as may be directed by the United States Joint Chiefs of Staff."

With this, Donovan's blueprint for the coordination of strategic intelligence collection with secret operations was realized.

"Special services" in intelligence terms meant unconventional warfare, commandos, support of partisans and guerrillas and the exploitation by covert means of all the weaknesses of Hitler's and Mussolini's empires. With the inclusion of this term "special services" in the OSS charter, an intelligence organization had been created for the first time in the United States which brought together under one roof the work of intelligence collection and counterespionage, with the support of underground resistance activities, sabotage and almost anything else in aid of our national effort that the regular armed forces were not equipped to do. Few of the people who today hotly debate the wisdom of this arrangement can recall the high auspices under which the decision was made some twenty-five years ago or the attention given the subject when the OSS and later the CIA were organized.

Donovan invited a variety of people from all walks of life to come and help him do the job: military men and civilian leaders, teachers, bankers, lawyers, businessmen, librarians, writers, publishers, ballplayers, missionaries, reformed safecrackers, bartenders, tugboat operators. He wanted people who already knew something that was useful. There was no time to learn the tradecraft of intelligence before these men and women started to work; the war emergency was urgent. He needed men who already had specialized knowledge, and he found them wherever he could. A bartender was hired not because he knew how to mix drinks but because he spoke perfect Italian and he was at home in the mountain passes of the Apennines; a missionary because he knew the tribes and the native dialects of Burma; an expert in engraving because his agents would need the most expert documentation to pass through enemy lines.

One of Donovan's earliest organizational plans called for setting up intelligence outposts in the important friendly and neutral areas in Europe. Without wasting any time he was able to push through an arrangement with our State Department which called for the placement of OSS officers in Sweden, Switzerland, Spain, Portugal, Tangier. Some of them were assigned to the American diplomatic establishments in these places, a proposal which naturally met with some resistance from the professional diplomats—but Donovan had his way. Some were under deeper and different cover.

I became one of Donovan's early recruits. Shortly after Pearl Harbor he asked me to join him, and he outlined his views about what the

OSS could accomplish to help win the war. We discussed the situation in Europe, particularly in the Nazi and Fascist occupied countries where there were signs of popular unrest under harsh dictatorship. In these areas his theories about unconventional warfare and psychological warfare could be put to a test. It did not take much persuading on his part, as I was thoroughly convinced both of the general soundness of his approach and of the importance of the work which lay ahead.

Donovan was an old friend. I had known him well during the days before World War II when he was working in Washington in the Department of Justice and, also, later as a lawyer in New York. Donovan knew that I had worked my way around the world teaching school during the early days of World War I and thereafter had served as a diplomat in Germany, Austria-Hungary and Switzerland. In my Swiss post my real activity was in providing Washington with intelligence about what was happening in Germany and Austria-Hungary and in the Balkans.

At first, Donovan wanted to me to go London to work with him and David Bruce there in cementing our relations with the British intelligence services. I finally persuaded him, however, to let me go to a less glamorous post, but one where I felt my past experience would serve me in good stead; namely, to Switzerland.

2

Mission in Switzerland

On November 2, 1942, I took off for Lisbon, the first lap on my journey to my post at Bern, where I was attached to the American Legation (now an Embassy) as a Special Assistant to the Minister. My real tasks, however, were to gather information about the Nazi and Fascist enemy and quietly to render such support and encouragement as I could to the resistance forces working against the Nazis and Fascists in the areas adjacent to Switzerland which were under the rule of Hitler or Mussolini.

Before I left, I was carefully briefed on the problems of my trip. Also, I was warned that there was a good chance that I might not make it to my post. The United States was already at war with Germany, and I had, of course, to avoid crossing territory under Nazi control. The only way for an American to reach Switzerland at that time was by flying to Lisbon and then crossing Spain and Vichy France to Geneva. But when I left New York I knew that Operation Torch, the secret American-British landing in North Africa, was planned for the early days of November. We estimated in Washington that as soon as the landing took place the Nazis would move immediately to occupy all of Vichy France. The military necessity for them to control the French ports on the Mediterranean would be urgent. Toulon could not be left to the French Navy.

Unfortunately, because of bad weather, my plane for Lisbon was help up a couple of days in the Azores. I had lost valuable time. The landing, I knew, was imminent. From Lisbon I flew to Barcelona. The rest of the journey across Spain and Vichy France was to be by train. It was already November 8th when I took the train from Barcelona. On the way from Barcelona to the French frontier I had met some Swiss friends and we were lunching together at Port Bou, the last stop in Spain before crossing over into Vichy France, when the Swiss diplomatic courier, who was well known to my friends, came up to our table. "Have you heard the news?" he exclaimed in great excitement. "The Americans and British are landing in North Africa."

I was still in neutral Spain and able to turn back if necessary, or I could go ahead and gamble on the possibility that the Nazis would take a few days to make up their minds about what to do. I had to assume, however, that at least they would occupy the lines of communication across France and would stop and search trains. I knew that my trip would be through an area close to where plenty of German troops were stationed. If I was picked up by the Nazis in Vichy France, the best I could hope for would be internment for the duration of the war. My diplomatic passport would be of little use to me. It was a tough decision, but I decided to go ahead. Across the frontier, in Vichy France, I received a reception in the town of Verrières as though I were a part of an American liberation army come to free them from the Nazis. The French were delirious. They had some sort of misconception that the American forces would be coming across the Mediterranean within a few days. As it turned out, they had to wait almost two years.

While my train made its way through France that night, I decided that if there were evidence of German controls I would try to slip away at one of the stops and disappear into the countryside in hopes of making contact with the French resistance, eventually perhaps to get over the border into Switzerland unofficially—or "black," as we used to call it.

At Annemasse, the last stop in France where all passengers for Switzerland had to alight to have their passports examined, I found that a person in civilian dress, obviously a German, was supervising the work of the French border officials. I had been told in Washington that there would probably by a Gestapo agent at this frontier. I was the only one among the passengers who failed to pass muster. The Gestapo man carefully put down in his notebook the particulars of my passport, and a few minutes later a French gendarme explained to me that an order had just been received from Vichy to detain all Americans and British presenting themselves at the frontier and to report all such cases to Marshal Pétain directly. I took the gendarme aside and made to him the most impassioned and, I believe, most eloquent speech that I had ever made in French. Evoking the shades of Lafayette and Pershing, I impressed upon him the importance of letting me pass. I had a valid passport and visa and there was no justification for holding me up. I assured him Marshal Pétain had many other things to worry about on that particular day besides my case. I also let him glimpse the contents of my wallet. Neither patriotic speeches nor the implied offer of a small fortune seemed to move him. He went off to make his telephone call, leaving me to pace the platform. I began to case the area in the hope of carrying out my plan of slipping away on foot to avoid being trapped there. It wouldn't have been easy.

Finally around noon, when it was about time for the train to leave for Geneva, the gendarme came up to me, hurriedly motioned for me to get on the train and whispered to me, "*Allez passez. Vous voyez que notre collaboration n'est que symbolique.*" (Go ahead. You see our cooperation [with the Germans] is only symbolic.") The Gestapo man was nowhere to be seen. Later I learned that every day, promptly at noon, he went down the street to the nearest pub and had his drink of beer and his lunch. Nothing, including landings in Africa, could interfere with his fixed Germanic habits. The French authorities had gone through the motions of phoning Vichy, as they had been ordered to do. But once the Gestapo man had left his post for his noon siesta, they were free to act on their own, and they did. Within a matter of minutes I had crossed the French border into Switzerland legally. I was one of the last Americans to do so until after the liberation of France. I was ready to go to work.

In Bern I found an apartment in the Herrengasse, in the delightfully picturesque and ancient section of the Swiss capital near its cathedral. This arcaded and cobblestoned street ran along the ridge high above the river Aare. It was near where I had lived and worked twenty-four years before in the last months of World War I. Then, as a young diplomat, I had received my first training in the work of intelligence in a neutral Switzerland, during a world war. Between my apartment and the river below grew vineyards which afforded an ideal covered approach for visitors who did not wish to be seen entering my front door on the Herrengasse. From the terrace above I had an inspiring view of the whole stretch of the Bernese Alps.

I had been in Switzerland only a few weeks when one of its most respected and widely read newspapers, alerted to the unusual circumstances of my entry, came out with an article describing me as "the personal representative of President Roosevelt" with a "special duty" assignment. This flattering designation, in all its vagueness, was widely circulated, and even if I had wished to do something about it there was little I could do. A public denial would merely have advertised the report. Of course, it had the result of bringing to my door purveyors of information, volunteers and adventurers of every sort, professional and amateur spies, good and bad. Donovan's operating principle was not to have his senior representatives try to go deep underground, on the very reasonable premise that it was futile and that it was better to let people know you were in the business of intelligence and tell them where they could find you. The unsolicited Swiss newspaper publicity put this principle into practice in short order, though not exactly in the terms I would have chosen for myself.

As my work expanded, and it did so rapidly, I badly needed reinforcements. I obviously could not get any from Washington now that all Swiss borders were closed by zones of Nazi or Fascist occupiers. So I borrowed a few aides from among the American officials already stationed in Switzerland whose original assignments had become more or less outdated now that Switzerland was isolated; men and women from various departments of the American government—the Board of Economic Warfare, for example. But most of those who worked closely with me during the ensuing years of my stay in Switzerland I found among the Americans who had been living privately in Switzerland for various reasons, or who had been stranded by the sudden closing of the frontier. Some had had jobs in the sadly dying League of Nations at Geneva. Some had been in Switzerland for their health. Some had simply been caught there while traveling, overtaken by the unexpected events of the war and the Nazi occupation of Vichy France.

One of these men, Gero von Schulze Gaevernitz, played a large part in the special undertaking to which this book is devoted. Gaevernitz is a naturalized American, German by birth, who had business interests and family holdings in Switzerland, but had remained there after the outbreak of the war largely because he foresaw that he might make himself useful sooner or later in a rather special way in the cause of liberating Europe from the Hitler dictatorship. Gaevernitz was a tall handsome man, then in his early forties. He had a beguiling personality and a great capacity for making friends. During my days in Switzerland in World War II we constantly worked together, and he was my closest collaborator in all my work with the anti-Hitler resistance.

Gaevernitz's father had been a well-known German professor and political scientist, a member of the former German *Reichstag* of the liberal wing. In pre-Hitler days he had helped draw up the Weimar Constitution, and had devoted much of his life to furthering the idea of an American-British-German *rapprochement* as the surest way to secure world peace. When I was attached to our Berlin Embassy in 1916, before we entered World War I, I knew him well.

Through his family and his personality, the younger Gaevernitz had developed excellent connections with the members of the underground opposition to Hitler within Germany. He had traveled frequently between Switzerland and Germany while America was neutral, and had built up these connections. His name alone was to stand us in good stead when we shortly began our contacts with the men involved in the major conspiracy against Hitler, which culminated in the unsuccessful assassination attempt of July 20, 1944. By temperament, conviction and association he was ideally suited to working with the Germans in the difficult psychological situations that prevail when one tries to talk sense to an enemy during wartime.

Gaevernitz was deeply motivated by the conviction that Germany had never been so thoroughly permeated by Nazism as many were inclined to believe and that there were people in Germany, even in high positions in both the civilian and military administration, ready to support any workable undertaking that would get rid of Hitler and the Nazis and put an end to the war. He had become friendly with many prominent Germans and Austrians who had sought refuge in Switzerland from Nazi persecution, as well as anti-Nazis still able to reside in Germany who visited Switzerland occasionally. Two of the most important men whom he introduced to me were: Hans Bernd Gisevius who played a dramatic and dangerous role as a link between my office and the anti-Nazi conspirators of the twentieth of July; and Dr. Wilhelm Hoegner, an invaluable adviser to me on internal German conditions, who, incidentally, had been the prosecuting attorney in the case against "one Adolf Hitler" after the unsuccessful Munich *Putsch* of 1923, and who, therefore, became one of the very first targets of Nazi persecution. Other Hitler opponents in Switzerland produced for us from their friends still located in enemy territory information on conditions in German-controlled Europe, including some vital intelligence on the location of the German secret V-1 and V-2 weapons arsenal at Peenemünde on the Baltic Sea.

Intelligence, however valuable intrinsically, is, of course, worthless if it cannot be put promptly into the hands of the people who need to make use of it. From the beginning communication between my mission in a country entirely surrounded by the enemy and the various OSS centers to which I reported—Washington, London and Allied Forces Headquarters at Caserta, Italy—was one of our major concerns. Our agents in France, Germany and Italy had ways of slipping in and out of Switzerland over the border, but the information they had risked their lives to gather for us, had to be forwarded at once to intelligence centers thousands of miles away.

The passage of secret written material from Switzerland to the United States was, of course, risky until France had been cleared of the Germans and our official couriers could travel again. Hence, we had to depend on coded diplomatic messages sent by Swiss commercial radio facilities. This was a speedy channel, but one that did not allow for lengthy essays and analyses since our few code clerks could encipher and decipher only a limited number of words a day. We also had a transatlantic radio-telephone connection to Washington, for which the Swiss provided a speech-scrambling device. My phone reports had to be limited mostly to newspaper summaries and other unclassified material. They were, of course, available to the Swiss themselves, although, we hoped, not to the Germans, unless they took the trouble to intercept and unscramble them, which we always had to assume they could do.*

A notable operation that eased our communications with the partisans in Northern Italy and the passage of men and supplies in and out of Switzerland was staged at a place called Campione. This is an Italian enclave of some fifteen square kilometers on the Lake of Lugano, reachable by boat from the town of Lugano and entirely surrounded by territory and lake waters under Swiss control. Its most lucrative business in normal times was the maintenance of a casino which the Swiss, who do not have legalized gambling in their own country, could patronize.

We learned that the garrison of Campione consisted of six carabinieri whose loyalty to Fascism was not so great that they would risk their necks

---

* I once had the experience at a dinner party of having a high Swiss official repeat, with a smile, a remark to me which I had just made in a telephone conversation with Washington. Knowing that the Swiss listened to my talks with headquarters, I usually managed to include a few remarks in my reports which I wanted the Swiss to hear.

to defend it against a non-Fascist population of six hundred, who, as we heard, would gladly throw them in the lake. One dark night in January, 1944, firearms for twenty men and some hundred hand grenades were smuggled over the water into Campione, and the surprised carabinieri surrendered without a murmur. Campione joyously celebrated its union with the South Italy of King Victor Emmanuel, which was working with the Allies, and our agents set up shop in the enclave, installing a radio station to keep in contact with the partisan units in the mountains and organizing a training school there for guerrilla activities we did not engage in on Swiss soil. After the guerrillas were trained, they slipped out of Campione, across about three hundred meters of Swiss terrain on the landward side and into German-held Italy to join anti-Fascist partisan groups hidden there.

The people of Campione, however, had not thoroughly studied the economic consequences of their revolution. Cut off from Fascist Italy, they ran into financial problems and turned to me for aid on a scale I had not bargained for. However, this crisis was met through a clever device which the Campione leaders themselves thought out. With our help they arranged to issue a special set of stamps to commemorate the union of the enclave with the Kingdom of Italy. The stamps naturally became collectors' items throughout the world. Enough were sold to carry more mail than Campione would send for generations and enough money was realized to meet the budget deficit. Residents of Campione were gainfully employed writing letters furiously to addresses in many nations, since collectors were anxious to have the stamps on postmarked envelopes.

By midsummer of 1944, the successful Allied invasion of France had brought to an end our work with the French resistance, who now had direct contact with the Allied military authorities. This had occupied a large part of my time since my arrival in Switzerland. My colleagues and I had spent days with the chiefs, fighting men and couriers of the Maquis and other resistance organizations who slipped in and out of Switzerland during the difficult months of 1943 and early 1944. We had passed them funds, arranged for parachute drops of arms and supplies and had formulated with them the plans which geared them into the Allied push across France. The groups we had worked with in the Haute-Savoie region adjoining Switzerland had been instrumental in clearing the way for the American thrust northward after the landings on the coast of Southern France in July of 1944.

Our work with the Italian partisans resembled what we had done in France. Partisan leaders slipped over the mountainous border into the Ticino, the Italian-speaking canton of Switzerland, to bring us requests and plans. We arranged for air drops of supplies to them in their mountain holdouts.

The Italian partisans were in a difficult spot. The long German stand at Monte Cassino and the stubborn attempts of the Germans to hold every foot of ground as they retreated after Cassino meant that the partisans in the North throughout two difficult winters (1943–44 and 1944–1945) could not act in direct conjunction with Allied armies that had still not reached the areas where the partisans were entrenched. Anything beyond sporadic raids against the German occupiers would have been tantamount to suicide.

Much of my work in this period involved giving the partisans the moral and financial support necessary to keep them intact until the Allies would finally arrive on the scene. The Italian temperament being what it is, this was not easy to do. In occupied Northern Italy all the anti-Fascist political parties, including the Communists, had banded together to form the Committee for the Liberation of Northern Italy (the CLNAI) and it was with the leaders of this committee that I dealt. Most prominent among these CLNAI chiefs and one of its top military planners was Ferruccio Parri, who became Italy's first Prime Minister after the war. His name in the underground was "General Maurizio," and I was known to him and his colleagues as "Arturo." Parri was a scholar and a politician with thick eyeglasses and an unruly head of hair that had turned prematurely white as a result of long imprisonment and mistreatment at the hands of the Fascists. Parri was a man Mussolini feared—uncompromisingly honest, passionately devoted to the cause of liberty but very temperamental. His headquarters were in Milan, and although we kept in touch through secret couriers, Parri thought nothing of coming himself to Switzerland from time to time and risking a trip through the German-Fascist border controls to see me and my British colleagues who worked with him.

In late 1944, at a time when partisan morale particularly needed bolstering, we arranged for a CLNAI mission with Parri at its head to be taken to Allied military headquarters at Caserta, Italy. Their route was the only one available at the time. After slipping illegally into Switzerland they were taken into France, where, since the Nazi evacuation, we had OSS bases and airfields. From one of our fields in France they were flown to Allied Forces Headquarters at Caserta. The Supreme Allied Commander in the Mediterranean officially authorized the CLNAI as a military force acting in coordination with the Allied armies and assigned it the task of maintaining law and order in territories from which the Germans would eventually withdraw.

The CLNAI mission returned to Italy over the same route considerably heartened by the show of Allied faith and support. But then misfortune struck. Despite all the security precautions taken to conceal the exit and re-entry of the CLNAI mission from and to Italy, the Germans had caught wind of something and swooped down on all suspected resistance centers in a series of raids in which regrettably they netted Parri. This precipitated a service crisis in the CLNAI. It had to be assumed that the Germans had got Parri's papers when they picked him up and it was therefore necessary, as so often in the past when resistance leaders were caught, to cancel all operational plans, since many of them were noted in documents in Parri's possession.

One of the more adventurous young activists of the CLNAI, Edgardo Sogno (now a member of the Italian diplomatic service), attempted to free Parri from the Hotel Regina in Milan by disguising himself and three companions in German SS uniforms and entering the hotel via a skylight from a neighboring roof. He was intercepted by guards in the halls, caught, beaten and interrogated and imprisoned himself. Parri was then moved to a more secure German SS prison in Verona. Any chance of rescuing him from there by force was out of the question. Other CLNAI officials with whom we were in contact appealed to me to try to approach the Germans via intelligence channels to propose exchanging some prominent German prisoner for Parri. This was not feasible, but shortly thereafter quite an unexpected opportunity for effecting Parri's release came to our hands. But that story will have to wait until later in this account.

Against Germany it was obvious from the start that our work would have to be of another sort. There were certain high-level resistance groups in Germany but no partisan activities of the kind we supported in France and Italy. Our best intelligence source on Germany materialized in the summer of 1943, in the person of a diplomat, one who had the kind of access which is the intelligence officer's dream. George Wood (our code name for him) was not only our best source on Germany but undoubtedly one of the best secret agents any intelligence service has ever had. He was an official in the German Foreign Office in

Berlin and his job there was to screen and distribute for action the cable traffic between the Foreign Office and German diplomatic posts all over the world. Since the messages to and from German military and air attachés in Tokyo were also generally sent through Foreign Office channels, he saw these, too, and they became of great value as the war in the Far East was still to be fought out. He was frequently sent by the Foreign Office as a courier to Switzerland as well as to other posts, and it was on one of his courier trips to Switzerland that he succeeded in making contact with us, having convinced himself that in this way he could contribute to the fall of the Nazis, whom he hated.

While at his post in Berlin, he would scour the files of official cables and copy or photograph (microfilm) for us everything he thought of importance. He would then bring the copies out in his locked diplomatic bag along with the material he was delivering to the German Legation in Bern or mail them to us by secret channels. It is impossible here to describe fully his coverage. He turned in to us some of the best technical and tactical information on the V-weapons, on the effects of Allied bombings on German planning, on the gradually weakening fabric of the whole Nazi regime. General Donovan thought highly enough of this material to pass much of it on directly to President Roosevelt.

Some excerpts from a message I sent to Washington in April, 1944, about Wood's material will give the reader an idea of the picture he was providing us of conditions within the Nazi hierarchy.

> Sincerely regret that you cannot at this time see Wood's material as it stands without condensation and abridgment. In some 400 pages, dealing with the internal maneuverings of German diplomatic policy for the past two months, a picture of imminent doom and final downfall is presented. Into a tormented General Headquarters and a half-dead Foreign Office stream the lamentations of a score of diplomatic posts. It is a scene wherein haggard Secret Service and diplomatic agents are doing their best to cope with the defeatism and desertion of flatly defiant satellites and allies and recalcitrant neutrals. The period of secret service under Canaris* and diplomacy under the champagne salesman is drawing to an end. Already Canaris has disappeared from the picture, and a conference was hurriedly convoked in Berlin at which efforts

* Admiral Wilhelm Canaris was chief of the German military intelligence and counterintelligence service known as the *Abwehr*.

were made to mend the gaping holes left in the *Abwehr*. Unable now to fall back on his favorite means of avoiding disconcerting crises by retiring to his bed, Ribbentrop has beat a retreat to Fuschl and retains a number of his principal aides at Salzburg. The remainder of the Foreign Office is strung out all the way between Riesengebirge and the capital. Almost impossible working conditions exist in the latter, and bomb shelters are being permanently used for code work. Once messages have been deciphered, a frantic search begins to locate the particular service or minister to which each cable must be forwarded; and, when a reply is called for, another search is necessary to deliver this to the right place.

The final death-bed contortions of a putrefied Nazi diplomacy are pictured in these telegrams. The reader is carried from one extreme of emotion to the other as he examines these messages and sees the cruelty exhibited by the Germans in their final swan-song of brutality toward the peoples so irrevocably and pitifully enmeshed by the Gestapo after half a decade of futile struggles, and yet at the same time sees also the absurdity of the dilemma which now confronts this diplomacy both within and outside of *Festung Europa*.

Since this message describing German disintegration caused some raised eyebrows in Washington, I was immediately queried whether or not on second thought I wished to modify or tone it down a bit. I answered that I stood by it and did not wish to change it. I pointed out, however, that I was not by any means indicating that the morale of the German armies was near collapse, solely that the psychological hold of the Nazis over Europe was beginning to crumble and the intelligence machinery of the Nazi state organization was beginning to creak.

Of direct practical value of the very highest kind among Wood's contributions was a copy of a cable in which the German Ambassador in Turkey, von Papen, proudly reported to Berlin (in November, 1943) the acquisition of top-secret documents from the British Embassy in Ankara through "an important German agent." This was, of course, the famous Cicero, the valet of the British Ambassador who had managed to procure the keys to the Ambassador's private safe and to photograph its contents. I immediately passed word of this to my British colleagues, and a couple of British security inspectors immediately went over the British Embassy in Ankara and changed the safes and their combinations, thus putting Cicero out of business. Neither the Germans nor Cicero ever knew what was behind the security visit, which was, of course, made to appear routine and normal. Thus our rifling of the German Foreign Office safes in Berlin through an agent reporting to the Americans in Switzerland, put an end to the rifling of the British Ambassador's safe by a German agent in Turkey.

In World War II Swiss neutrality meant that Switzerland would not willingly engage in the conflict on either side or support either side in any military or nonmilitary endeavor. It did not mean that Switzerland would not defend itself if attacked or that it had committed itself to be neutral in spirit where Nazism was at issue. It was clear from the beginning that the Swiss had nothing to fear from the Western Allies and everything to fear from Nazi Germany which on at least two occasions had considered the possibility of invading Switzerland, once in 1940 before the fall of France opened the door to the West, and in 1943 during the crucial days in the battle for North Africa.

At the peak of its mobilization Switzerland had 850,000 men under arms or standing in reserve, a fifth of the total population. The commander of this force was General Henri Guisan, an outstanding patriot. That Switzerland did not have to fight was thanks to its will to resist and its large investment of men and equipment in its own defense. The cost to Germany of an invasion of Switzerland would certainly have been very high.

After the country had been completely surrounded by the Axis, the defense of Switzerland was based on the strategic assumption that the areas in which its major cities and industries lay, could not be defended against German attack. The concentrated defense would therefore take place in the Alpine fastnesses into which the major portion of the Swiss Army would withdraw. A system of fortifications, tunnels, underground supply depots would have made it very difficult for any opponent to root out the Swiss defenders from this stronghold. Furthermore, the railroad tunnels under the Alps which the Germans needed for shipping supplies to Italy would be destroyed by the Swiss themselves. This was announced publicly and the Germans, if they invaded Switzerland, were thus given notice that they would lose rather than gain by an attack.

In the desperate days of 1940, when Switzerland became entirely encircled by the Axis, some elements of the Swiss government were inclined to look for compromises to avoid open conflict with the Germans. In the Swiss Army, however, there was a group of patriotic officers who stood firmly for the idea of resisting the Germans at any cost. Among them were some of the top military intelligence personnel of the Army who were well informed about German intentions toward Switzerland.

Under the leadership of Captains Max Waibel and Hans Hausamann an intelligence unit known as "Bureau Ha" (after the first two letters of Hausamann's name) had reason to believe that German agents were prepared, by the use of physical force, to prevent General Guisan from issuing orders to the Swiss Army to defend the country. Hausamann and other officers, including Max Waibel, who will later pay a prominent role in our story, went so far as to make a secret agreement among themselves that they would take over the higher commands if their senior officers showed any reluctance to oppose a German move into Switzerland. For this patriotic act of insubordination some of them were sentenced to short terms of arrest, a small price to pay for the strengthening of the Swiss will to resist which resulted from their firm stand.*

The official Swiss position in regard to my mission observed the proper decorum of neutrality, but it was a benevolent neutrality.

The Swiss had to be assured, of course, of my discretion and good sense, and my full understanding of their position. For example, the Swiss desired to forestall any action on our part which, if it came to the attention of the Germans, could be thrown up to the Swiss as an instance of favoring one belligerent over the other. There was fear that any blatant breach of neutrality would be taken by the Germans as an excuse for reprisals. I cooperated to the utmost, by making it clear to the Swiss that I had no interest in spying on any Swiss measures of defense. The stronger they were in their preparations against a German attack, the better we liked it. The Germans, on the other hand, had agents and saboteurs in Switzerland spying out Swiss defense secrets. Scores of German agents were arrested, and a few were shot.

We realized, of course, that the Swiss Intelligence Service, in the normal course of business, had contact with both German and Allied intelligence. Since the Swiss were neutral, they could maintain such connections with each group of belligerents, and in their own defense interest they were wholly justified in doing so. Misunderstandings were minimized by the fact that one set of Swiss intelligence officers worked chiefly with the Germans, and another with the Allies. Colonel Roger

---

* A fair account of these events can be found in a recent excellent book by Alice Meyer, *Anpassung Oder Widerstand* (Compromise or Resistance) (Frauenfeld, Switzerland: Huber, 1965).

Masson, of the Swiss General Staff, had contact with Walter Schellenberg, the head of Himmler's intelligence service, and Max Waibel and his close associates consulted with us. What went on between Masson and Waibel, both of whom reported to General Guisan, I do not know to this day. I put my confidence in Waibel and never had any reason to regret it. As we later proceeded to develop our secret and precarious relations with the German generals early in 1945, we would have been thwarted at every step if we had not had the help of Waibel in facilitating contacts and communications and in arranging the delicate frontier crossings which had to be carried out under conditions of complete secrecy. In all his actions Waibel was serving the interests of peace.

In any discussion of Swiss neutrality in World War II, it would be seriously remiss to omit the humanitarian role of Switzerland. It was a refuge and an island of humane and charitable undertakings for the persecuted, the homeless and the displaced. As the site of peace organizations and international institutions devoted to cooperation among nations, it was one place in Europe where both Allies and Germans could hope to find competent and constructive helpers in the quest for peace.

3

Roadblocks to Surrender

In the shrinking German Reich of the last months of 1944, and the first months of 1945, Hitler was still the master. By the fear he engendered, he remained so till the day of his death. The German generals who led his armies were his captives. There was no political leader in Nazi Germany who had real power and influence except the Führer. After the failure of the plot to kill Hitler on July 20, 1944, his position was stronger rather than weaker.

The generals on both sides, Allied and German, had long known there could be only one military outcome. It was merely a question of time and how the end could be brought about. Could there be an orderly surrender, or would it all end in chaos? From reports reaching us in Switzerland it was clear that when the German military defenses finally crumbled, Hitler hoped to drag all of Europe down with him. The German Army leaders might put into force orders to "scorch the earth," to wreck what was left of the industry and economy of the countries they had occupied, and even of Germany itself.

It was in March, 1945, that Hitler ordered Albert Speer, the czar of the Nazi economy, to destroy Germany's railways and bridges, factories and public utilities—to scorch the German earth. Speer recoiled before such an enormity and begged his Führer to consider what this would mean to future German generations. According to Speer's testimony at the Nuremberg trials, Hitler turned on him and said:

"If the war is to be lost, the nation perishes. This is inevitable. There is no necessity to consider what the people would require for even a primitive existence. On the contrary, it is wiser to destroy these things ourselves. For this nation has been proved the weaker, and the future belongs solely to the stronger Eastern nations. Besides, those who remain after the battle are the inferior ones. The good ones have fallen."[*]

Rumors were also spreading that there would be a last-ditch stand of the Nazi forces in an Alpine bastion in Bavaria and Austria. While there was little evidence that the Germans were actually building a new system of fortifications in the Alps worthy of the name of redoubt, there was reason to fear that bands of desperate SS troops might withdraw to the natural mountain fastnesses and there put up stubborn resistance. This could have prolonged the war by weeks or months.

What troubled any thinking observer of the European scene in these days was whether anyone would be left in Germany with whom the Allies would deal or who had the authority and courage to effect a surrender; the alternative seemed to be a battle for each German city. General Eisenhower, at the time, correctly estimated that the war would not end until the Anglo-American troops coming from the West and the Russians coming from the East met in central Germany like two bulldozers, closing over a ruined land.

The plot against Hitler which ended with the attempt on his life in July, 1944, led to the slaughter or imprisonment of scores of high German military and civilian leaders who had had the courage to try to liquidate the Nazi tyranny and by doing so to end the war.

In Switzerland, Gaevernitz and I had been in close touch with important members of the conspiracy. They had told us, in advance, of their plans to kill Hitler, of the leaders involved in the plot and of the approximate time set for the coup. Our experience with this courageous anti-Nazi opposition had convinced us that, even after the blood bath which followed the failure, there must be many people in Germany, besides those directly involved in the conspiracy, who were anxious to salvage what was left of their country before the Nazi war madness destroyed it utterly.

We also learned from our contacts with the military conspirators that our policy of unconditional surrender constituted a deterrent to German generals who might otherwise have been willing to act against

[*] Allen W. Dulles, *Germany's Underground* (New York: Macmillan, 1947), p. 195.

Hitler. Several of the top generals whom the conspirators approached had been unwilling to take part in the plot and to assume the political responsibility involved because the unconditional-surrender policy, as they understood it, meant that Germany would be treated with the same harshness by the Allies whether the surrender came early by action of the Germans who dared defy Hitler or at a later date by one of Hitler's henchmen. In April of 1944, before the actual assassination attempt, the conspirators had in fact sent a special emissary to me in Switzerland to see whether there was any hope of getting better terms than unconditional surrender from the West. The answer given was an emphatic no; the Allied position on unconditional surrender could not be changed. The emissary returned with the answer, to the despair of some of the conspirators, many of whom then began to feel that the Soviet, with a far more flexible attitude, was their main ally against Hitler.

In addition to the unconditional-surrender slogan and the hopes placed in a Nazi redoubt in the Alps, other roadblocks continued to bedevil our progress in promoting a Nazi surrender. One of these was the myth of the "stab in the back." This idea was originally generated after Ludendorff and other German generals in World War I claimed that they had been hoaxed into an armistice in November, 1918, by the promises of Woodrow Wilson and his Fourteen Points. Weakness and even treachery were attributed to some of the German political leaders of that day, who, the myth goes, had undermined the will of the German people to resist and had forced the German generals to surrender even when they were still undefeated on the battlefield. This myth played havoc in German political life after the war and, combined with the German view of the harshness of the terms of the Versailles Treaty, did a great deal to destroy the Weimar Republic and build up the spirit of revenge which bred the Nazi philosophy. Strangely enough, this myth affected not only the attitude of many German generals against taking any initiative toward peacemaking at the end of World War II; it also affected the thinking of the Allied political leaders in Washington and London toward a surrender. The war against the Nazis and German militarism, many of them said, must be fought to the bitter end this time. They did not want the Germans, the Nazis or the writers of their history books ever to be able to deny that Germany had been thoroughly defeated on the field of battle. Thus the World War I "stab in the back" myth tended to make Washington and London skeptical of any effort to work out an early World War II surrender through the use of German military leaders.

Another myth was the one about the new German miracle weapons, and Hitler used it effectively to discourage any move toward surrender. Up to the very end Hitler promised his troops that he had in reserve some new weapon of war besides V-1's, V-2's, and jets, which would change the whole course of the battle. No one can predict how much the war would have been lengthened and the slaughter increased if the Germans had been a year or two ahead of their schedules with these weapons and if the Allies had not succeeded in bombing out Peenemünde, where they were making and testing V-1 and V-2 weapons. So the idea of miracle weapons was not wholly a myth, and the possibility that they might be produced influenced many German generals to keep fighting when otherwise they would have gone along with the surrender.

The final myth I would mention was that of coming Allied dissension. Throughout the war Hitler nourished the illusion that the Anglo-American Allies and Russia would quarrel and that he could then make a deal with one or the other of them. This myth grew apace at the time of Franklin Delano Roosevelt's death on April 12, 1945. This, Hitler thought, would spur on Allied dissension. After all, we had lost our great leader, and what better time could there be for him to break up the Alliance and use the Russians as his secret weapon, either joining them against us or joining us against them? This may seem today just another evidence of madness, but such madness was the fuel which lit the flames of hope in the mind of a Hitler. While he knew little history, he is said to have been greatly influenced by the accounts of Frederick the Great's escape from an impossible situation when the sudden death of Czarina Elizabeth disrupted the alliance of Russia and Austria against Prussia in 1762.*

Some of the main obstacles to peacemaking had been created by Hitler himself much earlier. Of these, the Nazi oath of loyalty taken by every soldier and officer in the German Army was no doubt the most potent deterrent to any individual act against the Führer's orders. The oath read as follows:

"I swear before God to give my unconditional obedience to Adolf Hitler, Führer of the Reich and of the German people, Supreme Commander of the Wehrmacht, and I pledge my word as a brave soldier to observe this oath always, even at the peril of my life."**

---

* J. W. Wheeler-Bennett, *Nemesis of Power* (New York: Macmillan, 1953), p. 611n.
** Ibid., p. 339.

The distinctive feature of this oath was that it pledged the military to the person of Adolf Hitler, as leader and commander, and not simply to country and flag.

To us today, far removed from the scene in time and spirit, it is difficult to form a notion of the awesome power the Nazi oath had in the minds of the German officers. Both the ceremony of oath-taking and its words had overtones harking back to the sworn fealty of the medieval knight to his liege lord and the military aristocracy to the sovereign. To break the other for one sensitive to such traditions, then, presented a difficult matter of conscience. Only a man of earnest convictions and independent ethical judgment would be likely to do it. Some of the men who participated in the twentieth of July plot, aware as they were of many of the crimes of the Nazis, had to wrestle with their own consciences before they could justify disloyalty to the Führer—largely because of the binding power of the military oath. A number of generals invited to participate in the conspiracy, among then Jodl, Guderian and Manstein, refused to take part in it, at least so they claimed, because they felt they could not break the oath. For some no doubt, then and later, it was a convenient excuse for compliance, for a sweeping evasion of personal responsibility. As we shall see, it again played a role in our dealings with the German commanders in Italy.

Hitler's carrot-and-stick treatment of the individual generals had succeeded in strengthening his hold over some of them. When a general did well and pleased Hitler, he was rewarded with praise, decorations, promotion to Field Marshal and, in some important cases, with bonuses of money and even of large estates. With flattery and bribery these generals were thus bound to Hitler more deeply than the oath had already bound them. When the generals displeased Hitler, they were removed from command peremptorily, and if they disobeyed, they were court-martialed; in some cases sentenced to prison; in some executed or allowed the escape route of suicide, as with Rommel.*

---

* Twice during the weeks immediately following the Normandy landings, Field Marshals von Rundstedt and Rommel met with Hitler and frankly placed before him the ultimate outcome of the battle in the West as they saw it, hoping to reach the closed monomaniacal mind of the Führer and to persuade him to withdraw or negotiate. This was, of course, hopeless. Still, they tried. Hitler was already ranting about super-destructive miracle weapons and he could not be budged. Rommel then secretly conceived a plan to approach Eisenhower or

The leading role the military had played in the unsuccessful assassination attempt weakened any initiative the generals, singly or as a group, had ever possessed to influence the course of the war, either by direct representation to Hitler or by any action taken behind his back. Their treachery toward Hitler, exposed by the failure of the plot, turned Hitler fanatically against the military caste. Even generals who had no part in the plot had to fear that the slightest appearance of an unwillingness to carry out the Führer's orders might be taken as evidence of treason and that they would be punished accordingly.

After the twentieth of July, aside from close personal advisers like Bormann and Goebbels, Hitler relied almost solely on the SS for the execution of his policies and for his own protection. The military had been discredited and disgraced. He would not listen to a Wehrmacht general again or let one enter his presence until the general's side arms had been removed. After all, it was Colonel Klaus von Stauffenberg, a Wehrmacht officer, who had carried the bomb in his briefcase to the meeting at the bunker of July 20th. By Hitler's orders the investigation of this complex and widely ramified conspiracy was in the hands of SS Chief Himmler and his immediate subordinate, Ernst Kaltenbrunner, Chief of the RSHA (Security Office of the Reich) a congeries of SS security formations which included the secret police (Gestapo), the secret intelligence service both within Germany and outside it (the SD) and the security police in occupied territories (the Sipo).

In Berlin, Gestapo functionaries hanged Field Marshal Erwin von Witzleben, once commander of all the German armies in the West (1941–42), and seven other high-ranking officers for their part in the conspiracy.

The once proud and independent German military intelligence service, the *Abwehr*, had become subordinate to the secret foreign intelligence service of the RSHA under Walter Schellenberg. Its chief, Admiral Canaris, was thrown into a concentration camp for his part in the conspiracy and later executed by SS functionaries.

Montgomery on his own to seek a separate armistice in the West. A serious automobile accident resulting from the attack on his staff car by an Allied aircraft put him out of action in mid-July, so that he was unable to carry out his plan. Shortly afterward he committed suicide, at Hitler's invitation, because he had given his assent, even though at a distance, to the plans of the generals conspiring against Hitler. (Cf. Hans Speidel, *Invasion—1944* [Chicago: Henry Regnery Co., 1950], pp. 151–160.)

Gestapo informants predominated in all military headquarters. Bootlicking sycophants and personal favorites of Hitler, like General Walter Model, who took over on the Western Front after von Kluge, in August, 1944, invited SS officers into their staffs as proof of their loyalty to the Führer. Plans for scorched-earth and extermination policies, in case of the impending defeat, were entrusted to special SS units. Hitler well knew that he could not trust the "cowardly" sentimentalists of the Wehrmacht to carry them out. Reichsführer-SS Himmler had been made Commander-in-Chief of the home army, a new command for him which meant that in the last-ditch defense of Germany itself the SS was to play the major role.

This dominance at the end by the SS was primarily a matter of control by secret-police methods and by the overhanging threat of individual punishment. If the generals had felt bound by their oath, now they also lived in fear for their lives; if Hitler would ruthlessly destroy a Rommel, a Witzleben and a Canaris, who could feel safe?

Thus, the situation was fraught with mortal danger for those who might be disposed to work for peace. The surviving generals, who theoretically could have engineered local surrenders, were now powerless or too intimidated to try. The element in control of Germany, the SS, was precisely the faction which the Allies would be least disposed to recognize as spokesmen of a surrender and whose removal and punishment would be one of the prime considerations of Allied policy. In view of these conditions within the Nazi hierarchy, it was obvious in late 1944 that the German generals were not going to surrender against Hitler's orders or behind his back—not unless it was possible to do so without being liquidated in the attempt.

Despite this pessimistic outlook for a peace that could be achieved before the Germans fought to the last man, we came up with an idea in Bern in the fall of 1944 based on the conviction that there were still some German generals who did not believe in Hitler's promises and who would be glad to surrender if it was possible for them to do so with reasonable security for themselves. The central idea of the plan was to locate such commanders, to make secret contact with them and to create the circumstances under which their surrenders could be carried out, swiftly and silently, before the long arm of Hitler and the SS could descend on them and their staffs.

After the Germans had been cleared out of Southern France and the American forces had reached the Swiss border, our mission in Bern established liaison with the headquarters of the American Twelfth Army Group and the Seventh Army in France, and it was my habit to meet the chief intelligence officers of these units, General Edwin L. Sibert and Colonel William Quinn (now Lieutenant General), at points in France just over the Swiss border, in order to pass to them the latest intelligence we had on the situation in Germany.

At one such session in Pontarlier, in the Jura Mountains, Gaevernitz, who usually accompanied me to meetings of this sort, presented to General Sibert the idea which had been taking shape in our minds, to try to win bloodless victories by establishing contacts with generals in the enemy ranks. About ten days later we received a cable from Twelfth Army Group headquarters in Luxemburg asking Gaevernitz to visit them at once to pursue further the recommendations made in Pontarlier.

By the time Gaevernitz talked with General Sibert in Luxemburg, the Allied armies had captured a large number of German prisoners. Many of them were being held in France and Belgium, and some of the highest-ranking ones in England. Some of them we thought might be ardent anti-Nazis and, given the opportunity, might take an active part in helping to bring the war to a speedy conclusion. Our idea was to locate such men and enlist their aid in pinpointing German commanders on the Western Front who they thought might be willing to cooperate in such an undertaking. Besides this, our plan also contained a scheme for solving the problem of how physically to reach the German commanders thought to be open-minded regarding surrender. This was to send captured junior officers across the lines to them, posing as escaped prisoners of war.

Gaevernitz presented these ideas to General Sibert. The question was where to begin. It was next to impossible to remain well informed about the sentiments of the German generals then in command on various sectors of the Western Front. Many of them had been shifted and replaced during the gradual German withdrawal from France and as a result of the events of the twentieth of July. Gaevernitz, in his preliminary talk with General Sibert, put forward the name of General G. Count Gerhard von Schwerin as the kind of man we had in mind. He happened to know of Schwerin's opposition to the Nazis at the outbreak of the war, and had good reason to believe that he was somewhere on the Western Front. This rang a bell. Sibert recalled having just recently heard the name. He called in some members of his staff to check the matter out, and they reported that Schwerin had recently been in command of the 116th Panzer Division stationed at Aachen. There were rumors that he had declared Aachen an open city, but had somehow been removed from his command, after which the city had become the scene of a bitter battle. It sounded as though there were facts here that fitted in with Gaevernitz's original surmise about Schwerin and might be worth pursuing. Sibert agreed. He assigned one of his staff, Lieutenant Colonel (now Colonel) E. C. "Bud" Lee, to work with Gaevernitz and take him over to Aachen, then in American hands, to get the story.

In the ruins of Aachen, Gaevernitz and Lee interviewed a large number of surviving German inhabitants and pieced together the following facts.

Aachen was the first major German city on the route of the Allied advance into Germany. It may have been for this reason that Hitler had ordered a last-ditch defense of the city, to make of it an example of German fortitude and to give the Allies a taste of what was to come. Despite his orders, Schwerin announced to the citizens of Aachen that he intended to declare it an open city and to withdraw without fighting to spare its destruction. This he was able to do because the Nazi officials, thinking the city was about to be overrun by the Americans, had fled, so that Schwerin was in full control.

The population, who had first been ordered by the Nazis to evacuate the city, received the news of Schwerin's decision with an outburst of joy. To carry out his plan, Schwerin tried to get word of his intentions to the American First Army, which had stopped just short of Aachen. When the Americans, after three days, gave no sign of advancing, the Nazi bosses returned, arrested those citizens who had cooperated with Schwerin and denounced him to his military superiors. As a result, Schwerin was ordered to relinquish his command and to report to the headquarters of his Army Corps.

He did so but, realizing what fate might be in store for him, asked permission to return to his troops to take leave of them, which was granted. What he really hoped to do was to stall for a few days until the Americans arrived on the scene. The following day a German military-police detachment suddenly turned up and surrounded the farmhouse where Schwerin had his headquarters. They obviously intended to arrest him. All around the farmhouse Schwerin's officers and men took up defensive positions with machine guns. Had the police detachment attempted to arrest Schwerin, his troops were prepared to open fire on them. The whole incident, even though it did not come to a head, was without precedent in German military annals of any fighting front in the Second World War.

When the expected American advance still did not materialize after three days, Schwerin relinquished his plan and his command and reported, as ordered, to his Corps headquarters. He was fortunately spared any serious punishment because one of the principal investigating officers in his case was in sympathy with Schwerin's aims and likewise in opposition to Hitler's policies of last-ditch stands at the expense of the civilian population.

From the time the American VII Corps finally broke into Aachen on October 13, 1944, the battle within the city itself lasted eight days before the Germans would surrender, and this only after the last of the defenders took refuge in a single building in the center of the city, which the Americans proceeded to blow to bits, piece by piece, by firing 155-mm. weapons at its walls at point-blank range. The city lay in ruins. Hitler had had his way.

Gaevernitz could hardly have found a better example to support the argument for our proposals. Had Schwerin only been able to make contact with the Americans, a battle could have been avoided and a city and thousands of lives saved on both sides. The problem was to locate men like Schwerin and make it possible for them to take the required steps successfully.

General Sibert understood, and offered his full support. Recently captured German generals would be the only reliable sources of information about their colleagues still fighting at the front. If we could find captives of anti-Nazi conviction, it should be possible to get them to indicate men like Schwerin among the still-active German generals. Gaevernitz thereupon proposed that he, with Colonel Lee, go to several of the large prisoner-of-war camps to look for suitable German officers. At the camp in Revin, Belgium, Gaevernitz, after careful screening, singled out two good prospects, Generals Hans Schaefer and von Felbert. Both were outspoken in their dislike of the Nazis and volunteered to draw up lists of their colleagues who they thought might be sympathetic to surrender. Both were willing to become members of a sort of advisory committee of anti-Nazi generals, acting in concert with the Allies.*

---

* Although our plan was quite a different one, it may bring to mind the von Seydlitz Free Germany Committee which the Soviets sponsored, made up of captured German generals and officers in Soviet hands who had "gone over" to the Soviet way of thinking. The Russians finally used this group as a clever propaganda mouthpiece for the future Sovietization of Germany, and not in order to persuade anyone to surrender. Von Seydlitz had been one of generals under Field Marshal Paulus captured at Stalingrad.

Gaevernitz put forward a plan to try to assemble five Generals as an advisory group. Two had been found. We had now to look
for three more. Sibert suggested that Gaevernitz and Lee go to England,
where a considerable number of high-ranking German generals were
being held.

To the British the idea of our project was not altogether new. Of the
many German generals who had passed through the screening of British
intelligence, they had already selected a handful whose determined anti-
Nazi attitude seemed well established.

This small group of prisoners had been assembled near London. According to the British, General Bassenge, who frequently acted as
spokesman for the group, was without doubt the ablest and the most
determined to cooperate in any action against the Nazis. He had already
assisted the British in an attempt to induce the commander of the German-
occupied British Channel Islands to surrender. In a British naval craft he
had approached the shore of the island of Jersey and had tried to speak
to the German occupiers with the help of a megaphone. Unfortunately,
the German commander had answered Bassenge's overtures with a blast
from his heavy guns. The attempt at least had shown Bassenge's willingness to act, though it obviously had not proved the enemy's readiness
for surrender. Of course, in this instance both sides had to act too much
in the open. The incident proved what we already knew—that any surrender moves would have to be accomplished with the greatest secrecy.
One could not expect success by megaphoning one's intentions or flying
white flags, both of which exposed a delicate undertaking prematurely
and could not fail to wreck it.

When Gaevernitz saw Bassenge, he struck him as the likely man to
head up the project. Bassenge had already formulated his own plans for
overthrowing Hitler and inducing the German armies to lay down their
arms. These were somewhat more romantic than ours, calling for radio
proclamations, air drops of liaison personnel and mass showerings of
leaflets proposing surrenders and explaining how to carry them out. But
the important aspects, from our point of view, were Bassenge's willingness to cooperate, his conviction of the senselessness of continuing the
war and his intellectually superior position among the captured generals.

The next step, the one most difficult to accomplish, was to secure
the support of the highest Allied military and political authorities for
carrying out the project. Thus, a few days later, at a meeting at General
Eisenhower's headquarters early in December, 1944, Gaevernitz, with

the support of General Sibert, submitted his plan. It proposed the establishment of a committee of dissident German generals from among those captured, headed by General Bassenge, to advise the Allied commanders on the ways and means of making contact to those German commanders still fighting who were believed to be thoroughly anti-Nazi and to be sympathetic to the idea of surrendering. And it suggested the use of captured junior officers posing as escaped prisoners to play the role of intermediaries.

Several weeks went by and finally a reply was received from Washington that the project had been considered at a high level but had been rejected.

The Western Allies did not propose using German militarists to defeat German militarism. This was understandable to us even though it was not a very practical approach to the German surrender problem. Another reason for the negative answer was that the Battle of the Bulge had intervened between the initiation of our talks with General Sibert and the final answer we received. Washington was now pretty well convinced that the Germans would fight to the bitter end and that voluntary surrenders were most unlikely—and, in the war psychosis which then gripped Allied military thinking about the Germans, maybe not even too desirable if it gave the Nazis an easy way out.

However, the attempt was not wasted. Our experiences with Schaefer, Felbert and Bassenge showed at least that, despite the slaughter of German generals after the twentieth of July, there were still some German military men who saw that surrender was the only answer. Who they were and where they might be found remained the questions—one we were shortly to have answered, but not at all in the fashion we expected.

4

Peace Feelers

During the autumn of 1944, while we were pursuing the idea of surrender by persuasion on the Western Front, we were also becoming aware of certain stirrings to the south of us, certain changes in the political weather in North Italy. We had had no indications up to that time that the German forces on the Italian front were any less under the influence of the last-ditch mentality prevailing in Berlin than those in the East and the West. On the contrary, we had assumed that they would play an especially important role in safeguarding any Alpine redoubt the Nazis chose for a last stand, and that this was one of the main reasons for their holding on so tenaciously in the northern Apennines. Yet rumors and feelers began to reach us, originating in Italy, and the word "peace" began to crop up. We were rather suspicious from the start, and what made us so was the fact that the SS rather than the Army was most often named as the interested party behind the feelers. This being so, we were not exactly enthusiastic, but we were willing to listen, particularly because churchmen frequently appeared as intermediaries or emissaries. One did not question their sincerity but only wondered what the initiative was behind their action.

The first feeler was relayed to me by a high Catholic dignitary in Switzerland whose acquaintance I had made through diplomatic circles in Bern. Early in November of 1944, shortly after I returned from a Washington conference with Donovan the dignitary came to me with a story about a serious attempt on the part of the Germans in Italy to discuss peace, which unfortunately, he thought, had come to nothing. Perhaps, he suggested, the Americans would be able to salvage something from it.

He then recounted that a well-known Italian industrialist, Franco Marinotti, had been in Switzerland for the last month and had made certain proposals to the British on behalf of the Germans. Marinotti, as I knew, was the president of a major rayon company, the Snia Viscosa, which had large factories in Italy. When last heard of, he had opposed the attempts of Mussolini's German-sponsored Fascist government to socialize the big industries of North Italy, a rather vague plan which had made no headway, and for his pains he had been put in jail.

The Germans—behind Mussolini's back, so I was told—had released Marinotti and had sent him to Switzerland to sound out the British in a scheme involving the same German dream we had met before and were often to meet again; namely, that the Germans would cease fighting in the West if the Allies would join them in a common front against the Russians. As proof of the high-level German protection Marinotti was enjoying, I was shown a document purporting to come from Wilhelm Harster, the German SS police general in North Italy, which guaranteed Marinotti safe passage in and out of Italy.

The British, after hearing Marinotti's story, had closed their doors to him; on advice from London, it appeared. Thus, according to my church contact, the desired channel between the Germans in Italy and the British did not materialize. He had come to me to see if I would not be interested in picking up the pieces and bringing Washington into the affair. On reporting the matter to headquarters I was not surprised to receive the comment that Washington was not convinced of German good faith in feelers of this sort. Neither was I.

Several factors puzzled us in this strange collusion between Marinotti and the SS official. Harster had assured Marinotti that no less a person than Heinrich Himmler himself was behind this peace move. Whether this assertion was true or not is impossible to ascertain, but we do know now from certain German documents captured after the war that Harster reported the results of Marinotti's efforts to Schellenberg in Berlin, who stood two notches below Himmler in the SS chain of command. Also, Harster was still not the highest-ranking SS officer in Italy. Over him stood General Karl Wolff, who was Himmler's personal representative and commander of all the SS forces in Italy. Despite this, Harster claimed that Himmler was dealing through him and not through Wolff, whose name in fact had not yet entered into the matter at all. We were, of course, at the time not able to understand these refinements in the secret operations of the SS hierarchy.

The captured German documents showed too that Harster had eventually reported on my contact with the church dignitary. Presumably the churchman had reported his visit to Marinotti, who had told Harster. It is interesting to note how this SS General distorted the facts in his report to Berlin, probably to arouse the interest of his superiors. He claimed that "Dulles wished to be consulted [in peace matters] because he had returned with a mission from Roosevelt to make contact with the appropriate German spokesman. This spokesman should be sought in SS circles since only a contact to the SS seemed of value to the United States. The contact should be taken up after the re-election of Roosevelt. The purpose of the talks would be to free American troops in Europe for use in Asia. An anti-Bolshevist interest would be less important for the Americans. . . ."

A little later, through Signor Olivetti, of the famous Italian typewriter company, who sometimes came to Switzerland on business, I met another churchman, the Reverend Dr. Don Giuseppe Bicchierai, the secretary of Cardinal Ildefonso Schuster of Milan, who had just arrived in Switzerland on a secret visit. His purpose was twofold: to see me, and to communicate through the Papal Nuncio in Bern with the Vatican, in the name of the Cardinal. This the Cardinal could not do from Milan since the battle lines then separated Milan from Rome. The Cardinal, it was reported, wished to act as mediator between the Germans and the Italian partisan forces in order to avoid further bloodshed and destruction in Italy. Since the partisan forces were now (ever since the visit of the CLNAI chiefs to Allied headquarters) an officially authorized fighting arm of the Allied forces, their actions could presumably be controlled by Allied headquarters. Don Bicchierai was, therefore, anxious to have me communicate the Cardinal's plan to Allied headquarters in Rome and he was asking the Vatican to do the same on the theory that the more pressure brought to bear the better. The substance of the proposal was that the Germans would agree not to destroy Italian industry, public services and power installations or anything not of immediate military importance, provided the partisan forces on their side would agree not to obstruct the German withdrawal by armed or terroristic raids. The ecclesiastical authorities offered to act as middlemen between the two parties.

Don Bicchierai gave me a copy of the "project" as it was called, a rather unusual document. I passed along his request through my communications facilities to Rome and was informed shortly afterward that the CLNAI wouldn't hear of it. They were working for a general uprising against the Germans and could not renounce it. They had suffered and fought, had been hounded, outnumbered and given no quarter. Now the Germans were getting a little worried about what might happen if they were trapped between the Allies forcing them north and the partisans falling on their backs and their flanks.

The CLNAI intended to do everything possible to show the world that the Italians themselves would make a major contribution to their own liberation and had not sat by while the Allies did the job. Allied headquarters in Rome, having no reason to differ with the CLNAI in this matter and not being anxious to let the Germans save themselves by using their threat of a scorched-earth policy to buy safety from the partisans, did nothing to persuade the CLNAI to change their minds.

It was not clear to us where the incentive for this probe had originated. It was clear, however, that the Cardinal of Milan, a powerful figure in the church, would not have lent his name to this venture if he had regarded it solely as a shot in the dark. He would not have proposed, as the document suggested, that General Wolff and Field Marshall Kesselring sign the agreement for the Germans if he had not had some indications from their side that they might be interested. Whatever the full meaning of this proposal was, it gave us, at the least, further indications that something was brewing in high Nazi circles in Italy such as we had not encountered in any other battle area.

Shortly after Don Bicchierai visited me at the end of November, Gaevernitz returned from his secret mission to Belgium, France and England fully aware of the obstacles to be encountered in trying to put over a plan for achieving German surrenders in the West. Above all, the technical difficulty of making contact with anti-Nazi German commanders was a major stumbling block. But Gaevernitz was not the kind of man to give up easily. If the problem of making contact across the fighting front in the West was insoluble, why not, he thought, try to reach the generals from the rear, from our own home base in Switzerland?

The opportunity to explore this line materialized toward the end of December when Gaevernitz learned through contacts in Switzerland that the German Consul in Lugano, von Neurath, was discreetly taking soundings. While the job of German consul in Lugano was by no means an impressive one, Neurath himself was a man of some potential for our plans because he was the son of Baron Konstantin von Neurath, former German Foreign Minister in Hitler's Cabinet. Furthermore, we had the impression that the younger Neurath was in German intelligence. Because of the geographical position of Lugano, if for no other reason, he seemed to be trying to play some liaison role between the German leaders in Italy and the Allies in Switzerland. It was known to us, for example, that he had somehow been involved in the Marinotti affair and had in fact been present when Marinotti met with General Harster in Italy to discuss his overtures to the British.

Gaevernitz met Neurath just before the end of the year. Neurath claimed that he was in direct touch with Marshal Kesselring, and Generals Wolff and Harster of the SS in Italy. What seemed even more promising to Gaevernitz, who was still thinking in terms of the Western Front, was the fact that Neurath personally knew Field Marshal von Rundstedt, who had for the second time become German Commander in Chief on the Western Front, as well as Chief of Staff, General Siegfried Westphal, and the commander of German Army Group G on the Western Front, General Blaskowtiz. Here was a tempting array of high-ranking generals of the German Army. Further, Neurath said he was convinced that the war was lost for Germany and that it was a crime on the part of the Nazis to continue it. He declared to Gaevernitz that he himself was prepared to take any personal risks to bring an early end to the war.

In January, 1945, Neurath went to Italy and saw Kesselring who informed him that the German armies in Italy were not to be weakened in order to bolster the Eastern Front and that neither he nor Rundstedt on the Western Front was prepared to come to terms with the Allies at the moment. Kesselring was, however, willing to have Neurath follow up the possibilities for peace through persons in less exalted positions than his own. In early February he sent a message to Neurath, who was then visiting his father's estate near Stuttgart, and told him that he had arranged for Neurath to meet secretly with Westphal and Blaskowtiz for discussions. This meeting took place on the night of February 10th in a small village inn near Stuttgart, the two generals traveling incognito. The report of the meeting which Neurath gave Gaevernitz afterward summed up the attitude and the dilemma of the German military leadership at the time. Continuation of the war was futile. Everybody agreed. But many of the German soldiery on the Eastern Front, whose homes had already been overrun by the Russians, had nothing to look forward to and would just as soon keep fighting. Perhaps on the Western Front some German divisions could let themselves be overrun by prearrangement, rather than resist or retire farther into central Germany. But how was such a thing to be arranged? And would any general who consented to this receive assurance that he would not for his pains and his treachery to Hitler still be tried later as a war criminal by the Allies? What were the terms for Germany? What part of Germany would be occupied by the Russians, what part by the Western Allies? What was the meaning of the Allied formula of unconditional surrender? Would the German generals be allowed to demobilize the Wehrmacht themselves? From all this, Gaevernitz held out the lone hope that through Neurath it might be possible to get Westphal to come to Kesselring's headquarters in Italy and from there be smuggled into Switzerland for face-to-face talks. Neurath himself as negotiator could not carry the matter any further.

In the meantime, during these first two months of 1945, further evidence of special deals of many kinds emanating from Italy were accumulating. The Catholic church again seemed to be playing a leading role. In January, we were informed that a group of German diplomats at the Vatican who had been permitted to stay on at their posts after our armies took over Rome, were proposing to make contact with Field Marshals Guderian and Rundstedt via Switzerland to discuss peace. At the same time, a Benedictine priest from Milan turned up in Rome, having crossed the German and Allied lines safely. He claimed he was carrying a message for the Pope to be transmitted through the Abbot General of the Benedictine order. An excerpt from his message gives the flavor of the affair:

> In the sixth year of the war Germany finds herself alone in the fight against Bolshevist Russia. In the interests of saving mankind, Germany now looks to the highest ecclesiastical authority to intervene with the Anglo-Americans and guarantees absolute secrecy in any negotiations with the Vatican.

In February, other quarters were heard from. At the beginning of the month a high official of the Swiss Intelligence Service informed me that an envoy from Schellenberg, the head of the German foreign intelligence department of the SS (Amt VI of the RSHA) had arrived in Switzerland

and wanted to see me. The message he carried contained an interesting but quite improbable switch from the theme we had been hearing so far. It was that the stiff German resistance on the Western Front and the maintenance of the front in Italy, as contrasted with the rapid withdrawal of German forces on the Eastern Front, was part of a plan to open Germany to Russia. However, if the Anglo-Saxons were disposed to modify the unconditional-surrender policy, the Germans would be interested in talking things over. Needless to say, I had no interest in seeing this envoy. It looked as if Schellenberg was trying a new ploy.

In the middle of February, an official from the German Embassy in Northern Italy, Hitler's mission to Mussolini, turned up in Switzerland. To a source of ours this official stated that Kesselring was ready to quit if the Allies would offer acceptable terms. A few days later a story appeared in the London *Daily Dispatch*, stating that Kesselring had made secret overtures to the Allies. He was allegedly willing to withdraw his troops from Northern Italy, leaving its cities intact, if his soldiers would be allowed to return to German territory to maintain order there.

Just at the end of February we heard from still another quarter. An Austrian agent arrived in Bern from Vienna, having been sent by Kaltenbrunner himself, Chief of the RSHA, and the most powerful man in the SS after Himmler. The Austrian had been acquainted with Wilhelm Hoettl, one of Kaltenbrunner's intelligence officials in Austria, and through him had met Kaltenbrunner. The message rang a new change and, if it were true, gave some inkling of the conflict within the Nazi leadership. Kaltenbrunner wanted him to tell us that he and Himmler were anxious to end the war and were contemplating liquidating the warmongers within the Nazi party, especially Martin Bormann. They wanted contact to the British and Americans. Kaltenbrunner's name had not previously cropped up in the probes that had reached us from Italy, although Himmler's name had. But this message was clearly from Kaltenbrunner, and though it was hardly the opening through which we would be willing to work on the problem of peace, the idea that there was a powerful person who did not intend to go along with Hitler, Bormann and the die-hards in a plan to hold out in an Alpine redoubt was significant.*

* We did not know at the time that the supposedly all-powerful Himmler was being gradually displaced at the center of power around Hitler in these last months by Bormann and his clique. Bormann had suggested to Hitler that

No doubt Kaltenbrunner was doing this in an attempt to maneuver himself and his fellow-SS criminals into a favorable position as peacemaker, perhaps even under the illusion that the Allies would allow his group to take the lead.

Thus matters stood at the end of February. We had talked primarily to churchmen and to industrialists. Our connections to the Army had been a result of our own initiative. They had sent us no one and we had got nowhere with what we had tried to do. And among the SS feelers, it was still impossible to ascertain, with the sole exception of the Kaltenbrunner probe, whether the men who had allowed their names to be used were acting on their own or on higher authority, and above all whether any of them had anything to deliver. As we saw it, the SS appeared to be chiefly trying to get some good marks with the Allies to offset what was otherwise an unmitigated record of black criminality. It is no wonder, then, that when still another probe bearing all the same earmarks of the earlier ones reached us at the end of February we were not especially enthusiastic or optimistic about it. But before taking up the story of the probe that did turn into a surrender, we should have a look at the situation in that part of Italy which was still held by Marshal Kesselring's armies at the end of February, 1945.

Himmler take over the command of the German Army Group Weichsel (Vistula) from the Wehrmacht generals who had failed to make a successful stand against the Russians. Hitler accepted the suggestion, which was not made in good faith but was solely a trick of Bormann's to distance and discredit Himmler. Himmler had no choice but to accept the command, where his troops promptly suffered serious losses. He had no special magic for turning the military tide. His presence did not arouse any enthusiasm with the fighting men to make up for his lack of military experience.

5

Background of a Surrender

The Allied decision to invade Italy via the stepping-stone of Sicily, and to make Italy the base for one of the major thrusts against Hitler's forces in Europe, was taken at the Casablanca Conference in January, 1943. It was at this same conference that the Allied policy of unconditional surrender was announced.

When the invasion of Sicily started in July, 1943, the Germans had about four divisions there to bolster the Fascist garrison, with three more on the Italian mainland. By mid-October, shortly after the Allies took Naples, the Germans had nineteen divisions in Italy, eight more than the Allies. Obviously, they intended to hold Italy if they could, and Hitler assigned to this theater two of his ablest generals: Field Marshal Albert Kesselring as commander of the German forces fighting the Allies south of Rome and Field Marshal Erwin Rommel to command German Army Group B in Northern Italy. There was continuous quarreling between Rommel and Kesselring, and Rommel was eventually recalled to Germany. Kesselring then took over the command of all the German forces in Italy. He had made an excellent record as a soldier on the Russian front, and had also commanded the German Air Forces in the Mediterranean during the African campaign. He was a man Hitler felt he could trust. In this instance, Hitler was not making a mistake.

By October, 1943, the Allied Fifteenth Army Group in Italy consisted of eleven divisions. It comprised the British Eighth Army commanded by General Sir Richard McCreery and the American Fifth Army under General Mark W. Clark. The headquarters of the Fifteenth Army Group was set up at Caserta, just outside Naples, in a regal building that had been the summer palace of the kings of Naples, sometimes also called the Bourbon Palace. Allied headquarters remained at Caserta until the very end of the war in Italy. An OSS mission was attached to these headquarters, and we maintained direct radio communications with it from Switzerland.

Ever since Mussolini's ouster in July, 1943, at the time of the successful Allied invasion of Sicily, the Germans had expanded their forces in Italy politically as well as militarily. With their proclivity for puppet governments, which they fondly hoped would give a semblance of popular support and save them some of the administrative headaches of a full occupation, they had installed Mussolini as the chief of a *pro-forma* government in that part of Northern Italy which the Germans controlled militarily. The Germans well knew the real sentiments of the Italian people, and that they could expect even less from this rootless North Italian Republic of Mussolini's, which they had created out of the shambles of Fascism, than they had secured from Pétain's Vichy France.

But as Hitler saw it, to let Mussolini go by the board entirely would foster the idea that dictators could be dispensed with—a thought that Hitler feared might become contagious. By mid-October, 1943, Mussolini and the nucleus of his regime had settled in various hotels on the southwestern shore of the picturesque Lake of Garda in North Italy, a famous resort area almost as far removed from the battle scene as from the political and military realities of the period. The new government was popularly known as the Republican Fascist Government of Salò after the tiny town where its main offices were located.

The contribution of Mussolini and his Armed Forces Minister Graziani to Hitler's war effort was to consist chiefly in an attempt to raise new Fascist military forces who would fight at the side of the Germans. At the same time, Italian Fascist militia for the keeping of law and order in the area nominally under Mussolini's control were to be recruited and trained.

Hitler assigned a trusted German diplomat, Rudolf Rahn, as his Ambassador to Mussolini's government, and he was given the additional title of Plenipotentiary of the Reich (*Reichsbevollmächtigter*). As Hitler's personal emissary, he was not only to convey to Hitler Mussolini's never-ending problems and gripes but to keep a close eye on the whole enterprise of this rather inauspicious experiment in political puppetry. Rahn, as we shall see, became one of the main supporters of the peace movement during the last year of the war and played a helpful role behind the scenes in the surrender negotiations.

The real power in North Italy was, of course, in German hands. Not so much in those of the military, who were largely engaged in holding off the Allies farther south, but in the hands of that same ruthless and highly trained instrument of suppression which the Germans used for policing all territories they conquered—the SS.

Long before the fall of Mussolini, in the days when Italy was a full-fledged Axis partner, there had been close collaboration between the German and the Italian secret-police organizations. For this purpose, the Germans had in 1938 placed in their Embassy in Rome several trained and selected SS police and intelligence men whose daily business was to keep in touch with the Fascist secret police. Between the Germans and the Italians there was a steady exchange of experiences in the penetration and crushing of dissidents. There is no doubt also that these German secret-police officials were under orders from Himmler to watch the political moods and look for signs of disaffection. Typical of the SS men in the German Embassy in Rome was their chief, Herbert Kappler, whose name will live in infamy as the perpetrator, on orders from Berlin, of the massacre of three hundred and thirty-five Italians in the Ardeatine Caves in March, 1944, in reprisal for the bombing of a bus full of South Tyrolean Germans who belonged to a police unit.

Of quite a different cut among the German SS in Italy was SS Colonel Eugen Dollmann, who was to figure prominently in the German surrender. Dollmann, after completing his university education in Germany in 1927, had gone to Italy to carry on research in Renaissance history. He remained in Italy earning his living as a translator and writer. Because of his good manners and cultured interests, he found entrée to the aristocratic families of Rome as well as to German aristocratic and clerical circles there. He was an intellectual, highly sophisticated, somewhat snobbish and cynical.

Dollmann had managed to stay clear of military service in Germany when an unexpected opportunity brought him rather suddenly onto the stage of history. In 1937 he went to Germany as guide and interpreter for a group of Italian Fascist youth on a tour of Germany. This was the period of enthusiastic Italo-German cooperation. The high point of the visit was to be a personal reception of the group and an address by the Führer. At the last minute Hitler's interpreter was suddenly taken sick, and Dollmann was asked to step into the breach. He did so well that Hitler commended him, and Himmler, who was also present, asked him to serve as his interpreter during a trip he was going to make to Italy in the fall. On the latter occasion Himmler apparently saw how valuable Dollmann's intimate knowledge of the Italian scene could be. In the future Dollmann was usually the official aide and interpreter to important Nazi visitors to Italy, as well as to Italian officials who went to visit Hitler and Himmler in Germany.

Dollmann hardly filled the bill as a blond Germanic hero. He had long black hair, combed Italian style, and almost effeminate gestures. Himmler, however, sensed that his manners and his ability to make high-level contacts were important for the job at hand. Soon the expert on Renaissance history became Himmler's private diplomat-observer in Rome, though he had not attended the SS training schools and rarely even appeared in Germany except when accompanying Italian dignitaries there. It is said that he seldom wore the SS uniform, aware no doubt that it would be offensive to his Italian aristocratic and clerical friends. He was rapidly promoted and by 1944 had become a colonel (*Standartenführer*) in the SS.

As the situation in Italy changed in 1943 with the fall of Mussolini and the occupation of the larger part of Italy by massive German forces, Dollmann's position became even more important. He had been there before the troops and the run-of-the-mill SS that accompanied them arrived on the scene. He was the man who knew everybody. From having been primarily Himmler's eyes and ears in Rome, he now became a kind of top liaison officer between the Germans and the Italian officials, and the church. There was no longer much need for spying, since the Germans had taken over the place, but there were many touchy relationships to be ironed out between the German High Command and the neo-Fascist government of Mussolini, between the SS and the Italian police. Dollmann seems to have played the middleman with his excellent command of Italian, his diplomatic suaveness and his thorough knowledge of the scene. He gradually got to know Field Marshal Kesselring himself exceedingly well, and soon, in addition to his other duties, he was acting as an intermediary between the two main and sometimes not so cooperative components of the German occupation of Italy—the military and the SS. In short, he was everybody's man, but only in high places, and seems in some measure to have created the functions he had, or to have taken them over by default, rather than to have been assigned them. It is no wonder, then, that later he was also one of the first Germans to appear as emissary to the Allies in Switzerland.

The German occupation forces had had little or no forewarning of Mussolini's ouster by his own Grand Council on July 25, 1943, and a shake-up in their diplomatic and intelligence units in Italy followed. The German Ambassador to Italy, Mackensen, was in fact removed from his job and sent home in disgrace, reportedly for having wired the German Foreign Office two days before Mussolini's fall that "his position and that of Fascism in Italy was firmer than ever." (Dollmann, who had his finger on the pulse, tried to warn Mackensen that all was not well, but Mackensen had his own Italian sources, who assured him that nothing could dislodge Mussolini.)

The Germans naturally did not intend to be taken by surprise again, and to prevent this and to police the Italians was, of course, the job of the SS—with such Italian help as could be mustered. Dollmann fitted well into this picture.

On September 9, 1943, the same day Marshal Badoglio and the King fled Rome to set up a new government in South Italy under Allied sponsorship, two men arrived in Italy from Germany. Their assignment to Italy doubtless was made before the defection of Badoglio and the King was a certainty.

The defection only increased the importance of their mission. The two men were SS-Obergruppenführer Karl Wolff and SS-Gruppenführer Wilhelm Harster. Himmler had been responsible for Wolff's appointment, Kaltenbrunner for Harster's, presumably with Himmler's O.K. *Obergruppenführer*, the rank held by Wolff, was almost the highest rank in the SS hierarchy. Even Kaltenbrunner held no higher rank, and only Himmler, as *Reichsführer*, ranked above Kaltenbrunner and Wolff. Harster, as *Gruppenführer* and as a Commander of the Security Police, was one step below them. In the Nazi system SS ranks were parallel to military ranks, and Wolff was roughly equivalent to a full general of the Army and Harster to lieutenant general.

To supervise all SS activities, both police and military, a position existed in most German-dominated areas which was called the Higher SS and Police Leader (*Höherer SS und Polizeiführer*). Normally, this is what Wolff's title should have been, but he had very special duties. He was too big a man in Himmler's hierarchy to be just another Higher Police Leader. Himmler wanted him to have standing in the eyes of both Mussolini and Kesselring. Accordingly, a new title was created for him, the only one of its kind in the whole Nazi system. If the other bosses of SS and police were Higher SS and Police Leaders, then Wolff would have to be superlative and he was named Highest SS and Police Leader (*Höchster SS und Polizeiführer*) and became Himmler's personal representative in North Italy.

Wolff was responsible directly to Himmler himself and, of course, to the Führer. He was the man who was to safeguard and keep order in an area which, at the time of his arrival in Italy in 1943, stretched from north of Naples to the Brenner Pass. He was to be Mussolini's adviser in police matters as Rahn was Mussolini's adviser in political and diplomatic matters. There is no doubt that he was also to keep a close eye on Mussolini and his Salò government for Himmler's benefit. But Wolff was also to work with Kesselring in coordinating the disposition of his SS forces with those of the Army and to advise and consult with Kesselring in the maintenance of order and the pacification of that part of Italy still held by the Germans.

To do all this, Wolff was given still another title—Plenipotentiary General of the Armed Forces for the Rear Combat Areas of Italy (*Bevollmächtigter General der Wehrmacht für das Rückwärtige Frontgebiet Italiens*)—to add to his title of Highest SS and Police Leader. As the Nazi power dwindled, their titles grew. This new title meant, of course, that if any question of authority between SS police and military forces should arise in the North Italian area, Wolff could act as coordinator. This responsibility of Wolff's was of importance later in the efforts we made to protect Northern Italy from Hitler's scorched-earth policy. Here the Wehrmacht and the SS each had separate special assignments during the German retreat, and Wolff was able to exercise a restraining influence.

Who was this Karl Wolff? Since his official position in Italy combined with his singular personal attributes enabled him to play a major role in the German surrender to come, his powers and the reasons for his presence on the scene are crucial for our story. Before he arrived in Italy in 1943, he had been the Chief of Himmler's personal staff and one of the liaison officers between Himmler and Hitler; that meant between the SS top command and Hitler's headquarters. He was also for some time the liaison officer between Himmler and Ribbentrop; i.e., between the SS and the Foreign Office. He was not concerned with the organization and administration of the SS itself. He was not in its chain of command which ran on one side from Himmler directly to Kaltenbrunner, as head of the RSHA or combined SS police organs, and on the other from Himmler to the chiefs of the military (*Waffen*) SS and other subsidiary SS organizations. Wolff was thus not primarily either a commander of troops or a police official. Rather, he was a kind of diplomat or political adviser to the SS leaders. He had unobtrusively slipped into very high places as a man who could manage other men by dint of his personal qualities and an ability to deal with people. Apparently he could soothe ruffled tempers and, as a result, found himself a special berth in the Nazi constellation of temperamental and violent personalities, a sort of minister without portfolio. He was naturally resented by the more typical Nazi and SS types. Kaltenbrunner and Schellenberg in particular disliked him and were also envious of him.

Before coming to Italy, he had broken one rule of the SS which Himmler could not lightly forgive. He was married and had four children, but early in 1943 he had decided to marry another woman, a countess by marriage, and he needed a divorce to do so. He went to Himmler with his request (as every marriage and divorce in the SS, even in lower SS ranks, required Himmler's approval). Himmler turned him down; his own Chief of Staff, his personal adjutant, could not be allowed to set such an example for the rest of the SS; an exception could not be made for him. But Wolff persevered, and he then did something which riled Himmler more than the request for a divorce. Without a word to Himmler, Wolff went to Hitler and asked for his permission. Hitler gave it and that was final. So Wolff got divorced and married the countess. According to many accounts, this incident was one of the reasons Himmler sent him to Italy. Apparently the rift was not long in healing. A top SS official was needed in Italy, and while there were other, more experienced SS administrators who might have qualified for the job, Wolff had the rank and the personal qualifications for it and Hitler apparently liked him. For Hitler, Mussolini's fall had been a traumatic experience. To calm the Führer required a man on the spot he trusted. Thus, a number of problems were solved at once in this assignment.

Shortly after Wolff arrived in Italy, he put Dollmann on his staff. It was Dollmann and the German diplomats at the Vatican who introduced Wolff to the main ecclesiastical authorities in Italy whom he seemed anxious to meet. The churchmen in turn, as soon as they realized that this SS General was no ogre, began to funnel their requests to him, usually through Dollmann, for lenient treatment of their colleagues or contacts who had fallen into the hands of the Gestapo.

Of the wild notions current in SS circles in Berlin, one was that the Pope and the main members of the Vatican Curia should be taken from Rome and held hostage by the Germans if the Allies tried to force the Germans out of Rome. Allegedly one of Wolff's first acts as he got in touch with the Vatican was an assurance that this would not happen. Later, on May 10, 1944, he had an audience with the Pope at his own request, having given evidence of his good faith by releasing from jail certain prominent Italians whom the Gestapo had arrested and whom the Vatican wished to help. The audience reputedly was arranged by Dollmann and the German Ambassador to the Vatican, Ernst von Weizsaecker. After the war Wolff wrote briefly of this interview in an Italian magazine, and various other accounts of it have appeared in print, written by persons who were not present but claim to have learned of the course of the interview from churchmen close to the Pope.

Here is Wolff's bland description of his interview, as translated:

> His Holiness Pius XII had been informed by cardinals and bishops of the way I carried out my duties, my efforts to avoid pointless harshness, and my efforts toward shortening the war. He then had me invited to come to an audience with him, provided this would not involve too many difficulties in connection with my position. And thus, early in May, 1944, Pius XII received me in private audience. The conversation, which was cordial, lasted an hour, and was couched in terms of complete frankness. On this occasion, His Holiness showed an astonishing familiarity with the most secret circumstances and the most minor problems. During the course of this meeting—an unforgettable one for me—I declared my readiness to do whatever was in my power for the rapid conclusion to the war, should an honorable opportunity present itself.*

Wolff was to see the Pope again to explore the possibilities of an armistice on the Italian front; however, after the May interview he went to Berlin and then to Hitler's headquarters in East Prussia, and before he returned to Italy the Allies had already taken Rome. He therefore never saw the Pope again.

To return to the military situation, after the fall of Rome on June 4, 1944, the Germans pulled back gradually to their prepared line of defense, the Gothic Line, north of Florence, fighting rear-guard actions all

---

* *Tempo* (Milan), XIII, No. 8, February 24, 1951.

the way and making every inch north of Rome costly to the Allies, who finally entered Florence itself on August 4, 1944. Another series of Allied attacks in the fall breached the Gothic Line, and by the end of the year the Allies had reached a point just south of Bologna, where they then dug in for the winter. The Germans held the industrial northern rectangle of Italy, including the major cities of Genoa, Milan and Turin.

The Allied Mediterranean command, still based at Caserta, outside Naples, saw some changes at the end of the year. Sir Henry Maitland Wilson, Supreme Allied Commander, was transferred to Washington as Chief British Military Representative with the Combined Chiefs of Staff. Field Marshal Sir Harold Alexander took his place as Supreme Commander. General Mark W. Clark succeeded Alexander as Commander-in-Chief of the Allied armies in Italy. Under him were General Lucien Truscott, commanding the American Fifth Army, and General Richard McCreery at the head of the British Eighth. The Allied armies had been depleted by seven divisions (three United States and four French) earlier in the year to bolster the landings in Southern France which followed the invasion of Normandy. Allied forces now consisted of seventeen divisions and some additional combat units and brigades, representing many nationalities besides American and British and including some Italian units (100,000 men) we had rearmed and trained to fight alongside our own troops. The Allies had almost complete control of the air. Field Marshal Alexander described the aims of the campaign being prepared for the spring of 1945 in these words:

> First of all, I was to ensure that the present front was solidly held; secondly, to do my utmost, by means of such limited offensive operations as might be possible, and by measures of deception, to contain the German forces now in Italy and prevent their withdrawal to other fronts; and thirdly, to take advantage of any withdrawal or weakening of the enemy forces. These were modest aims, and appeared to limit me to a mere offensive-defensive, but I already considered that in spite of the reduction of my forces, I might yet be able to do something more drastic and decisive.*

* *The Italian Campaign, 12th December 1944 to 2nd May 1945. A report to the combined Chiefs of Staff by the Supreme Allied Commander Mediterranean Field Marshal the Viscount Alexander of Tunis* (London: His Majesty's Stationery Office, 1951), p. 32.

On the enemy side, Marshal Kesselring was now in command of the entire Italian front up to the Alps. German Army Group C (Southwest) under Kesselring was made up of the German Tenth and Fourteenth Armies under Generals Herr and Lemelsen, comprising twenty-three German divisions plus the so-called Army Liguria, consisting of four Italian divisions. This army had been raised by Marshal Graziani, Mussolini's Armed Forces Minister, as Mussolini's contribution to the German effort. They had been trained in Germany and then returned to Italy in October, 1944. According to a German report, the men deserted after their return in numbers ranging from ten to twenty-five per cent per division. Their officers complained to the Germans that the men were insufficiently armed and were not combat-ready. Maybe the Germans didn't want a too well-trained and too well-armed Italian combat force in their midst. However, in October, 1944, Mussolini wrote an anguished letter to Kesselring asking what had happened to the Italian divisions that had been trained in Germany. "What are they doing? Why are they not used? Why are the enemy armies using the people of five continents to attack Italy, while the Italians, the best Italians, are not allowed to contribute to her defense?"[*]

These were the German forces under Kesselring facing the Allies. In addition to the forces deployed on the fighting front itself, there were substantial forces under General Wolff's command whose task was to fight the partisans and to maintain order in the rear of the fighting front.

The motley components of Wolff's police army are worth enumerating, since they show how the Germans collected the pro-Nazi riffraff of all the countries they had invaded (those who were "ethnically" acceptable to them) and tried to organize them into SS-type blood-brotherhood fighting organizations. Wolff had, first of all, about 150,000 Italians organized into the National Republican Guard; in addition, the so-called Mobile Black Brigades, and one SS grenadier division, the 29th, as well as lesser legions, flotillas and brigades of Italian nationals. Beyond this, he had an SS division made up of ethnic Germans (*Volksdeutsche*) from the Alpine regions of Italy that also included some Spaniards left over from the Blue Division which had fought alongside the Germans in Russia, Franco's contribution to that campaign. And besides, there were an SS division of Czechs, another of Slovaks, and some

---

[*] F. W. Deakin, *The Brutal Friendship* (New York: Harper, 1963), p. 732.

battalions of Ukrainians and other Russian anti-Soviets, who had joined with the Germans in Russia and come west.

After the fall of Rome in June, 1944, two men were assigned to Kesselring's staff who later figured prominently in the eventual surrender. Looking at their courageous and independent acts in the last days of the war, one must single them out as the chief exceptions in that lengthy roster of subservient and equivocating commanders whom I mentioned earlier.

One was General Hans Roettiger, who became Kesselring's Chief of Staff the very day Rome fell. Largely because of disagreements with Hitler over the conduct of the war in Russia, he had been placed on inactive service and was sitting around at his home in Württemberg during the spring of 1944 with no commission and no assignment.

At the same time that Roettiger joined Kesselring's staff, a new commander was appointed as chief of the German Air Force in Italy. This was General Max Ritter von Pohl, a Bavarian of noble descent and a professional flier who, like many of the top officers in the Luftwaffe, saw the handwriting on the wall at an early date. With the destruction of the major striking power of the Luftwaffe by the end of 1943 and the absolute superiority of the Allies in the air over the major battle fronts, it is not surprising that the Luftwaffe officers became discouraged about the war's outcome before their colleagues on the ground. On the other hand, von Pohl's stand shows him to have been possessed of independence of mind and moral courage. He might have done nothing. Instead, his outspoken efforts in favor of taking secret steps to end the war in Italy invigorated the men who were in a better position than he to arrange a full-scale surrender.

To set the stage for the account of the surrender negotiations, we need now only to indicate where the main participants were located by the beginning of 1945. General Wolff and his staff had taken up quarters on the shore of the Lake of Garda, where Mussolini had chosen in 1943 to establish his neo-Fascist Republic of Salò and where the German Embassy of Ambassador Rahn had been functioning ever since. Clustered along the lake in requisitioned hotels and villas, this dwindling remnant of Fascism and the chief representatives of Nazi Germany assigned to work with it were all housed in the shadow of the Alps— Rahn and Wolff at Fasano, with offices in neighboring Gardone, while Mussolini and some of his ministers lived and worked at Gargnano and at Salò. Working headquarters of the SS was at Verona, where Wolff had an office and where General Harster, the SS Police Chief, was stationed. To carry out its police and intelligence work in the area for which it was responsible, the SS had established large units in Genoa, Milan and Turin. The SS inspector for this area, Colonel Walter Rauff, plays a role at the end for a number of reasons. Milan, the major city in North Italy and the most important Italian industrial center, is only an hour's drive from Switzerland. The German threat to devastate North Italy was chiefly directed toward the industrial and economic complex in and around Milan, and it was here in December of 1944 that Mussolini made his last public appearance and threatened the Milanese with the wrath of the Germans. As the civil authority collapsed in the area, Cardinal Schuster of Milan was to become the person to whom Germans and Italians alike could turn in their attempts to prevent a holocaust in Italy. In Wolff's own attempt to avoid unnecessary bloodshed and destruction in the area, he gave Rauff the job of maintaining contact with the Cardinal. Both Mussolini and Graziani in their last attempts to save themselves also turned to the Cardinal.

Being acquainted with the leading personalities and their assignments on both the Allied and the enemy sides, the reader now knows much more about them than we in Bern did as the surrender discussions began. To us in early 1945, Wolff, Harster, Dollmann and their subordinates were only names, principals in a chain of command. In our minds all of them shared the black reputation of the SS. We saw them to a great extent through the eyes of our friends in the Italian resistance, who feared them and hated them and had frequently suffered at their hands. Generals such as Roettiger and Pohl we had not yet even heard of.

6

An Uncertain Beginning

By the end of 1944 the Allied invasions through the Normandy beach-head and the Mediterranean had brought about the liberation of France, except for a few pockets here and there of isolated Nazi resistance. The Allies had cleared the French side of the Swiss border from Geneva to Basel, and this had enabled me to establish an OSS post in the small Alsatian village of Hegenheim, near the Rhine and not far from the Swiss frontier. I used to visit this post from time to time to meet with the intelligence chiefs of the American Army Groups operating in liberated France, particularly those of the Twelfth Army Group under General Omar Bradley, and the Sixth Army under General Jacob Devers. American intelligence officers, having experienced a nasty surprise at the Battle of the Bulge, were vitally interested to get any information we had gathered about German troop movements.

In this area of Alsace the Germans had retreated across the Rhine, except around the Colmar pocket, and were holding out in the Black Forest not many miles away. From time to time they would lob a shell across the river to pick off Allied military convoys, or perhaps just to let us know they were still there. To be on the safe side we generally shut off our car lights as we drove at night over the Alsatian roads.

On February 25, 1945, a Sunday, and a particularly cold and sunless day, Gaevernitz and I went to Hegenheim to meet General Gene Harrison, the Chief Intelligence Officer of the American Sixth Army. He had told us he had a special problem to discuss with us. During the confusion of the fighting around the Colmar pocket, as the Germans were being driven out of Alsace, an American Army truck carrying a safe filled with highly important military papers had mysteriously disappeared. The General asked our help in recovering it. In those days we made it a point never to be out of radio or telephone communication with our Bern headquarters. While we were working on this problem, an urgent message reached me from my office. Major Waibel, of Swiss Military Intelligence, wanted to see Gaevernitz and me in Lucerne that same evening.

I knew Waibel would not have requested that this message be relayed across the border to me unless it was of some importance. After assuring General Harrison that we were on the trail of his lost safe, we drove to Basel and caught the first train to Lucerne.*

For many months we had been working closely with Waibel in matters of mutual concern, and a strong bond both of friendship and professional trust and understanding had grown up between us. Naturally we shared a common desire to know what the Germans were planning.

Waibel, Gaevernitz and I had dinner together in a quiet restaurant near Lake Lucerne which served excellent trout. Waibel came to the point immediately. That day he had been talking with an Italian and a Swiss, and he believed that what they had to say would interest us. It was another peace feeler from the Italian front. I must admit that my immediate reaction was not enthusiastic. This approach had many of the earmarks of earlier feelers from Italian industrialists who were concerned about the German scorched-earth policy. The name of the Italian, which meant nothing to us at the time, was Baron Luigi Parilli, a businessman. The Swiss was Professor Max Husmann. He was a man of very different character, a schoolmaster who ran a well-known private school on the Zugerberg, not far from Lucerne. One of Baron Parilli's relatives had attended Husmann's school, and this was the slender link that had brought him to Parilli's attention and now into this adventure.

Early in January, Parilli had written Husmann asking his help in procuring a Swiss visa if it was possible. It was possible to the tune of ten thousand Swiss francs, a deposit to guarantee that he would stay in Switzerland for only a limited time. This Husmann provided. But one needed not only a Swiss visa to get into Switzerland. At that time German

* The safe was soon found with its contents intact, half sunk in an Alsatian stream. The thief had shown no interest in the safe and never even bothered to try to open it. All he had wanted was the truck.

permission was necessary to leave Italy, and we knew it was usually granted only when one had excellent connections with the Germans or could perform something useful for them in taking the trip.

Husmann, hearing what Parilli had to say after his arrival, had come to Waibel, whom he had known before, and Waibel had turned to us. It was a matter, Waibel explained, which could not be handled by the Swiss, but only by the Allies. At the same time, he assured us, the Swiss had a very deep and natural interest in any project which brought an early peace and would spare North Italy from destruction. Switzerland's economic health was closely bound with that of North Italy. The devastation of Italian industry and power plants and any impoverishment of the area would be a serious economic blow to the Swiss, particularly if it affected the port of Genoa, through which vital foodstuffs and supplies were imported into Switzerland.

While the Swiss no longer had reason to fear a German invasion, they faced the possibility that thousands of defeated Nazi and Fascist troops would be driven up against the Swiss border and seek asylum there, or passage through Switzerland, rather than surrender. The Swiss already had all the refugees they could care for, and they wished at all cost to avoid a new flood of them. Waibel felt he was justified in helping to the limit any serious move toward a peaceful surrender, as this was in his country's interest, but he acted strictly unofficially.

What did Parilli want? What was he offering? For the details Waibel suggested we talk directly to the two men who would be available that evening. I considered this for a moment and decided it would be premature to entangle myself personally with an unknown emissary who might have little to offer and was acting on his own—or, worse, was the agent in a German attempt to penetrate our mission. Gaevernitz was ideally suited for the task. He had been working very closely with me for a considerable time, knew my views and methods and was eminently capable of forming an accurate opinion on the genuineness of peace probes of this kind. After all, he had been dealing with this type of problem for many months. I thanked Waibel and caught the next train back to Bern.

Waibel took Gaevernitz to a room in the Hotel Schweizerhof in Lucerne where the two men, Parilli and Husmann, were staying. What they had to say and the impression they made on him Gaevernitz reported to me the next day when he returned to Bern. At first glance the two men had struck him as rather unlikely contacts to the armed forces

of Field Marshal Kesselring and the black-booted SS in Italy. The Italian
Baron was a short, slight, bald gentleman with ingratiating manners—as
Gaevernitz put it, a bit like the keeper of a small Italian hotel who is trying to persuade you to take your dinner there. The Professor was a rather
talkative gentleman, given to sweeping generalities and a little pompous
in the delivery thereof. During the pauses in Parilli's account the Professor lectured on the themes of peace and international understanding,
which were as dear to our hearts as to his, but to which the session in the
hotel room in Lucerne did not seem to be bringing us any closer. Parilli
hedged when pressed for the names of the people he was representing.
He kept on the theme of the coming horror of German vengeance in
North Italy, and related his shock when he had heard Mussolini's last
public address in Milan in December, when the aging dictator had
threatened the faithless Italians with all kinds of doom at the hands of
the Germans for their disloyalty to Fascism. This, Parilli declared, had set
him frantically looking for a way to avoid the impending disaster. He had
an inspiration that he had been chosen to find the solution, to be the intervening "angel" for North Italy. He was now a man with a mission.

Finally Parilli began to elaborate on the idea that all was not as it
might seem with the SS in Italy. It was the SS, not the German Army, that
was capable of some independent thought and action. It did not favor the
scorched-earth policy and could be used to sabotage it—certain people in
the SS, anyway. Who? How did Parilli know this? Gaevernitz kept pressing for names, for some proof of what Parilli claimed. Finally the Baron
mentioned his close relationship (which by now had extended over considerable time) with a young SS captain (*Obersturmführer*), a certain
Guido Zimmer, who had been chief of counterespionage in the SS intelligence office in Genoa where Parilli had first met him. Recently Zimmer
had been transferred to Milan, and Parilli, who also had offices in Milan,
had continued to see him. Zimmer, despite his membership in the SS, was
a devout Catholic, according to Parilli, who himself ranked in the Vatican order as a Knight of Malta. In talks with Zimmer, Parilli had learned
that Zimmer was deeply troubled by the possibility that the SS might be
ordered by Berlin to scorch the Italian earth. Zimmer, somewhat of an
aesthete and an intellectual, was moved by a desire to save the art and
religious treasures of Italy. Parilli was convinced of Zimmer's sincerity
because Zimmer had on occasion protected Italians whom the Gestapo
had orders to arrest. The talks between Parilli and Zimmer had finally
reached a point at which Zimmer, prompted to some extent by Parilli's

anxiety to act in the cause of saving North Italy, had carefully broached the whole problem to a top SS official whom he knew, Colonel Eugen Dollmann. To Zimmer's great relief Dollmann had listened to him with apparent sympathy, and had said that he would pass Zimmer's views to his chief, General Karl Wolff, commander of all SS units in Italy. Parilli did not know what had happened after that. He and Zimmer, he said, had developed the plan of trying to get to Switzerland and, through Husmann, to search out a connection with the Allies. On his own, Parilli had applied to the Italian authorities for an exit permit for a trip to Switzerland for "economic reasons." This had been approved by the Germans. Somewhere in the German SS command the word must have been given to let Parilli take his trip.

Gaevernitz was not overly impressed by all this. A lowly SS captain did not seem to be the key to the capitulation of the German armies in Italy, an objective which Gaevernitz had exhaustively followed up at a far higher level on the Western Front in the fall of 1944. Zimmer seemed to be a misfit in the SS, a man who, at a rather late date, discovered that he had thrown in his lot with the wrong party. As for Dollmann, Gaevernitz had once met him years before and the name aroused his interest— that of Karl Wolff even more so. But were Parilli and Zimmer important enough to influence either of these men to work for the capitulation of the German armies? Gaevernitz was skeptical. He thanked Parilli for informing him of his contacts and his good intentions and said that a talk with Dollmann, or Wolff, or preferably Marshall Kesselring would be worth while. Beyond that one could not go at the moment.

Gaevernitz left more or less convinced that this was the last we would see of Baron Parilli. Waibel, who had a further talk with Parilli and Husmann the next day, was a bit more optimistic and he gave Parilli a password to be used with the Swiss border guards if he should return. As a high officer of the Swiss Intelligence Service and a member of the General Staff, Waibel had authority to instruct the border police to let persons who were of interest to Swiss intelligence cross into Switzerland on giving a prearranged password. With his usual foresight Waibel thought of the possibility that the negotiators might wish to return to Switzerland, and that any incident at the border might risk the security of the enterprise and any publicity might cause a fatal setback.

After making his report to me on his meeting with Parilli and Husmann, Gaevernitz went off on a skiing trip, as we all felt that we had reached a breather and that it would be some time before we heard from the men again. We made a report of these meetings and dropped them into our "Peace Feelers" file, which had been growing fat in the last few months but still seemed rather futile.

But we were wrong. Only five days had passed since the meeting when we had an urgent call from Waibel. Parilli had returned to Switzerland. Not only that; with him were the two SS officers, Colonel Eugen Dollmann and Captain Guido Zimmer, from Milan. Waibel had quietly arranged for their admission to Switzerland and would find safe quarters for them in Lugano. Their presence in Switzerland could be kept secret. They would have to return to Italy in a few days. The rest was up to us.

I did not feel that the affair yet looked promising enough to call Gaevernitz back from Davos. Besides, it struck me as a good idea to try out another intermediary on these emissaries, one who so far had had nothing to do with this particular operation. The man I had in mind was Paul Blum, a trusted member of my Bern staff. He had proved in the past to be an excellent judge of people. He would come to the scene with no preconceptions, and would give me a fresh point of view on how he sized up Parilli, Husmann and Dollmann and their project. Paul had some other business to take care of in the Lugano area. An Italian agent had just been picked up in Campione and had to be interrogated. So the trip would not be wasted, whatever the Germans were up to.

For the meeting Waibel had reserved the private dining room on the upper floor of a Lugano restaurant, Ristorante Biaggi, which was normally used for meetings of the local Rotary Club, an ironic touch considering the clandestine business that was to be taken up on this occasion. The room had a low timbered ceiling and a fireplace, and was entered through Gothic archways. Its carved wooden furniture and the embossed metal plates on the wall were products of native Ticino craftsmen, all heavy and somber and providing a fit meeting place for our purposes.

On the afternoon of Saturday, March 3rd, Waibel had gathered the participants in the *sala*. Besides Parilli, Dollmann and Zimmer, Professor Husmann was again present. Waibel himself had to go on urgent business to Zurich and left a Swiss senior lieutenant, Fred Rothpletz, in charge of the visitors. Paul's interrogation of the Italian at Campione took longer than expected, and thus the strange group was left on its own resources for several hours. The Germans had been informed by Waibel that an emissary from my Bern office would meet with them. This was, after all, why they had come. But until my emissary arrived there was no real business which could be discussed. To the curious they would appear to be just a group of tourists who had happened to choose this well-known Lugano restaurant. They ate and drank and discussed the weather and the scenery and other noncommittal subjects, such as trips each of them had taken in the pleasant days before the war. Then, over the table of cold meats and half-empty wineglasses, when the conversation began to lag, Professor Husmann, who never lost a chance to make a speech, stepped into the breach. He took up the war-and-peace issue and, entirely on his own, switched from the role of professor to that of international politician and negotiator. Since no one from my office was yet present, I only learned what he said and did from later accounts, but, knowing the man and having heard him often, I can well imagine the impassioned lecture he gave on the total defeat which Germany obviously faced at the hands of the unshakable Alliance between the Western democracies and Soviet Russia. The Germans, he said, were merely deluding themselves. If they had any notions, as Hitler did, that they could break the Alliance, they were wrong. There was only one way out for the Germans: surrender. . . . unconditional surrender. Dollmann, at whom this tirade was directed, seemed to be somewhat taken aback by Husmann's blunt remarks. When he recovered, he told Husmann that was all very well, but that any surrender by German generals without orders or permission from Hitler would be treason, and that Kesselring—if it was Kesselring whom Husmann was talking about—would so view it. This mention of treason had an effect on Husmann like a red flag on a bull. He charged. Parilli, who had placed his hopes on Husmann as a mediator, rather than as a protagonist, became alarmed at Husmann's vigorous attack.

Dollmann wrote later that this speech of the Professor's could easily have been published verbatim as a lost oration of Cicero's. Husmann's theme was that Europe was at the mercy of a mad dictator, Hitler; that the survival of society was at stake. To the men now gathered around the table secretly in Lugano, the thought that a betrayal was involved was not worthy of consideration.

The conversation calmed down somewhat after this, but Husmann, though not acting on any advice from us, had cleared the air. Dollmann may very well have thought Husmann was speaking for me and was empowered to do so. His message was ours, although we probably would not have thrown it on the table like a gauntlet at this stage of the meeting. But its effect was good.

It was after four o'clock when Paul Blum arrived. As he entered the room, he was to face the problem that all Allied representatives faced each time we met with the Germans during the later negotiations. Should he shake hands with them? Paul's decision was: if I am willing to speak to a man and want to get his candid views, I see no point in refusing him my hand. He shook the hands of the Germans.

Dollmann, with his dark look, his long black hair combed straight back and curling a little over his ears, struck him as a slippery customer who no doubt knew much more than he was telling. Captain Zimmer, obviously in a very subordinate position to Dollmann, hardly opened his mouth. He was good-looking, clean-cut, not the way one pictures the typical SS officer. The conversation was carried on in French, in which all were fluent. It was mainly between Paul and Dollmann.

Paul was very conscious of the delicacy of the situation. He knew that he would be looked upon by the Germans as a spokesman for the Allies. It could easily be a trap, after all, to drive a wedge between the Soviets and the West, to throw the Allied armies in Italy off guard by talking of peace just as they were planning their major spring offensive to end the war. Paul carefully avoided any mention of military matters. On his way to the meeting he had jotted down what he intended to say in opening the meeting. This was how he began:

"The material and moral destruction in Europe caused by this war is so gigantic that the Allies will need the help of every available man of good will in the work of reconstruction. Everyone who helps shorten the war gives us proof of his good will. . . ."

This set the tone for what followed. At one point only did he break into English, as he told me later. Dollmann had asked him if the Allies would be willing to treat with Himmler if Himmler backed a separate action for peace in North Italy. To this Paul suddenly blurted out in good American, "Not a Chinaman's chance."

Paul's instructions from me were to find out whom these men really represented; did they impress him as serious? I did not intend to get into an argument about peace terms. We were bound by the policy of unconditional surrender. That was what we wanted. This was no time for negotiations. What did the Germans have to offer?

Paul learned that Dollmann was in touch with General Wolff, Chief of the SS in Italy. Dollmann did not say that he represented Wolff in what he was doing, but he said that he was attached to Wolff's staff. He would try to persuade Wolff to come personally to Switzerland to continue the talks if there was any hope of establishing contact with the Allies. No claims were made that he spoke for Kesselring, nor did he promise to produce him.

Before the meeting I had told Paul that I felt it was high time, if we were to continue the conversations with the German emissaries, that we should have concrete evidence both of their seriousness and of their authority. I had given Paul a slip of paper on which two names were written which he was to hand to Dollmann before the meeting was over. The names were those of two Italian patriots, members of the Italian underground with whom I had been working across the lines for some time. One was Ferruccio Parri; the other was Antonio Usmiani. Parri, as I have explained earlier, was one of the heads of the Italian resistance. Usmiani had been doing military intelligence work for me in North Italy and had rendered gallant services. Both had been caught by the SS police and both were being held in prison. Parri, I understood, was held in Verona, and Usmiani was jailed in Turin. I proposed, therefore, that General Wolff, if he wanted to see me, should give evidence of the seriousness of his intentions by releasing these two prisoners to me in Switzerland. In asking for Parri I realized that I was asking for probably the most important Italian prisoner the SS held. My friends in the Italian resistance had put great pressure on me to try to arrange his liberation, and various attempts to free him by the Italian underground had been made; all had been unsuccessful. I knew that in asking for his release I was asking for something that would be very difficult for Wolff to do, and in fact I was putting the stakes high—almost too high, as it later turned out. Yet if these men could be released, the seriousness of General Wolff's intentions would be amply demonstrated. Also, I had deliberately chosen two men who were imprisoned in different places in Italy to test out the extent of Wolff's authority.

Paul at no time had promised that the release of these men committed me to meet Wolff or other German emissaries; but it was implicit in this request, made in my name, that I certainly would not do so unless I had solid evidence of Wolff's seriousness and of his ability to get things done. Paul later told me that when all this was explained to Dollmann he was obviously startled at the thought of their giving up a prisoner as valuable as Parri. But after he got over his initial shock Dollmann agreed to do everything in his power to meet the demands. We would hear from him again in a few days, he assured Paul.

When I told Gaevernitz later what I had done, he thought it would be difficult for Wolff to comply because of Parri's prominence. Also, it was almost certain that Mussolini and probably Hitler knew of Parri's arrest. "Don't worry," I told him. "We can always ask for less." Both of us were of the opinion that we had probably seen the last of Dollmann. Paul wasn't so sure. He did not particularly like Dollmann but nevertheless was impressed with his earnestness. Anyway, if we had called the German's bluff and put an end to proceedings which were not serious, I need have no regrets; and at least I had done what I could to free Parri, who had bravely fought Hitler in Italy.

Had we known at that time the state of mind of the German chieftains in Italy, we would have been less surprised at what came next. Many of them were willing to pay a price to achieve a sure line of communication with the Allies, but they knew they were risking their lives in going after it and they were deeply split among themselves.

The three representative components of German power in North Italy—the Army, the SS and the diplomats—had little reason to like or trust each other. And within the ranks of any of these three groups everyone had to expect (certainly after the July attempt on Hitler's life) that his closest associates out of fear or loyalty to Hitler might betray to the Gestapo the least sign of wavering from Hitler's order to fight to the finish.

Even with the historical records we now have, it is difficult to reconstruct an accurate account of how the idea of a separate surrender grew and how the various partners to it gradually approached each other. There was no doubt something in the atmosphere of Italy that nurtured it. The people involved were remote from the main European fighting front and from the German heartland. Then there was the mollifying influence of the church. All this, combined with the particular character of the men who happened to be on the scene (men I have already mentioned, like Roettiger, Pohl, Rahn, Wolff and others), must account for it. Kesselring himself, who held the key to military action, remained the great question mark to us as well as to his associates. But even he was no bitter-ender by conviction.

Eventually Wolff was the prime mover; yet for some time he kept his counsel, waited and watched and let the threads gather in his hands. Reportedly he had told the Pope in May, 1944, that he was ready to commit his own life to the cause of peace. Few knew he had seen the Pope, and almost no one knew what had been said between them. One of the few was Dollmann, and it was the ubiquitous Dollmann who, knowing

Wolff's frame of mind, seems to have been the eyes and ears of Wolff in sounding out like-minded, potential supporters in a conspiracy for peace.

When Dollmann, according to a report he wrote after the war, was in Florence in July of 1944, he received an invitation to visit the commander of the German Air Force in Italy, General von Pohl, at his headquarters at Monsummano, outside Florence. Since Pohl, like Dollmann, came from Munich, where he had been acquainted with Dollmann's mother, Dollmann thought the invitation was purely social. To his surprise, Pohl opened up at once with a hard-hitting statement on the absurdity of continuing the war and the hopelessness of convincing Hitler that it had to be stopped before Germany was smashed to bits or Sovietized. Dollmann soon realized that Pohl was not just sounding off, dangerous as it was, but had chosen to talk to him for a purpose. The idea, which was really the key to the whole surrender in Italy, was clearly formulated by Pohl on this occasion, almost a year before the event. He told Dollmann that an agreement would have to be made with the Western powers without Hitler's knowledge. The Army, with its cast-iron notions of loyalty to the Führer's oath, could not be called on to take any action. There remained only the SS as the one organization left with sufficient authority to carry out negotiations to stop the war, yet Himmler would be an unsuitable and unacceptable spokesman. Therefore—and here Pohl turned to Dollmann with a question—wasn't there an energetic and uncompromised leader in the SS who could approach the Allies? Pohl quickly added that he was far from approving the political coloration of the SS, but this seemed to be the only way out. Dollmann said that Wolff was the man, whereupon Pohl expressed a desire to meet him as soon as possible. Dollmann brought Wolff and Pohl together in September, 1944. The meeting was secret. From then on, Wolff knew that he had Pohl behind him in whatever he might try to do—a fact of some importance during the climactic days to come.

Dollmann was also Wolff's contact to the churchmen of North Italy, to the Cardinals of Milan, Turin and Venice and to the bishops of the smaller cities. Dollmann knew of the visit made to me by Cardinal Schuster's secretary, Don Bicchierai. So did Wolff. They watched and saw that nothing came of it. It was Dollmann to whom Zimmer came with his story of Parilli's eagerness to go to Switzerland, but, as we later learned, Dollmann had met Parilli twice before this on social occasions. He already knew that Parilli was dreaming up his one-man campaign to save the Po Valley from destruction. All this Wolff undoubtedly also knew. But he was not ready to act, not ready to commit himself before he had found a connection on the opposing side high enough to warrant taking any risks.

As Wolff told us much later, he had believed in the possibility of a compromise peace until the beginning of 1945. He believed it because he thought that Hitler was really going to produce the new weapons he had been boasting about. After the failure of the Ardennes offensive (the Battle of the Bulge, in December, 1944–January, 1945), Wolff heard that the Germans had almost no air support. For the first time he realized that Hitler's promises were lies. He went to Hitler's headquarters on February 6, 1945, on one of his regular trips, but this time he made it his business to find out whether or not there were any secret weapons forthcoming. No one would give him a straight answer, and he saw that it was all a delusion. He persuaded Himmler to take him to Hitler, telling him he was going to propose to Hitler that the war be stopped before it was too late. Himmler warned him against bringing up the subject, but Wolff said there was no other way open to him.

According to his later account, he had hoped to see Hitler alone, as he was usually able to do, but this time Ribbentrop was present and Wolff couldn't shake him. He talked to Hitler in front of Ribbentrop about the need for Germany to find a way out of the situation. Hitler remained unruffled by the proposal, didn't say no, but didn't actually give Wolff permission to do anything. At that time, of course, Wolff still had no contact with the Allies. Ribbentrop apparently agreed with Wolff in front of Hitler, and said that he would look for a channel on his own.

Two days after Wolff returned to Italy from Berlin—this was in mid-February, 1945—he called his commanding officers together (both the SS and the military) and told them that he wanted to be kept informed personally of any possibilities of contacts to the English and Americans. If any were of sufficient importance, he said, he would deal with them himself. He evidently intended to make the widest use of the fact that Hitler had not said no.

At this same meeting, having just received in Berlin a basic briefing regarding the scorched-earth program for Italy, Wolff was obliged to explain its workings to his subordinates. Not to have done so would have brought Wolff under suspicion of opposing the Führer's decrees. Wolff got around the matter, however, by instructing his commanders that no act of sabotage or destruction whatever was to be carried out without his personal consent.*

At the same time, one other man of highest rank in the German establishment in Italy was thinking about surrender and was perhaps as ready to act as Wolff. This was the German Ambassador Rahn, Hitler's personal emissary to Mussolini. While Rahn commanded no troops himself, and had none of Wolff's police powers or military titles, he was closer to Kesselring than Wolff was and had known him far longer. And Kesselring was the man who had the real power to stop the fighting. Rahn had been in Africa until just before the final capitulation of the Afrika Korps, when Kesselring was in command of the Air Force there, and he had been in Rome with him. Rahn felt that since he was a diplomat, and not a militarist or a secret policeman, the Allies should not object to dealing with him.

After Wolff moved up to quarters on the Lake of Garda in the summer of 1944, he became a neighbor of Rahn's and the two men carefully sounded each other out. Rahn should probably be given some of the credit for influencing Wolff's way of thinking. In any event, there is no doubt that by the beginning of 1945 Wolff knew he had Rahn on his side in any effort he might make to secure a peace in Italy. Rahn himself may not have realized how ready Wolff was to take over the operation. He undoubtedly saw himself as the prime actor in what might come. He also had his agents in Switzerland. One of them had come into Switzerland in February, 1945, and had dropped the rumor that Kesselring was anxious to be kept advised of any Allied peace feelers. There were others.** We know that Rahn was disappointed when the initiative for peace passed into Wolff's hands. He continued to cooperate, however, and will play a role in our story often. Wolff was clever enough to keep him posted on developments and to draw on his advice.

All of this, which at the time was entirely unknown to us in Bern, explains why Dollmann and Zimmer turned up with Parilli in Lugano

---

* The basic plan was that destruction of heavy industry, power plants and port installations were to be carried out by units of Wehrmacht engineers under Wolff's command shortly before the Wehrmacht relinquished each major area. Destruction of bridges and tunnels was to be carried out by the fighting forces under Kesselring as they retreated.

** A certain Dr. Gumpert, a member of Rahn's staff in Italy, had twice been sent to Switzerland by Rahn in 1944 for "reasons of health." The real purpose was on the third of March, only six days after Parilli had talked to Gaevernitz in Lucerne. Wolff and his friends, who had been watching and waiting, apparently thought they had hit upon the channel to the Allies they wanted, despite our reticent handling of Parilli.

Parilli had returned to Italy from Lucerne on February 27th. He had gone immediately to Zimmer, his mentor in the SS, who was not stationed in Milan. When he reported what had happened in Lucerne, Zimmer got hold of Dollmann, who came to Milan the following day and talked to Parilli himself. Dollmann thought the contact of such importance that he tried to phone General Wolff on the spot.

Wolff was at that very moment attending a meeting at Kesselring's headquarters at Recoaro, the very purpose of which was to discuss means of ending the war in Italy. Besides Wolff and Kesselring, the meeting was also attended by Kesselring's Chief of Staff, General Roettiger and Ambassador Rahn. Dollmann telephoned General Harster in Verona and gave him the news of Parilli's contact with the Americans and told him it was important to report it to Wolff *at once*. When Harster then learned that Wolff had already left Recoaro for his post at Fasano, he drove in a police car himself to a point where the road from Recoaro enters Verona, flagged down Wolff's car when it came in sight and gave Wolff the news in the middle of the highway.

Parilli's report, as relayed to Wolff via Zimmer, struck Wolff as so promising that he asked Harster to get hold of Zimmer and his superior, Rauff, in Milan and to tell them to meet him as soon as they could at Desenzano, a small town at the southwestern tip of the Lake of Garda which was midway between Verona and Milan. He also asked Harster to come along with him to be present at the meeting.

At six o'clock in the evening, on the twenty-eighth of February, the four SS officials, Wolff, Harster, Rauff and Zimmer, converged at Desenzano and discussed the opportunity to contact the American Intelligence Service which Parilli had opened for them. The discussion lasted

---

to contact a member of the German Legation, Federer, whom Rahn suspected of having contacts to the Allies. Rahn was right. Gaevernitz knew Federer. Had Wolff's approach following Parilli's visit not served to call off Rahn's own probes in our direction, "Sunrise," or something like it, might very well have come about with Rahn as the principal German contact. Federer gave Gumpert a letter for Rahn claiming that he, Federer, could establish contact to me. Rahn showed Wolff this letter at the time. I learned of these facts only recently.

about an hour and a half. The decision to follow up the lead was taken almost at once, but there was a question about who the emissaries should be. Dollmann, though he was not present at the meeting, was the man on whom the choice fell. He was the natural diplomat of the SS contingent. He had the suaveness and the polish, and he knew the situation and the minds of both the Wehrmacht and the SS. It was also decided that Zimmer should accompany him.

Gaevernitz's parting words to Parilli at Lucerne had been taken at face value. Parilli was to go to Switzerland on the second of March and make arrangements with the Swiss for the two SS men to get over the border. When Parilli was told this and realized that his talk with Husmann and Waibel and the explanation of his motives to Gaevernitz had caused such major action, he could hardly believe it. His fondest dream was suddenly coming true. He could just be the man to save North Italy. But what would happen to him if the Americans in Bern refused to talk to the SS? To the Germans he would look like a swindler, perhaps like a spy for the other side. He had dropped Wolff's name in Switzerland as a peace seeker, and the Allies, if they were only playing a game, could use this against Wolff. And if anything happened to Wolff . . .

In the meantime other wheels began to turn. General Harster, who had been present at Wolff's council of peace on February 28th, sent a radiogram to Berlin that same night via his own channels and informed his chief, Kaltenbrunner, of what was going on. We know this from testimony that Harster gave many years after the war.* It will be recalled that while Harster was under Wolff's command locally in Italy, his boss in Berlin was Kaltenbrunner, who whom Wolff didn't get along. Whether Harster did this with the consent of Wolff, who might himself have felt it was necessary for the moment to keep Berlin in the picture, or whether he did it behind Wolff's back has never been entirely clear to me. Either way, this was the beginning of a development that was extremely dangerous for Wolff and almost finished off the possibility of a surrender in Italy.**

When Wolff made his decision to act, he confided in Rahn and had Rahn talk to Dollmann before he left for Switzerland. Rahn says in his memoirs that he advised Dollmann against any foolish attempts, in talk-

---

* Renato Carli Ballola, *"1953" Processo Parri* (Milan, 1953), p. 185.

** Within the intelligence organization of the SS (in which Harster and Zimmer, though not Wolff or Rauff, functioned) it was no crime to have contact *per se*

ing with the Americans, to drive a wedge between the Western Allies and the Soviets. Rahn knew the Germans liked to keep thinking this was possible, but he, Rahn, realized it was nonsense. The Alliance could not be broken. If this is correct, then what Professor Husmann told Doll-mann in Lugano could not have come as a great surprise.

After Dollmann left for Switzerland, Rahn and Wolff went deeper into the prospects. Only Kesselring could bring about an armistice, and he would have to be won over. Rahn offered to talk to him, since he knew him best. A few days later Kesselring, on a visit to Mussolini, dropped in to see Rahn, who was sick in bed at the time. Rahn never-theless did not let the opportunity go by. He drew Kesselring into a dis-cussion of the hopeless military and political outlook for Germany; turning to Kesselring at the end, he told him bluntly that the last mo-ment had come to save the remnants of the German nation from total destruction. As far as Rahn could see, Kesselring, the only undefeated German Field Marshal, was now called upon to play a role somewhat similar to the one Hindenburg had played at the end of the First World War. He alone, commanding the respect of the entire German Army, could act independently of Hitler, and he alone could call for peace and achieve it. Rahn waited. Kesselring seemed unperturbed. Outwardly he was cool and dispassionate, not given to outbursts. He quietly referred to his oath as a soldier and added that he thought the Führer would still pull them all through. To this Rahn said, "Field Marshal, this is no time for either of us to resort to propaganda slogans for each other's benefit. If you cannot make a decisive move now, I hope you will be ready to the moment we hear that the Führer is dead." Kesselring said nothing to this. He rose from Rahn's bedside to leave. Just before he went out the door, he said in an unmistakably friendly manner, "I hope your political plans succeed." Rahn had the impression that the first hurdle had been crossed. Maybe an obstacle had been removed even if an ally had not yet been gained.

---

to American intelligence; i.e., the purpose could have been to penetrate it, to find out about it, even to make some kind of deal with it. Only when and if this contact might become the channel for peace talks not approved by or known to Hitler and Himmler would the situation become highly dangerous for the par-ticipants. Harster's message, however, could not have failed to arouse Kaltenbrunner's suspicions.

7

The General Pays a Visit

An intelligence officer in the field is supposed to keep his home office informed of what he is doing. That is quite true, but with some reservations, as he may overdo it. If, for example, he tells too much or asks too often for instructions, he is likely to get some he doesn't relish, and, what is worse, he may well find headquarters trying to take over the whole conduct of the operation. Only a man on the spot can really pass judgment on the details as contrasted with the policy decisions, which, of course, belong to the boss at headquarters.

In view of my skepticism regarding the likely outcome of a meeting with General Wolff, I had no desire to stir up exaggerated hopes in Washington that we were about to engineer a German surrender, or to create the impression that we were engaged in any kind of high-level negotiations requiring policy decisions in Washington.

Sooner or later I would probably be faced with the decision of whether or not I should meet personally with General Wolff, but I knew that if I put this question up to headquarters in Washington they would be forced there to make a high-level decision which would probably cramp my freedom of action and decision. Too many people would have to be brought into the act at too early a stage. After all, I reasoned, an intelligence officer should be free to talk to the Devil himself if he could gain any useful knowledge for the conduct or the termination of the war. So for the moment I limited my reporting to the bare facts that Dollmann, who claimed to be on General Wolff's staff, had made

contact with us and that useful information about developments in Italy
might be forthcoming as a result. I had also sought from headquarters
their information about Wolff, Dollmann and Parilli, and, in answer,
they gave me all the background they had in their files, most of which
we already knew.

On Parilli they contributed something we did not know. Before the
war he had represented the Nash-Kelvinator Company in Italy. Washington checked with the firm and quoted its reassuring comment that
"you can count on him if he gives his word." This was comforting to
know but it did not take into account the fact that Parilli was no longer
exactly a free man, since he was acting on behalf of an SS General and
was often expressing the General's views rather than his own.

Feeling it was, at any rate, best to be forearmed, I directed to our
mission at Allied headquarters in Caserta, a very general question about
what course we should follow if it turned out that the Germans indicated
they seriously wanted to talk surrender. They came back with solid military advice. If Kesselring wanted to get in touch with the Allies, all he
had to do was send an envoy through the lines with the usual white flag.
I wired back explaining that this was out of the question. Kesselring was
undoubtedly surrounded by Gestapo informants on his own staff. By
the time an envoy could be cleared to cross to the Allied lines, Kesselring, in all probability, would be on his way to a concentration camp in
Germany. On the other hand, if Kesselring or his representative could
be brought secretly into Switzerland—and we now had the facilities for
arranging his passage in and out and keeping him under wraps while
there—Hitler and Himmler would never find out about it, or at least not
until it was too late. Caserta caught on immediately; they dropped the
idea of local envoys across the lines and agreed on Switzerland as the
desirable preliminary meeting place in case the Germans meant business
and wanted a meeting.

This response from Caserta, which settled what I then thought
was probably a hypothetical question, was hardly in my hands when
a telephone call from Gaevernitz, who was still in Davos, made it star-
tlingly clear that the Germans did mean business. To avoid giving sensitive information over the telephone to my office, Waibel had called
Gaevernitz in Davos and had asked him to pass a message to me.
Gaevernitz, in ski costume, had just come off the famous Parsenn run
and was fortunately in his hotel room where Waibel phoned him.
Waibel opened the conversation in a unique manner: "Gero, are you

standing or sitting? Because if you're standing you might fall over when you hear the news."

It was now the eighth of March. Parilli, Dollmann and Zimmer had only started back to Italy on the fourth with their report on the Lugano meeting at which I had asked for the release of two prisoners. Waibel's news for Gaevernitz was: "Parri and Usmiani are here. They were delivered safe and sound a few hours ago to my man at the Swiss-Italian frontier at Chiasso. SS Captain Zimmer has driven them up from Milan." Once over the border, Waibel said, he had consigned them to one of his Italian-speaking lieutenants who was now driving them up to Zurich. It was typical of Waibel to think of this detail; neither Parri nor Usmiani spoke much German. That was one thing. The other was that Wolff and his party, accompanied by Baron Parilli, had crossed the border shortly after the two released prisoners and were en route to Zurich by train. Parilli had arrived at the border the night before and had called up Husmann. Husmann had jumped the first train down to Chiasso in order not to miss a trick. He was now accompanying the Wolff party back to Zurich. The Highest SS and Police Leader evidently was not traveling like a thief in the night. He had three officers with him: Colonel Dollmann, Captain Zimmer and his adjutant, Major Wenner (*Sturmbannführer*)—all in civilian clothes, of course. Waibel had assigned to the group the Lieutenant Rothpletz who had been in charge of security at Lugano the week before.

What a security risk, I thought, Wolff and his three officers, Parilli, the talkative Husmann and the Swiss lieutenant; seven of them—in wartime—all together on a Swiss train for the five-hour ride from Chiasso to Zurich. Wolff's picture had occasionally appeared in the Italian press. He was known to the public, and certainly to any newspaperman who was on his toes, as Commander of the SS forces in Italy. What would he be doing in Switzerland?

As I learned later, the group remained in two compartments reserved for them on the train, with the doors closed and the curtains drawn. Waibel also had arranged a cover story for them in case interested strangers happened to ask a question. They were a German-Italian commission which had come in to discuss with the Swiss the use of the port facilities of the harbor of Genoa.

Gaevernitz was going to catch the first train out of Davos for Zurich. I told him I would meet him there around six o'clock, although I had still not made up my mind that I would talk to Wolff.

Wolff had acted with astonishing speed. In the four days since Doll-mann had brought him our message, he had ordered the release and de-livery of the prisoners, had arranged for his own trip and that of his staff, for documentation and for stories to cover his absence. How many people knew? The authorities of two separate prisons, chauffeurs, com-municators, SS border guards. How did he do it? Did he regard himself as invulnerable? Was his power so great that he had nothing to fear? Was he perhaps foolhardy? How would he have survived so long and reached such high rank in the SS if that was the answer? Or did Himm-ler know—had given his approval—and therefore there was nothing to hide? These were a few of the questions that filled my mind as I drove up to Zurich late that afternoon.

I met Gaevernitz at an apartment which we had rented in Zurich and used only for meetings of the touchiest nature. It was located on the ground floor of a rather bleak building at the end of the Genferstrasse, facing a corner of the Lake of Zurich. From the street, one entered a passage by a heavy portal that was opened by an ancient, massive key about four inches long. Beyond the passage another portal let one into the vestibule, and it took still another key to open the apartment door just beyond. Waibel, who was now also in Zurich, called to tell us that the German party and Baron Parilli were being entertained by Husmann and his wife, who had an apartment in Zurich, and that Husmann would like to come over and tell us how things were going. He also in-formed us that he had, for the moment, installed the two Italians, Parri and Usmiani, as patients in a fancy clinic in an elegant section of Zurich. It was the safest place for them.

Shortly thereafter the Professor arrived. This was the first time I had met him. He was very proper, almost stiff, a short stocky man with a head of thick gray hair; and, like Waibel, he was a cigar smoker. He did not make any of his well-known speeches on this occasion. He sug-gested that for reasons of security I should call on Wolff at his apart-ment. I declined this invitation and said that if Wolff wanted to see me he would have to come to me, at the Genferstrasse apartment, and alone; that is, Professor Husmann should bring him over, make the in-troduction and then leave us.

I had decided that it was worth the gamble to see Wolff, in full recognition of the fact that considerable risk was involved. If Wolff was trying to trick me, the consequences could be unpleasant. He would learn nothing from me, but he could perhaps make political capital of the fact that I had compromised myself by talking to him. I could see the headlines: "ENVOY OF PRESIDENT ROOSEVELT RECEIVES HIGH SS OFFICER." At least I had the alibi that already, through Wolff, I had secured the release of two Italian prisoners of importance to the Allies.

These thoughts prompted me to tell Husmann that Wolff would have to wait. On further consideration I had decided I wanted to see Parri and Usmiani first. I wanted to be sure we had the right men, that they were unharmed and that there was no deal involved. Husmann at first demurred, but acquiesced when I told him my reasons. We would call his apartment when we were ready.

I told him I wanted Wolff to understand before he came that all I expected to hear from him were proposals for ways and means to effect an unconditional surrender of the German armies in Italy. Nothing else. Husmann said he thought this was abundantly clear to Wolff. Husmann had been talking to Wolff for hours all during the long train ride and afterward at his house. He thought Wolff now recognized the facts of Germany's hopeless military position, of the solidity of the Anglo-American-Soviet position, and he was moreover, Husmann thought, acting wholly on his own.

Husmann then told us of an almost disastrous incident during the train ride. As bad luck would have it, an avalanche had chosen that day to block the railroad line near the Gotthard Pass. The party had had to leave their closed and curtained compartments, descend from the train, march up the tracks along with all the other passengers and then get into another train which the Swiss Federal Railways had provided to take care of the emergency. Some Italians Wolff knew were in the crowd and only by considerable ducking and stalling had he been able to let them pass him, as they all walked the tracks, without his being noticed. If he had been recognized, the news that Wolff was in Switzerland would surely have got out, and if it had appeared in the press it would have caused a sensation. High SS generals were not traveling around Switzerland, and at this particular juncture it was well known that Wolff had every reason to be at his post in Italy. At least we would have had to start all over again, and Wolff would have been "blown" as a possible negotiator.

Just before he left us, Husmann handed me some papers which he said General Wolff wanted me to see. They were surprising documents, written in German and with Wolff's official card attached. It was clear that they were notes of recommendation for the man whom I was about to meet, and they had obviously been prepared for the occasion. They were somewhat like the material that a man applying for a job prepares for the company he hopes to serve. They were, in effect, Wolff's references and an outline of his career. The covering page, in translation, read as given below:

KARL WOLFF

SS-Obergruppenführer and General of the Military SS, Highest SS and Police Leader and Military Plenipotentiary of the German Armed Forces in Italy.

Commander of Rear Military Area and of the Military Administration. Information about the above person can be given by:

1. The former Deputy of the Führer, *Rudolf Hess*, at present in Canada.
2. *The present Pope*: Visit in May, 1944; release of Professor Vasella at request of the Pope, who stands by to intercede, if desired, at any time.
3. *Father Pankratius Pfeiffer*, Superior of the Salvatorian Order in Rome . . .

There followed seven or eight more names of churchmen, Italian aristocrats, and so on, with details of how Wolff had been helpful to them, in most cases by releasing them from prison. On the next page were claims of a different sort. Here Wolff set forth that on his orders several hundred of the most precious paintings of the Uffizi Gallery, in Florence, had been removed to safety in North Italy when Florence was bombarded, along with various sculptures and the famous coin collection of the King of Italy, which was said to be worth many millions of dollars. He claimed also, along with Kesselring, to have been responsible for saving Rome from German bombardment, to have settled without bloodshed the general strike in Turin, Milan and Genoa, involving some 300,000 workers in 1944, and to have negotiated with the partisans in November of 1944, with the result that an amnesty had been declared and the Italian population of North Italy no longer needed to fear being drafted into Mussolini's armies or into German labor forces. There were attachments in support of the claims made. One was a personal letter to Wolff from the Cardinal of Venice thanking him for the release from prison of a nun of Jewish origin. In short, General Wolff wanted to show us what kind of fellow he was and who would vouch for him in case we had the wrong idea about him.

Then Gaevernitz and I drove off to the clinic where Waibel had deposited Parri and Usmiani. We were directed by a nurse up a long corridor to the room where the two "patients" had been installed. I shall never forget the scene. Parri, who within a few months would become Prime Minister of liberated Italy, was so excited that he broke into tears and threw his arms around me. He had not the slightest idea why and how he had suddenly been rescued in Verona to be conducted to the Swiss border by the SS, who up to then had been his jailers and interrogators. When he had been taken out of jail, he quite naturally assumed that he was to be shot or possibly deported to Germany, where he would suffer a more lingering fate.

His first question to me was typical of the man: "What sort of deal have you made with the Germans to get me out? I want you to know that I won't accept any restrictions on my freedom of action. I want to return immediately to Italy and continue the fight against the Germans and the Fascists."

I assured him I had not made any deals, and added, "Parri, my friend, you are free to return to Italy at any time. But please accept my word that it would be harmful to the cause you represent if you returned immediately. It would even block action which may help to end the war and save your own country from destruction." I then asked him to be patient for a week or two at least, and I gave him my promise that he would return to Italy before the day of liberation.

I was naturally apprehensive that if Parri returned to Italy and was picked up by the Germans or the Fascists again it would be difficult to explain his escape. Meanwhile his disappearance from the Verona jail could be passed off by Wolff as an exchange of prisoners, or as a transfer from one jail to another. I also told Parri that it was essential that no one in Switzerland should know of his escape.

Reassured that I had not bought his release on terms which tied his hands, he agreed with my suggestions.

He then told me, as recounted earlier, how Edgardo Sogno, one of the partisan daredevils, had tried to enter the Hotel Regina in Milan—where he was first kept prisoner—in SS uniform in order to free Parri by main force, but had been caught, wounded and was now himself in jail. Could I get Sogno released, too? Parri would not rest easy until Sogno was safe. To impersonate a German soldier was itself a capital offense in Italy. I told Parri I would do what I could. After a few words with Usmiani, who was as baffled as Parri at the events of the day, and equally grateful, we left them still wondering how they had been freed.

The first thing Gaevernitz and I did after returning to the apartment on the Genferstrasse was to build a fire in the fireplace in the library where we intended to talk to General Wolff. I have always tried to have important meetings around a fireplace. There is some subtle influence in a wood fire which makes people feel at ease and less inhibited in their conversation; and if you are asked a question which you are in no hurry to answer, you can stir up the fire and study the patterns the flames make until you have shaped your answer. If I needed more time to answer, I always had my pipe handy to fill and light.

Shortly before ten o'clock Husmann arrived with General Wolff. I learned later that the atmosphere at Husmann's apartment had become tense as the hours went by. Having exhausted the subject of politics, the guests, over their canapés and wine, had got into a long discussion about music with Mrs. Husmann, who had formerly been a singer at the Munich Opera—Bruno Walter, Richard Strauss, *Rosenkavalier*. They had reminded each other of various arias and leitmotivs, humming and singing them—chiefly Dollmann, who was musical, and Zimmer, the aesthetic SS Captain, and Mrs. Husmann. Wolff had tried to be genial and relaxed, I was later told, but SS generals were not accustomed to waiting and he had finally begun to drum his fingers on the table, in time to the music perhaps, impatiently waiting for the telephone to ring signaling my return from seeing Parri.

On the way over to the apartment, Husmann had asked Wolff a question which he had already asked him several times before. "Did Himmler send you here or did you come on your own initiative?" "Himmler knows nothing about my trip," Wolff answered.

Gaevernitz opened the doors for the two visitors while I remained in the library. As he shook hands with Wolff, Gaevernitz, in order to relieve the tension, told him that they had a friend in common, the beautiful Countess Mechtilde Podewils. Gaevernitz hinted to Wolff that he knew the Countess had come to Wolff in Berlin some years before to ask his help in protecting Romano Guardini, a well-known Catholic philosopher whom the Gestapo had threatened to put in jail. He also knew Wolff had succeeded in saving Guardini. At this, Wolff seemed to relax and the tense look on his face disappeared.

Gaevernitz led him into the library; Professor Husmann followed. We nodded and took seats around the fire. Scotch was offered around. Wolff was a handsome man and well aware of it—Nordic, with graying, slightly receding blond hair, well-built and looking no older than his age, which was in the middle forties. He sat rather stiffly and said very little at first. Our conversation was in German. Wolff spoke no English. My own German was passable. Husmann asked my permission to summarize the discussion he had had with General Wolff during the five-hour train ride from the Swiss-Italian border to Zurich. I consented and Husmann, in his professorial manner, ran down the list of topics discussed, occasionally turning to Wolff, who nodded his agreement. The crux of the matter was that Wolff had conceded that the war was irrevocably lost for Germany, and that the Western Allies could not be divided. He also had assured Husmann that he was acting without the knowledge of Hitler and Himmler. When Husmann had finished, he left us, his role for the moment completed.

I then asked Wolff to state his own position fully and frankly.

He started out by admitting that from the early days of Nazism until the previous year he had had faith in Hitler and had been completely attached to him. Now he realized that the war was lost and that to continue it was a crime against the German people. Therefore, as a good German, he felt compelled to do everything in his power to bring the war to an end.

"I control the SS forces in Italy," he said, "and I am willing to place myself and my entire organization at the disposal of the Allies to terminate hostilities." However, he emphasized that in order to end the war in Italy, it was not sufficient for the SS to work toward this goal; it was also necessary to win over the commanders of the German armed forces.

For a long time he had been on very good terms with Field Marshal Kesselring, he said. He had discussed with him the possibility of approaching the Allies and had found that Kesselring hadn't been altogether opposed to such an idea, but had not yet been completely won over to this view.

Wolff had acted at times as Kesselring's political adviser; he felt he had considerable influence on him and was confident that he could win him over. He felt, also, that Ambassador Rahn would be helpful. If we could assure Wolff that a secure line of communication reaching the top level of the Allied command was available through his contact to us, he would do his best to arrange that either Kesselring or his deputy would come to Switzerland with him to discuss a surrender. I assured Wolff that we were in direct contact with Allied headquarters. Wolff accepted this and seemed to be immensely relieved to know that a channel was now established.

He concluded by telling me that he would later outline the steps he could take to prevent unnecessary bloodshed and destruction of lives and property in North Italy.

Neither at this meeting nor later did Wolff suggest that his action would be contingent upon any promise of immunity for himself. He did say that he did not consider himself a war criminal and was willing to stand on his record. In an hour we had progressed as far as we could go at the moment. Until we knew Kesselring's attitude, we could not safely plan our future course. Wolff left us to rejoin Dollmann and his other aides.

I returned to Bern late that night to notify Washington and Allied headquarters in Caserta of this meeting. Gaevernitz remained behind and had a detailed talk the following morning with Wolff and Dollmann. In that conversation Gaevernitz was assured that Kesselring and Wolff between them controlled the German and Fascist situation in North Italy. Wolff explained also that his SS command included the approaches to the Brenner Pass. His action would thus frustrate Nazi hopes for a last stand in an Alpine redoubt. If he and Kesselring took joint action and Rahn joined them, Hitler and Himmler would be powerless to take effective countermeasures, Wolff said. Also, such action could have vital repercussions on the German armies elsewhere, as many German generals were only waiting for someone to take the lead.

Wolff then outlined in further detail the procedure which he contemplated:

1. He would see Kesselring over the weekend to obtain from him a definite commitment to joint action.

2. He would draft with Kesselring a declaration to be signed by them, by Rahn and others, setting forth the uselessness of the struggle, their responsibility toward the German people to terminate it, and calling upon the military commanders to dissociate themselves from Hitler and Himmler. The statement would also announce that hostilities in North Italy would be terminated by the Germans.

3. Radio and leaflet action would be prepared to get the message over to the people of Northern Italy, Germany and to the German Army and its commanders.

4. Provided Kesselring could be won over, Wolff believed that Kesselring would come clandestinely into Switzerland within a week to meet our military representatives and coordinate the technical military surrender measures.

As evidence of his ability to act, in addition to the steps he had already taken in releasing Parri and Usmiani, he stated he was prepared to take the following steps immediately:

1. Discontinue active warfare against the partisans, merely keeping up necessary pretense pending the execution of the plan.

2. Release to Switzerland several hundred Jews interned at Bolzano.

3. Assume full responsibility for the safety and treatment of 350 American and British prisoners at Mantua, of whom 150 were in a hospital and 200 in a camp on the southern outskirts of the city. He claimed these were all the American or British prisoners then held in Northern Italy; others had been transferred to Germany.

4. Release to Switzerland, if he could be found, Edgardo Sogno, the man who had been caught trying to free Parri.

5. Facilitate the return to North Italy of Italian officers held in Germany who might be useful in the post-hostilities period.

Wolff once more assured Gaevernitz that he was acting entirely independently of Himmler, and that neither Himmler nor the Führer had any information whatever about his trip to Switzerland. Then he left.

Meanwhile in Bern, I was waiting with something more than curiosity to learn the reactions I would get from Field Marshal Alexander, in Caserta, and from Washington. In my radio messages to Caserta I had suggested that if we received word that Kesselring or his deputy was prepared to come to Switzerland with Wolff to surrender their forces, it would be well for AFHQ (Allied Forces Headquarters, Caserta) to be ready to send some officers to Switzerland to meet them. I made it clear that we could not yet judge how much weight could be placed on Wolff's assurances or promises. This was subject to test.

This word of caution did not deter Field Marshal Alexander, who was a man of action. The very next day after the meeting with Wolff a radio message came through from Alexander that two senior staff officers from AFHQ were coming to Switzerland at once. The OSS office at Caserta was making preparations to provide guards, clerical assistance, special communications facilities and all the personnel and paraphernalia required for a complex operation which must remain absolutely secret and secure. It was at this point that we decided upon a code name for the whole undertaking—"Sunrise."* The code name reflected the

---

* In some of the military records, however, it is called Operation Crossword, the designation which Churchill gave it, as noted earlier in this book. Possibly

optimism of the moment. If events proceeded as Wolff hoped, there was no reason that the sun of peace should not rise over Italy in a matter of a few weeks at most, possibly sooner.

Wolff and his party had returned to Italy on the afternoon of March 9th, a Friday. Wolff intended to go to Kesselring over the weekend. Gaevernitz and I waited, anxious yet hopeful, not stirring from our post at Bern. If all went well, within days emissaries could be converging on Switzerland from the two massive armies that had been locked in battle in Italy since July of 1943. The arrangements for their secret passage into Switzerland and their secret rendezvous alone would require the assistance of all the personnel that both Waibel and I had at our disposal. We were already pondering the question of a suitable place for the meeting.

Waibel never told me whether he informed his superiors in Bern of the negotiations as they progressed. His participation, even unofficial, in conversations between belligerents might have been regarded as a breach of neutrality by literal-minded Swiss.* I never asked Waibel whether he even told his chief, General Guisan, for whom I had the highest respect. Most certainly I never put any injunction on Waibel against telling him. Waibel would have resented it, and properly so.

At the time I wished, above all, to prevent any leak to the press, as it might have been disastrous. I had no doubt whatever that what I was attempting to do was in the best interests of the Swiss, and that they as well as I knew it and wished to protect the secrecy and the success of the operation.

On the afternoon of Sunday, the eleventh, Waibel phoned me that Parilli had just crossed the border at Chiasso and had called him from there. He was alone. Waibel had told him to take a train to Lucerne and

---

he realized that this operation was indeed to be a puzzle, and he reveled in finding appropriate and resounding code names for the great operations of World War II. But before we knew that Churchill had baptized the Italian surrender operation as "Crossword" we had already given it the code name of "Sunrise," and that is how it will be called in our story.

* In the intervening years some writers have contended that the Swiss government was informed at higher levels of the Sunrise negotiations as they developed. Jon Kimche, in his book *Spying for Peace* (London, 1961), claims that General Guisan knew what was going on, "though officially he remained in total ignorance" (p. 127). Waibel himself made the following statement in a short article he wrote on the subject: "Switzerland's policy of neutrality pro-

asked us to come to the Hotel Schweizerhof in Lucerne in time to meet with him. Professor Husmann was on the spot, as always. Waibel evidently felt he was an important psychological cog, and I think he was right. Gaevernitz and I drove over in the evening. Parilli's train got in shortly before midnight.

This was the first time I had met Parilli face to face. I felt as if I already knew him well from the descriptions Gaevernitz and Paul Blum and Waibel had given me. He was bundled in a large handsome overcoat with a fur collar (it was bitter cold outside) which made him look twice his size, as I discovered when he removed the coat. He spoke a variety of languages with equal speed, Italian, French and German, and said a few words to me in English when we were introduced. He often interlarded whatever language he happened to be speaking with phrases from another. One of the phrases he enjoyed throwing in my direction was, "You are the boss." He was likable. He had a sense of humor. He had a tendency to dramatize things a bit, but certainly the affair in which he suddenly found himself an actor was highly dramatic, if a little out of his usual line.

Parilli was very hungry, as we expected. He sat at a small table on which a big platter of cold meats, bread and salad had been set out for him and talked to us while he ate.

The bare and disappointing facts did not take long to tell. No sooner had Wolff and his three officers, accompanied by Parilli, crossed into Italy on March 9th and entered the Italian customs station than a message was handed to Wolff by Colonel Rauff, the SS Chief Inspector from Milan, who was there to meet him. It was from Kaltenbrunner. Wolff read it, frowned and asked Parilli to come along with him in his

---

hibited the favoring of one or the other warring parties and, also, therefore, the conduct of armistice talks with personalities not authorized by their governments to negotiate. . . . Neither the Federal Council nor the Commander-in-Chief [Guisan] of the Armed Forces could have approved such negotiations. . . . I was, therefore, faced with a conflict of conscience: either to renounce the venture to bring about an armistice or to violate orders and take the entire responsibility on myself. . . . Was it not precisely the possibility of maintaining a stronghold of human dignity, even in the midst of world conflict, that was in its deepest sense the very heart of our country's neutrality? . . . For me the answer was clear-cut: I had to follow my conscience and act against orders." (Translated from *Die Schweiz im II. Weltkrieg* [Thun, Switzerland], 1959, p. 123.)

car as he drove back to his headquarters at Fasano. The message to Wolff stated, according to Parilli, that Kaltenbrunner was pressing Wolff to meet him in Innsbruck. When the party reached Fasano, Wolff learned that during his absence Kaltenbrunner had been trying to get in touch with him. Harster had wired Kaltenbrunner that Wolff had gone to Switzerland.* The fact that Wolff himself had failed to inform Berlin of his trip and the reasons for it immediately aroused the most hostile suspicions in the mind of a man like Kaltenbrunner. Late that night Wolff sent a teletype message to Kaltenbrunner in Innsbruck begging off because of the pressure of work. He had to assume the Kaltenbrunner might try to arrest him if he left his own territory.

Wolff had not heard from Himmler yet, but he knew now that he would have to straighten everything out with Himmler soon. What he proposed, and this was one of the messages he sent us through Parilli, was that we, the Allies, should turn over to him a German prisoner of high rank, equal in importance to Parri, so that Wolff could say he had only wanted to arrange an exchange of prisoners. Wolff asked us to locate and deliver to him, if possible, Obersturmbannführer Wuensche, a personal friend and favorite adjutant of Hitler's who had been taken prisoner in France. Hitler's birthday was coming up soon and Wolff could say he had personally and quietly engaged in the Parri affair in order to give a birthday surprise to the Führer. If we could not release Wuensche, then couldn't we get hold of some other high-ranking Nazi in the prison cages of France or England?

What amazed me about this, if it was a correct account, was the impulsiveness it revealed in Wolff. He had released Parri through Harster, expecting no doubt that word would somehow leak to Berlin, and he had done nothing at the time to cover himself. Now that word had leaked and he was or would be in trouble, he was hastily trying to devise a belated pretext for what he had done. He either considered him-

---

* Harster's behavior throughout this period is difficult to analyze without looking closely at the ambiguous position in which he was placed. It is easy to accuse him of betraying Wolff to Kaltenbrunner and acting behind Wolff's back, but the fact seems to be rather that, being subordinate to both these rivals, he had no choice but to appear to be obedient to Kaltenbrunner while covering Wolff as best he could, protecting himself at the same time if possible. It seems that Wolff understood and sympathized with his quandary and told him as little as he could of his true intentions.

self even more powerful than he was or thought his stock with Himmler, or possibly Hitler, was so high that he could do no wrong. Or, worst of all, he simply didn't think ahead.

That was one problem. The other was simpler but still more disturbing. As soon as Wolff had returned to his headquarters at Fasano, he had put through a call to Kesselring's headquarters, which at that time was located at Recoaro, farther to the east. From General Roettiger, Kesselring's Chief of Staff, Wolff heard the startling news that Kesselring had been summoned to the Führer's headquarters the same day (March 8th) Wolff had left to see me in Switzerland. Everyone assumed Hitler had new orders for Kesselring. The rumor was that he would be told to take over command on the Western Front and do what Kluge, Rommel, Rundstedt and Model had all failed to do—stop the American and British steam roller which was now pressing across the Rhine. Roettiger did not know who would take over Kesselring's command in Italy.

Parilli brought us one further bit of news from Wolff: Mussolini was considering plans to flee to Spain.

Meanwhile, Parilli had finished his cold supper at about the same time he finished his report. I had noted down three or four questions for Wolff while he was talking. I now asked him if he was willing to go back to Wolff on the earliest train out of Lucerne in the morning. There were no more trains that night. He said he was. My questions were these: If Kesselring did not return, was Wolff prepared to try to persuade his replacement to surrender to us? If the replacement refused or was unapproachable, was Wolff prepared to act alone? What forces and what areas did he control that could be turned over to the Allies? What would he do if he himself were ordered to report to Berlin? Parilli memorized the questions. Then we parted.

Gaevernitz and I motored back to Bern in the early hours of March 12th. It was bleak and cold; the roads were covered with snow and we were depressed. To add to our troubles we became hopelessly lost. Swiss road signs had been taken down early in the war against the threat of German invasion. We could manage in daylight because we knew the landmarks on the way, but now we had to steer by the stars. At one small village we vainly pounded on door after door, hoping we could rouse some native who would give us directions. But the Swiss farmer is a sound sleeper and we got no response at all. Eventually—I am not sure how we managed it—we got back to Bern just before dawn.

There was no time for sleep. We had messages to send and problems to solve before we sent them. Our code clerks and secretaries, when they arrived at the office after a good night's sleep and a solid breakfast, were surprised to find Gaevernitz and me already on the job, unshaven, brewing coffee on a rather sluggish electric burner we had around for just such emergencies. Fate had turned things upside down since we had last walked out of that office. Reluctantly, I decided it was best to suggest to Caserta in my report that they hold up the dispatch of Field Marshal Alexander's military envoys. There was little use having them come just for the ride and for discussions with me. We then sent a cable to London and Paris asking them to try to locate Hitler's friend Wuensche, reportedly in captivity, so that if Parri's release stirred up too much talk we could consider an exchange.

The next morning, March 13th, there were two messages for me. Caserta wired that the decision had been made to send on the two military envoys of Field Marshal Alexander even though the Germans had not signified that they were ready to talk. They were, in fact, already en route and would arrive at Lyon that day by air. When I read the names and rank of the men who were being sent, I was astonished. I wondered if I had made sufficiently clear just how bleak the situation was with the possibility of Kesselring's change of command. The two emissaries were the American Major General Lyman L. Lemnitzer, then Deputy Chief of Staff to Field Marshal Alexander, and the British Major General Terence S. Airey, Alexander's Chief Intelligence Officer.

The other message, a prompt reply from London, informed me that Wuensche had unfortunately been transferred to a prisoner-of-war camp in Canada and was not available. I next had to arrange to get in touch with the party from Caserta who would be waiting in Lyon for instructions about the Swiss border crossing.

There was obviously no need at the moment to have the whole OSS contingent, guards, radio operators, couriers and all come into Switzerland, since apparently no major armistice conference was soon to take place. It would be impossible to bring in a busload of Americans, even in plainclothes, all at once. Accordingly, I sent a message to Lyon asking that only the two generals and the senior members of the OSS group proceed to the Swiss border at Annemasse, the others to wait at Lyon until we needed them.

I intended to go down to Annemasse the following morning to greet our guests and accompany them into Switzerland, if they wanted to

THE STARS AND STRIPES
MEDITERRANEAN

Vol. 1, No. 243, Thursday, May 3, 1945   Printed In Italy   TWO LIRE

NAZI ARMIES IN ITALY SURRENDER

By Sgt. HOWARD TAUBMAN
Staff Correspondent

AFHQ, May 2—The German armies in Italy and in part of Austria have surrendered—completely and unconditionally.

The long, bitter, back-breaking campaign of Italy has been crowned with victory. In the theater where the
western Allies made their first breach in Adolf Hitler's Fortress Europe, the fighting has come to an end with the
surrender of an entire front.

This front covers not only the rest of Italy where the routed Germans have been fleeing in disorder but the
western area of Austria. The Germans defending the Austrian provinces of Vorarlberg, Tyrol, Salzburg and parts
of Carinthia and Styria have surrendered to the Allied might of the Mediterranean Theater.

This means that vital cities like Innsbruck and Salzburg are ours without a fight. It means that Allied forces
take over Austrian territory within ten miles of Berchtesgaden, where Hitler built what he thought was a personal
fortress so deep in the fastnesses of the Alps that it would take months and years to approach it.

It means that the bankruptcy of German aggressive policy and German arms has caused an old line Prussian
military leader like Col. Gen. Heinrich von Vietinghoff and a convinced Nazi like SS General Karl Wolff, the two
commanders on this front who have surrendered, to ignore Hitler's and Himmler's injunction—to fight to the end.

It means that other fronts where the Germans have any sort of sizable formations may choose to follow suit.
It may be that here, in Italy, where the Allies have done their hardest and most sustained fighting, the way has been
shown to German commanders how to end the useless slaughter at once.

But above all else, the surrender in Italy means that the valorous fighters of the 5th and 8th Armies, who
have fought their way up the entire length of the relentless Apennines, need not begin the heart-breaking task of
conquering the mountains that lead to the Brenner Pass and into Austria.

It means, too, that the fliers of the Mediterranean Allied Air Forces need not go plunging into the flak alleys
around Brenner Pass or in the other narrow passages among the Alps where the Germans (Continued on page 2)

Gero von S. Gaevernitz and Allen Dulles.

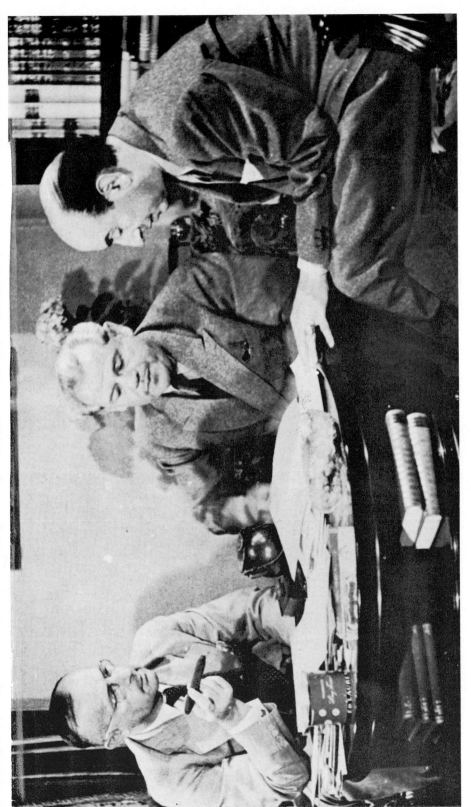

The three intermediaries: Major Max Waibel, Professor Max Husmann and Baron Luigi Parilli.

Discussing the plan for surrender, Ambassador Rudolf Rahn, Field Marshal Albert Kesselring, General Karl Wolff, General Hans Roettiger.

General Hans Roettiger, chief of staff to General von Vietinghoff.

General Karl Wolff, commander of all SS units in Italy.

The host, Gero von S. Gaevernitz, and the villa on the lake at Ascona, Switzerland, where the secret meeting between German and Allied generals took place.

At the Ascona meeting, Major Max Waibel, General Lyman L. Lemnitzer
and General Terence S. Airey.

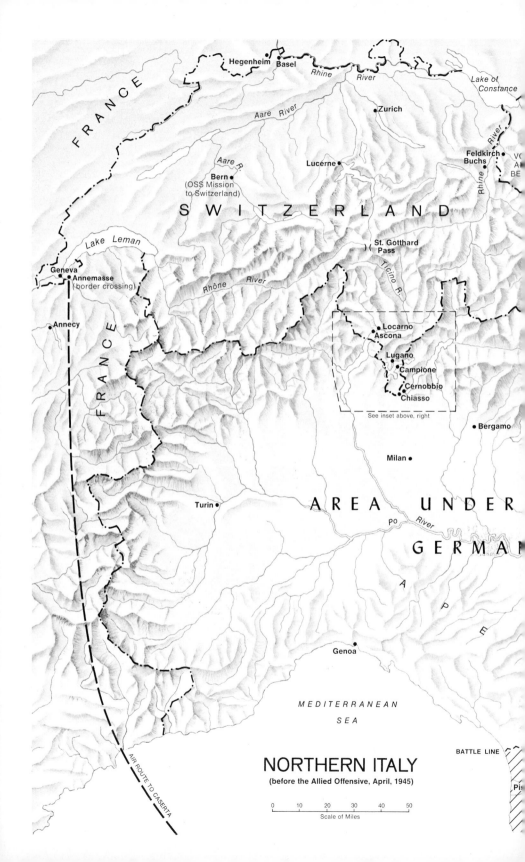

FRANCE

Hegenheim • Basel

Rhine River

Lake of Constance

Aare River

• Zurich

Rhine River

Aare R.

Feldkirch •
Buchs •

VO
A
BE

Bern •
(OSS Mission
to Switzerland)

Lucerne •

S W I T Z E R L A N D

Lake Leman

St. Gotthard
Pass

Ticino R.

Geneva •
Annemasse •
(border crossing)

Rhône River

• Locarno
Ascona •

• Annecy

FRANCE

Lugano •
• Campione

• Cernobbio
• Chiasso

See inset above, right

• Bergamo

Milan •

A R E A   U N D E R

• Turin

Po River

G E R M A N

A

P

Genoa •

E

MEDITERRANEAN

SEA

BATTLE LINE

NORTHERN ITALY

(before the Allied Offensive, April, 1945)

Pi

0   10   20   30   40   50
Scale of Miles

AIR ROUTE TO CASERTA

GERMANY
(BAVARIA)

SWITZERLAND

Ascona • Locarno

Inn River
Innsbruck
TYROL
AUSTRIA

Lugano
Campione

Brenner
Pass

Lake Maggiore

Lake
Lugano

Merano

Cernobbio
Chiasso (main border
crossing)
Como

Bolzano
(German military
and SS headquarters
at the end)

Lake Como

ITALY

0   3   6   9   12
Scale of Miles

Adige River

D O L O M I T E S

Piave River

YUGOSLAVIA

Fasano
Gardone
ò
Garda
enzano • Verona

Recoaro (Wehrmacht headquarters
for Italy)

Trieste

Venice

N

O N T R O L

Po River

Pola

ADRIATIC
SEA

Comacchio
Argenta

Bologna

GERMAN 10TH and 14TH ARMIES

RICAN 5TH and BRITISH 8TH ARMIES

Pistoia
River • Florence

EA UNDER ALLIED CONTROL

GERMANY
• Munich
FRANCE
AUSTRIA
• Bern
Bolzano •
Recoaro
YUGOSLAVIA
I
T
A
L
Y
Adriatic Sea
Florence •
Rome •
Caserta
Naples • • Salerno

Mediterranean Sea

Map by Harry Scott

General W. D. Morgan (*right*), chief of staff to Field Marshal Harold Alexander, addressing the German emissaries in Caserta, April 29, 1945.

Lieutenant Colonel Viktor von Schweinitz signing the surrender on the behalf of General von Vietinghoff. Behind him is General Wolff's representative, SS Major Max Wenner.

General Morgan signing the surrender for the Supreme Allied Commander of the Mediterranean Theater of Operations. Behind him are General Kislenko of Russia and General Lemnitzer of the United States.

General Morgan informing British and American newsmen of the surrender. The press kept the secret for three days.

INSTRUMENT OF LOCAL SURRENDER OF GERMAN AND
OTHER FORCES UNDER THE COMMAND OR CONTROL
OF THE GERMAN COMMANDER-IN-CHIEF SOUTHWEST

---

1. The German Commander-in-Chief Southwest hereby surrenders
    unconditionally all the forces under his command or control
    on land, at sea and in the air and places himself and these
    forces unconditionally at the disposal of the Supreme Allied
    Commander, Mediterranean Theatre of Operations.

2. All armed forces under the command or control of the German
    Commander-in-Chief Southwest will cease all hostilities on
    land, at sea and in the air at 1200 hours (Greenwich mean
    time) on 2 May 1945. The German Commander-in-Chief South-
    west undertakes to arrange accordingly.

3. The German Commander-in-Chief Southwest undertakes to carry
    out the orders set out in Appendices A, B and C and any fur-
    ther orders of the Supreme Allied Commander, Mediterranean
    Theatre of Operations. Disobedience of such orders or failure
    to comply with them will be dealt with in accordance with the
    accepted laws and usages of war.

4. This instrument will enter into force immediately on signature,
    and the orders in Appendices A, B and C will become effective on
    the date and at the time specified in paragraph 2 above.

5. This instrument and accompanying orders are drawn up in the
    English and German languages. The English version is the
    authentic text. If any doubt as to meaning or interpretation
    arises, the decision of the Supreme Allied Commander is final.

6. This instrument is independent of, without prejudice to,
    and shall be superseded by any general instrument of
    surrender imposed by or on behalf of the United Nations
    and applicable to GERMANY and the German armed forces as
    a whole.

VICTOR VON SCHWEINITZ,
Lieutenant Colonel in
  the General Staff of
  Army Group C,
for Colonel General VON
  VIETINGHOFF-SCHEEL,
Commander-in-Chief South-
  west and Commander-in-
  Chief of Army Group C.

W. D. MORGAN,
Lieutenant General,
Chief of Staff,
for Field Marshal The
  Honourable Sir Harold
  R.L.G. ALEXANDER,
Supreme Allied Commander
  of the Mediterranean
  Theatre of Operations

EUGEN WENNER,
SS-Sturmbannführer and
  Major in the Waffen-SS,
for SS-Obergruppenführer
  and General of the Waffen-
  SS WOLFF,
Supreme Commander of SS and
  Police and plenipotentiary
  General of the German Wehr-
  macht in Italy.

Signed at CASERTA, Italy.

29th April 1945

.... Hours

At German headquarters in Bolzano after the surrender, General Roettiger, Gaevernitz, Major Wenner, General Heinrich von Vietinghoff, Colonel Eugen Dollmann and General Wolff.

St. Leonhard, the Tyrolean village where the Uffizi and Pitti art treasures were stored.

Little Wally, the Czech radio operator, in his secret hide-out at SS headquarters, Bolzano.

Palace of the Duke of Pistoia, Balzano, headquarters of General Wolff.

come. They were to stay overnight at Annemasse in our OSS post, the same one where I had once spent a restful night just after the German withdrawal, ignorant of the fact that a time bomb, fortunately discovered in time, was gently ticking away in the cellar.

Late at night I received a phone call from Waibel. Parilli was back again. He had Wolff's answers to my questions. At least Parilli wasn't getting any more sleep than we were. He had returned to Italy on the morning of the twelfth and he was back again in Switzerland on the night of the thirteenth. I decided to hold off going to Annemasse until Parilli arrived in Bern, which would be early the next morning. I wanted to be able to give the generals from Caserta the latest word.

Parilli came the next day to my apartment in the Herrengasse in Bern. As I thought, he hadn't closed an eye for forty-eight hours and looked it. He told us that when he arrived back at Wolff's headquarters in Fasano Wolff was not there, but he returned around dawn. Wolff had gone to Kesselring's command post to feel out the situation. Kesselring definitely would not be returning to Italy. He was being transferred to the Western Front, and no one was yet certain who his replacement in Italy was to be. To my questions for Wolff, which Parilli put to him while they sat together in the garden as the sun rose, Wolff had given the following answers: If he was ordered to report to Berlin, he would refuse to go, stating that it was impossible to leave Italy during Kesselring's absence. A senior man had to stay in the area. He could try to win over Kesselring's successor for our plan or he could act alone. It depended on the personality of the successor. He was ready to act alone, if necessary, and would draw up a plan for us of the units and areas under his command. They were scattered, and although they would do as he ordered, such an action would not bring about the full cessation of hostilities he desired. One useful thing he could arrange would be the clearing of airfields and coastal areas for Allied parachute and seaborne landings. At least we could seize the major airfields and get a foothold in the north behind the German lines. This would hasten the end. Lastly, he wanted me to know that he was awaiting my instructions and was ready to come to Switzerland whenever I wanted to see him.

Having heard this, I was ready to leave for Annemasse but Parilli asked me for five more minutes because he had two stories to tell and something to give me. At this point he drew a folded and torn piece of fabric from his pocket and handed it to me. It was a burnt piece of cloth, Parilli said, from Wolff's overcoat. On the way back from Kesselring's headquarters an American fighter-bomber had shot up Wolff's car. It had been close. The chauffeur was injured and the car was put out of commission. Wolff wanted to know if we couldn't get the Air Force to take it easy east of Milan, at least against automobiles traveling singly.

The morning Wolff returned from Army headquarters a meeting of all SS chiefs was to take place. He had summoned them the day before. Since Parilli was on the spot, he invited him to attend, and Parilli accepted, though with some trepidation. All the top toughs of the SS were there: Harster, Rauff and the commanders from Genoa, Turin, Venice and the smaller posts. The little Baron sat at Wolff's right hand as a guest at this secret parley. The reason was clear from what Wolff had to say. According to Parilli, Wolff issued instructions that from then on in all Italian territory controlled by the SS there was to be no violence against persons or property of any kind without first referring to Wolff himself for further orders. It was very brief. Wolff then dismissed the generals and colonels of the SS and had breakfast alone with Parilli.

"Tell the General," I said to Parilli, "that we would like to see him in a few days. As soon as he finds out who is replacing Kesselring and has decided on his plan."

Then I went to Annemasse, met my guests in the evening and stayed overnight with them. Two finer officers than Lemnitzer and Airey could not have been found for the mission on which they had been sent. Lemnitzer, a career soldier from West Point, had been promoted to Major General while still in his early forties. He had accompanied General Mark W. Clark on the secret expedition to North Africa before the Allied landings in November, 1942, had fought through the African campaign and had helped to conduct the clandestine armistice negotiations of September, 1943, that made non-Fascist Italy a part of the anti-Hitler alliance. His wartime participation in these important covert operations in Italy and North Africa had well prepared him for his part in Operation Sunrise, where secrecy proved to be an important element in eventual success. He played a vital role in the beginning and end of the Mediterranean campaign. As Deputy Chief of Staff he enjoyed Field Marshal Alexander's full confidence.

General Airey had served with Alexander since the days before El Alamein. He was an experienced British intelligence officer, with a wide knowledge of Europe and keen insight into the German character. Besides these excellent qualifications, both men were delightful companions and, fortunately, they each had a good sense of humor which stood them in good stead during the semi-humorous, semi-dangerous predicaments of their mission. Together they made an excellent team, Lemnitzer's sound common sense being supplemented by Airey's understanding of European intelligence work.

I told them of the last news from General Wolff as reported by Parilli, and I painted a somewhat discouraging picture. With Kesselring's departure from North Italy and no word yet of his successor, we could not judge our chances of getting a man in charge of the German Army who would accept Wolff's view of the situation. Also, it would not be easy to get any new Wehrmacht commander to act with the required speed. Therefore, I asked the generals, did they want to come with me into Switzerland and wait for Wolff or return to Caserta?

To my relief they were not disturbed by my account. Caserta was under no illusions. Alexander had thought it important for them to hear firsthand of my contacts, to appraise the intelligence we were getting through Wolff and—most important, of course—to explore the surrender possibilities. The whole picture I had been reporting of the dissension and confusion within the German command was new to them and of great significance for their planning, even if a surrender was not immediately forthcoming. The Allied spring offensive in Italy was surely to begin quite soon. Whatever could be found out in Switzerland about the intentions and the morale of the German forces and their commanders could be of critical value in the final stages of preparing this offensive. They decided to come into Switzerland with me.

The generals then told me that Field Marshal Alexander's report of the surrender possibilities had been sent via the Combined Chiefs of Staff to Moscow. In one sense I was relieved to get this news. From the very beginning I had felt that the only real danger which could come from my meeting with Wolff lay in some maneuver on the German side to use it to drive a wedge between the Russians and us. It would have been a simple matter for the Germans to let word leak to the Russians that some secret negotiations were going on in Switzerland, that the Western Allies were running out on them. If the Germans had an ulterior motive and Wolff was being used as a tool by Hitler and Himmler, this would certainly be the way the game would be played. Now that the Russians had been given the information through official Allied channels, any news that leaked out to them through the Germans could do little harm. At the same time I was puzzled about what the Soviets would do with this information.

As we sat there in Annemasse on March 14th, a message came for General Lemnitzer from Field Marshal Alexander stating that the Soviets wanted to send representatives to any parley held in Switzerland. Lemnitzer sent a return message saying that there would be no objection to *one* Russian joining us if he could speak English. (Fortunately we did not know at the time that the Soviets were considering sending *three* generals into Switzerland.) For the moment the question was only a technical one. How to get a Russian general into Switzerland? Russia had no diplomatic relations with Switzerland at the time, and a Russian was not easy to disguise and pass off as a Britisher or an American. Any hint that even one Soviet officer had been introduced secretly into Switzerland would have caused a major sensation from one end of the country to the other and would have seriously embarrassed us all, Waibel in particular.

Since we had no definite word about the Russian decision we decided to put off this problem and to tackle the more immediate questions, one of which was the identities Lemnitzer and Airey would use while in Switzerland. It was not feasible for them to use their true names and ranks and to trump up some innocuous excuse for their trip, such as a prisoner-of-war exchange, an Army purchasing mission or the like. Any astute newspaperman would realize that these particular generals would not come into Switzerland on a mission of that nature. They had to be somebody else, but who? And with what identification? Caserta, as I have said, unaware of the touchiness of the situation in Switzerland, had not prepared for this problem. Finally, we hit upon the solution of giving them the identification tags of two senior sergeants in the OSS group, who parted with them somewhat reluctantly, seeing their chances of a holiday in Switzerland with lots of chocolate and Swiss cheese rapidly fading. But orders were orders. So Lemnitzer became Nicholson and Airey became McNeely, and they hung the "dog tags" around their necks which proved it.

But to get into Switzerland they had to do more than just wear the borrowed "dog tags." In those days the Swiss border authorities often questioned travelers closely and American soldiers on leave constituted no exception. It was known to the Swiss, for example, that every American soldier knew his serial number cold. Any hesitation in reciting it on request would be fatal. The hesitater would obviously be an impostor. As a result General Lemnitzer and Airey set about memorizing the serial numbers of the two sergeants so that they could recite them faultlessly.

They also memorized in brief the life histories of the two men they were impersonating. General Lemnitzer as Nicholson acquired several children and a domicile in Long Island City. What was more unlikely, General Airey, with his most distinctive British accent, had to hail from New York City as McNeely. When they finally lined up to go through the Swiss border post, General Lemnitzer went first and was rather closely questioned, which made General Airey, waiting behind him, somewhat nervous. General Lemnitzer passed muster, having recited his new serial number without a hitch. When they got to General Airey, to the latter's great relief, they only asked him two questions and then let him pass.

The senior OSS aides accompanying the generals were to come in under their true names. The party entered on March 15 and drove up to Bern. The two generals stayed with me in my apartment. Bern is a small place and we decided it was safer for them to spend the day looking out my windows at the beautiful view of the Alps or listening to the radio, and to take the air only when night fell. We waited for word from Wolff.

8

Secret Meeting at Ascona

For the duration of the war, Gaevernitz had the use of two unique pieces of property which belonged to his brother-in-law Edmund H. Stinnes, who because of his opposition to Hitler had emigrated to the United States together with his family. The property was located at Ascona, on Lake Maggiore, in the Ticino, the Italian-speaking canton of trilingual Switzerland. It comprised a villa directly on the lake and another at some distance above it on the hillside. It was from the quiet of this retreat that Gaevernitz carried on much of his secret work.

Not far away is Locarno, famous in post–World War I days for an attempt at peacemaking. It was no accident that Locarno was chosen in 1925 as the site for an international peace conference. The placid lake among towering mountains creates an atmosphere of security and calm. It was hard to believe as we arrived there in 1945 that a few hundred miles north and south of these mountains a war was being waged. All the surroundings breathed peace and mirrored beauty.

If a secret meeting was to be held between the Allied and the German generals, as we were then planning, here was the perfect spot for it.

We foresaw that the parleys would consist initially of separate meetings among the representatives of each side, Allied and German. Then, if progress was made, there would be a get-together of the two groups of belligerents. All this required careful handling. The two sides would have to be kept secure and at arm's length until there was agreement to meet. Thus, the two villas, one on the lake and one on the hillside, would suit our needs admirably. Trees, mountains and the lake provided the premises with a screen against intruders. Public hotels and inns were out of the question for a gathering of such a sensitive nature. So we went ahead with plans to get things in shape. Gaevernitz went down to make the necessary arrangements and to lay in provisions—not an easy matter for such a large group, since all food was at that time strictly rationed in Switzerland. Even a few guards were brought in, as tourists.

There was only one hitch. It has always amazed me how desk personnel thousands of miles away seem to acquire wisdom and special knowledge about local field conditions which they assume goes deeper than that available to the man on the spot. Washington, which by this time had begun to take a lively interest in Sunrise, objected at first to our proposal to hold the meetings in Ascona. Somebody back there had undoubtedly looked at the map and discovered that Ascona was less than five miles from the Italian border across the lake. What if the Germans stormed up the lake in speedboats and kidnaped the Allied generals off the veranda of Gaevernitz's villa or even dropped in parachutists? They had, after all, captured Mussolini right from under the noses of his Italian guards, and earlier in the year there had been a rumor of plans to kidnap General Eisenhower. It took a few cables to straighten this out. The Germans were not, at this late point in the war, going to break Swiss neutrality. They had enough troubles already. Besides, the Swiss patrolled their sector of Lake Maggiore in motorboats day and night. Besides this, it was hardly conceivable that the purpose of Wolff's protracted and laborious efforts and the release of Parri and Usmiani were all a build-up for a kidnaping operation. This argument with headquarters we finally won and Ascona was cleared for security. It was a minor skirmish compared to some that still lay ahead of us.

On March 17th Baron Parilli was back in Switzerland again. He phoned Waibel and Husmann from the border. He had two messages. General Wolff and his party would arrive at the Swiss border very early on the morning of the nineteenth. General-oberst Heinrich von Vietinghoff, whom Wolff regarded as a personal friend, had taken over Kesselring's command in Italy. Waibel and Husmann went to meet Parilli in Lugano on the eighteenth. They intended to wait there for the Germans. This time, in view of Kaltenbrunner's hostile interest in everything Wolff was doing, Waibel and I worked out special security precautions. In the early morning of the day of the proposed meeting, the German party would be taken in a car from the border to a private house in Lugano.

They would enter the house, and the car that had brought them would drive away. Then they would leave the house by the rear, where our cars would be waiting for them and would take them to Ascona.

What makes intelligence officers despair is the unexpected and usually silly accident that threatens to spoil everything after the most careful preparations have been made. While Waibel was out making these arrangements, Husmann and Parilli, sitting in an alcove of the empty lobby of one of the large hotels in Lugano, engaged in a whispered conversation. This attracted the attention of the concierge of the hotel, who, like many men holding that position, was a self-appointed detective. He decided the two were a couple of smugglers and reported to the police, who came to question them. Waibel returned in time to vouch for them and the police departed. It was merely a coincidence, just a not so comic interlude.

Several OSS officers from Bern went down to Ascona on the eighteenth in twos and threes on separate trains. Lemnitzer and Airey were to be Gaevernitz's guests in the villa on the hill while I stayed in a picturesque hotel on the lake near the other villa, where we planned to have the secret talks. For the rest off the group, Gaevernitz had found rooms in the hotels of Ascona and Locarno.

An amusing incident took place when the generals settled into the quarters Gaevernitz provided them in the villa on the hill. Gaevernitz had checked the premises in minute detail before they arrived, and, noticing a collection of German books on the shelves of the room General Airey was to occupy, he removed them, thinking that a British general would take exception to this blatant reminder of the foe in the peaceful atmosphere of Switzerland. No sooner was dinner over than Airey asked Gaevernitz if he had some copies of Goethe's and Heine's poetry around the house. He knew the German language well and enjoyed reading the German poets. Gaevernitz was glad to comply immediately. The books were in the next room, to which he had just temporarily exiled them.

The following day dawned clear and sunny. If one believed in omens, this was a good one. It was spring on the southern side of the Alps. After breakfast Gaevernitz, while going over the premises, was shocked to discover a number of tough-looking fellows in civilian clothes, heavily armed and at the ready, hiding behind trees. We had not realized that OSS guards intended to surround the place. But we did know that if just one of them thought he saw something suspicious in the bushes and fired a warning shot, we could close up shop and go home, because the Swiss police would arrive immediately to investigate the place. Since most of the "visitors" would be present under assumed names and without proper identification, our whole program could blow up in a highly embarrassing newspaper story, and most of the participants might have been arrested by the Swiss police.

We arranged to withdraw the unneeded guards but not before a distant cousin of Gaevernitz's, who lived in the vicinity, gave us another scare. He had borrowed an ax some days earlier from Gaevernitz and had chosen that day to return it. Luckily, Gaevernitz spotted him entering the grounds with the ax on his shoulder and hastened up the hill to intercept him before he could run head-on into the guards hidden among the trees.

General Wolff and his party, with Husmann, Waibel and Parilli, arrived from Lugano shortly before eleven. Wolff had brought with him his adjutant, Major Wenner, and Captain Zimmer, both of whom had accompanied him to Zurich. But this time he left Dollmann behind at his headquarters to keep an eye on the situation there during his absence. If any messages came from Himmler or Kaltenbrunner, he wanted Dollmann to know about it. The Allied generals were to remain at their villa on the hill during the morning while we prepared the ground with Wolff. Parilli, Waibel, Husmann and Wolff's two aides were invited to sun themselves in the garden, and Gaevernitz and I settled down with Wolff in the living room of the villa by the lake.

Wolff first reviewed for us the developments since the meeting in Zurich eleven days before. On hearing that Kesselring was to take over Rundstedt's command on the Western Front, Wolff had assumed that he would first return to Italy to make his adieus to Mussolini. This would have afforded Wolff a chance to talk to him. But the situation in the Western Front was too serious. Kesselring had been ordered by Hitler to go directly from his conference at the Führer's headquarters to his new command. His replacement, Vietinghoff, was expected in North Italy on the very day we were meeting, March 19th.

I pressed Wolff to tell us something about Vietinghoff. What sort of man was he? How well did he know him? Vietinghoff, he replied, was an old hand in the Italian campaign. He had been Commander-in-Chief of the German Tenth Army defending Monte Cassino, and had taken over Kesselring's top command in Italy during a short period late in 1944 while Kesselring, injured in an automobile accident, was hospitalized.

When Kesselring returned to his post, Vietinghoff had been transferred to Latvia, which Hitler was stubbornly trying to hold. It was no surprise that he had turned up again as Kesselring's replacement. Wolff said that his relations with Vietinghoff in the past had been close and friendly, and he felt that he had been of considerable help to him during his periods of command in Italy. However, Vietinghoff was a rather stiff and proper aristocrat of Baltic origin, as nonpolitical a German general as one could find. He was not the sort of man who would be likely to take independent action or to understand the political and ethical implications of Germany's position at the present stage of the war. He would not be easy to win over unless he felt that he had the backing of other senior officers in the Wehrmacht. Furthermore, Wolff, having had no way of foreseeing Vietinghoff's assumption of the Italian command, had never discussed the idea of surrender with him. If he could be brought around to the idea of surrender at all, Wolff feared it would take some time to do it.

Kesselring had now been gone from North Italy for ten days, and Wolff had not been in touch with him and could not risk talking with him over the telephone when the Gestapo would be listening in. Knowing that Kesselring's attitude about the German situation was pessimistic, Wolff assumed that he had taken over his new duties on the Western Front without complaint, as a soldier obeying the Führer's orders—but probably with a heavy heart.

Did this mean, I asked, that we would have to dismiss Kesselring entirely from our surrender plans? No, Wolff answered, not entirely. As he saw it, there were three possible alternative courses of action. The one to be chosen depended upon how long a time he, Wolff, had in which to act. If there was practically no time available, he could simply act with the forces under his own command. This might not be very effective. The next possibility was to go directly to Vietinghoff and see if he could enlist his aid. The third possibility, which he would strongly recommend, was for him to go immediately to Kesselring's headquarters on the Western Front and try to get his support. Kesselring, he thought, could swing Vietinghoff into line.

It turned out that the element uppermost in Wolff's mind in regard to these choices—the controlling factor, namely, time—touched on a sensitive question. "The German command," he said, "had information which led them to believe that a big Allied offensive in Italy would be staged by the end of March." I must say that I could not help wondering at this point whether Wolff was trying to find out the date of the offensive for reasons other than those we had met to discuss. But there was no fear that I might inadvertently give him the answer to his question. I did not know it myself, though the two generals on the hill certainly did. His point was, of course, that once the offensive began, the chance of talking surrender with any success was minimized, at least until the first clashes were over.

"If you can give me five or possibly seven days to act," Wolff said, "I would favor an immediate visit to Kesselring. I would need this time as I would have to go by car. To arrange an airplane trip would be too conspicuous, and, as a matter of fact, we have no airplane gas to spare. But since I control the police forces up to the Brenner Pass, I could motor over the Brenner Pass, unless your bombing interrupts communications, proceed to Germany and talk with Kesselring. I have laid the groundwork with Kesselring, and, what is more, I have a perfectly legitimate reason to visit him. There are many unfinished matters affecting the Italian theater which I would discuss with him."

Wolff's reasoning, then, was that if Kesselring went along with his plan, Vietinghoff would be easier to handle. Whether Kesselring could be talked into surrender on the Western Front itself was not discussed. We learned later that Wolff secretly cherished hopes of this possibility, but for the moment our concern was the Italian front.

At this point Gaevernitz and I told Wolff that we had available for consultation two competent Allied military advisers. (We gave no names.) During the lunch hour Gaevernitz and I would talk over with them the entire picture as Wolff had presented it. Offhand, it seemed to us that he should follow his own best judgment and visit Kesselring. I did not know and could not tell how much time was available for action. All I knew was that if the Germans wished to surrender, they should do so quickly. Any coming Allied offensive might so dislocate the Nazi armies that an orderly surrender would be impossible.

Wolff was disappointed. He had hoped for more definite advice.

We then turned to the alternative of acting on his own. What troops were directly under his command? What use would they be? He described the mixed and motley forces which the SS had assembled in North Italy: Italians, Russians, Serbs, Croats, Czechs, *et al.*, which I have enumerated in a previous chapter. They were armed only with light weapons and had a few rather ancient tanks. They were widely scattered, the Slavic elements posted toward the Adriatic coast. Besides these units, which he commanded as Highest SS and Police Leader, he had over

50,000 Germans assigned to him as General of the Wehrmacht, the other title he carried. Of these only about 10,000 were tactical units, the rest supply and transportation companies. Realistic prospects for any major support to our cause from these troops seemed slight, though they might be useful, we were told, in securing airfields and coastal areas for Allied takeover.

One thing was now very clear. In any surrender, General Wolff's contribution would have to be primarily as the persuader, as the man who would talk the Army generals into realizing the futility of further fighting. The question was, therefore, whether Wolff should try to see Kesselring or should just concentrate on Vietinghoff, who didn't sound like an easy man to persuade now that we had the facts about him.

We asked Wolff about Mussolini's position. Wolff said he was largely under the influence of the women around him—his wife, Donna Rachele, and his mistress, Claretta Petacci, and her relatives. He was, in any event, now of no consequence in the matter of a surrender. Kaltenbrunner? Wolff showed signs of disgust. Kaltenbrunner was merely trying to develop his own line through Switzerland for peace negotiations. He did not want to encourage or permit any competition. What about the Alpine redoubt, we asked. "Madness," said Wolff. "It would only bring additional suffering to the German people. Everything possible must be done to prevent such last-ditch resistance."

I told Wolff that before talking with my military advisers I wanted to clarify one or two additional points. To carry out any program of surrender there were complicated and technical military matters to be settled. It would be necessary to have conferences between qualified military spokesmen, and they could best take place at the headquarters of the Allied forces in the theater, at Caserta. Wolff recognized this and said that as soon as the plans materialized he would be prepared to send competent persons to Allied headquarters. In reply to my inquiry whether this should be through the lines or via Switzerland, he said that secrecy could be infinitely better preserved if we could arrange for parliamentarians to be met at the Swiss-Italian frontier and conducted from there via Switzerland and France to Allied headquarters in Southern Italy.

There was one other technical matter. We appreciated very much the services of Baron Parilli, who was going back and forth as courier between Italy and Switzerland, but wouldn't it be advisable, especially if a surrender began to look promising, to have instantaneous and absolutely dependable communications channels between us in Bern,

Allied headquarters at Caserta and Wolff in Italy? I proposed to supply a wireless operator who spoke German like a native and who could pass for German to be placed at Wolff's headquarters. Wolff agreed. He would have to be kept under wraps and abide by the rules Wolff would set, but Wolff would take responsibility for his safety. Arrangements, of course, would await Wolff's return from his trip to Germany to see Kesselring, but in principle our suggestion was accepted. It proved to be one of the decisive steps to the success of our enterprise.

I remarked to Wolff that my military friends had never understood why the Germans had continued to maintain a large force in North Italy, given the present German military situation. Wolff said that the orders had been all prepared and approved by Hitler for an evacuation of a large part of North Italy in September, 1944. Under this plan nine divisions would have been available for other sectors. However, both Wolff and the German military experts in North Italy felt that the line could be held for some time to come and had opposed the move. The food supplies available in North Italy were considerable; Italian industry had some value; a great deal of food and commodities was then being taken out of North Italy; advance Allied air bases in the Italian plain would be a serious danger to Germany. These in effect were the arguments they used at the time, and Hitler swung over and subsequently had been against evacuation for the same reasons that impelled him to hold on in Norway and other such areas. Hitler was afraid of what the Germans called a *Räumungspsychose* (withdrawal complex), fearing that it would become epidemic after the complete defeat in France and would lead to a general breakdown.

It was now twelve-thirty. Gaevernitz and I had talked with Wolff for an hour and a half. Lunch had been laid on the terrace for Wolff and his aides and the others who had been sunning themselves near the lake. Gaevernitz and I went up to the villa on the hill to join the two generals. We found them sitting in the garden which commanded one of the most charming views in Switzerland, over part of Lake Maggiore, with the Alps glistening behind in the sun. They were impatient to hear our report on how things stood. Over a picnic lunch, out-of-doors, we gave them a full account of our talk with Wolff. While the meal was being served, the bell at the portal below rang loudly; Gaevernitz jumped up to see who was trying to invade our hide-out. Nobody with an ax this time. Just two friendly priests who wanted to look at the roses in the garden and wondered if they might pick some to decorate the altar of their church.

Lemnitzer and Airey, after hearing Wolff's story and his recommendations and discussing them with us point by point, were inclined to feel that Wolff should proceed immediately to Germany to see Kesselring. They felt that there would be time to do it. As yet, they had not decided whether they themselves would meet and talk with Wolff. But now their curiosity was aroused. They wanted to see what sort of man this character Wolff was. If he really was willing to undertake a peace mission to Kesselring and Vietinghoff, they thought it would be a good idea for them to size him up, to see him with their own eyes in order to judge whether he was the kind of man who had the ability to carry through the enterprise on which we were embarking and which could have a profound influence on history. We all realized that this was a major decision.

Now some questions of protocol and procedure arose. Should the names and military roles of the generals be disclosed to Wolff? It was agreed not to do so at the time and to introduce them simply as my military advisers. Then General Airey spoke up, "I'm quite willing to meet Wolff and to discuss with him the means of getting a German surrender, but you must understand that I will not shake hands with an SS general." I understood Airey's attitude.

The room in the lake house, where the meeting was to take place, was small and almost entirely taken up by an antique octagonal table. There were entrances into the room, facing each other, one from the spacious terrace on the lake and the other from the kitchen.

To meet General Airey's point, Gaevernitz suggested that he and the two generals enter the room on one side through the kitchen door while Wolff and I would enter from the terrace. Thus, Wolff and the Allied generals would be at opposite sides of the table, too far away from each other for handshaking. But it just didn't work that way. The formal introductions had hardly been made when Wolff stepped briskly around the table, squeezing his large body through the narrow gap between the table and the wall, grasped first Airey's and the Lemnizter's hand and shook them. But the handshakes were merely a reflex action; a man puts out his hand and you take it spontaneously without thought. To have done otherwise would have been an unnecessary slight and disturbed the progress of our meeting.

After I had introduced the two generals as my military advisers, no names being given, and stated that I had already given them the substance of General Wolff's report of that morning, I called on General Lemnitzer to open the meeting. He spoke in English and Gaevernitz acted as interpreter. The situation was unique and solemn. It was the first occasion during the entire war when high-ranking Allied officers and a German general had met on neutral soil to discuss a German surrender and talked peacefully while their respective armies were fighting each other.

Lemnitzer, after an appropriate reference to the purpose of the meeting, said that the report he had just received of the morning meeting had given him a good picture of the problems which Wolff faced as a result of Kesselring's departure for the Western Front. The early defeat of Germany was inevitable, and it was understood that all concerned accepted this fact. He had hoped that action could be taken quickly, but he realized now that there had to be a slight delay, since some preparatory work had to be done. Wolff, as a solder, would understand that speed, in any operation of this character, was a vital factor. Wolff was in a good position to assess the German position in North Italy, and it was now up to him, in collaboration with the appropriate military commanders, to produce the specific plans to achieve the desired end of unconditional surrender. From the technical viewpoint, it would be necessary to arrange for qualified military representatives on the German side to meet with the Allied military representatives. If the German representatives could be brought to Switzerland, arrangements would be made to take them from there to Allied headquarters in Southern Italy. Wolff replied that there should be two representatives, one for the Wehrmacht and one for the SS. General Lemnitzer emphasized that once these representatives reached Switzerland, we, the Allies, would assure their security and protect the secrecy of their passage to Allied Forces Headquarters and their safe return to Switzerland. The Allies, Lemnitzer went on to say, were interested only in unconditional surrender, and there would be no use in the Germans coming to Caserta unless they agreed to such terms. Furthermore, he told Wolff, conversations at Allied headquarters would be limited to methods of military surrender, and would not include political issues.

I asked Wolff to give in his own words his reasons for desiring to talk to Kesselring before he approached Vietinghoff. "I have been close to Kesselring," Wolff replied, "and I have in the past often talked with him about ways and means for ending the war. What I would say to him now would be neither new nor startling. On the other hand, I have never talked this problem over with Vietinghoff, and, knowing the conservative nature of the man, and his military training, I doubt whether

I would have, at first, much success with him unless I could assure him that both Kesselring and possibly General Westphal, Kesselring's new Chief of Staff and a friend of Vietinghoff's, would back him up."

Lemnitzer asked Wolff what he thought Kesselring could do, and to this Wolff replied that if his mission was successful, Kesselring would tell Vietinghoff to go ahead. Then he, Wolff, would go directly to Vietinghoff, and what he could say to Vietinghoff would have the added weight of the support of the Supreme Commander of the German Western Front.

"I cannot tell how long this will take," Wolff said in reply to Lemnitzer's question. "I am no prophet. With good luck, and if the Allied bombers do not get me, I might make the trip in five days, or a maximum of seven."

"Possibly Kesselring, too, would feel the urge to surrender on the Western Front if he had a good chance," Gaevernitz suggested. To this General Lemnitzer replied that since this related to another theater, it would be referred to General Eisenhower's headquarters for decision, but undoubtedly a method could be arranged to deal with it promptly if the occasion arose.

My "military advisers" withdrew, and before Wolff set out for the Italian frontier Gaevernitz and I had another brief talk with him. It was decided that if on the German side any questions were raised about the purpose of Wolff's trip to Switzerland, he would say he was negotiating an exchange of prisoners. I explained to Wolff then that it was going to be impossible to produce Wuensche in exchange for Parri, as he had suggested some time ago. Wolff took this in good grace but said his position would be considerably easier if we could at least produce somebody to explain his otherwise inexplicable action of releasing Parri. It needn't be a general officer; a lower one would do, as long as he had a decoration or two. I said I would keep trying.

Gaevernitz then took Wolff aside and had some questions for him. "How many political prisoners are being held in concentration camps in Italy?" he asked. Wolff didn't know precisely. Several thousand, he thought, of many nationalities. "What will happen to them?" Gaevernitz asked. "There is some danger that they will be killed," Wolff replied. We had heard this rumored. Secret orders had gone out from Hitler or Himmler to kill all political prisoners rather than let them fall into Allied hands alive.

"Will you obey these orders?" Gaevernitz asked. Wolff got up and walked up and down the terrace. Then he returned, halted in front of

Gaevernitz and said "No" and gave his word of honor, taking Gaevernitz's hand. When the time came, he kept his word, but that, like the
surrender, was farther off than we thought. He left then, intending to see
Kesselring at once and to report to us again immediately thereafter.

In the hope that Wolff would soon be back, perhaps in a week, with
news that he had swung Kesselring and Vietinghoff over to the idea of
surrender, Lemnitzer and Airey proposed to wait in Switzerland and received permission from Allied headquarters in Caserta to do so. On one
of the following days Gaevernitz said to his guests that he would like to
provide them with a souvenir of their visit to Switzerland. What was it
to be? A watch? A cigarette lighter? Switzerland was the place to find
such things. No, General Airey said, a dachshund.

Since we represented an intelligence organization, there was nothing, supposedly, that we could not do or find. But this project presented
problems. We put Gaevernitz's secretary, Nancy Leslie, on the job, as
she was a dog fancier herself, and she soon located a lady on the Lake
of Lucerne who raised the desired breed. Then, because General Airey
couldn't expose himself on such a trip, Nancy had to go and look at the
dogs herself. The dachshund lady, when Nancy honestly admitted the
dog wasn't for her, began to be suspicious. She always insisted on meeting in person the future owners of her dogs. She didn't want her dogs
taken out of the country. She particularly didn't want any of her dogs to
go to Germany. Nancy was evasive but assured her the dog was going
to Ascona, which was true, although it wasn't to be his last stop. The
lady finally sold her a little beauty which was promptly christened
"Fritzel" by its new owner.

In May, when news of the surrender broke, the British press got
hold of the Fritzel story and made the most of it, with slight distortions
of fact. The London *Daily Express* of May 7th had Fritzel's picture on
the front page with the following caption: "Fritz, the dachshund that
led to the surrender. A British and an American general went to
Switzerland, dressed as tourists, ostensibly to buy a dachshund. The
real purpose of their visit, however, etc., etc." When the war was over,
I gave Nancy permission to tell the dachshund lady where the dog had
really gone. We thought she might have been brooding over her miss-
ing pet. When Nancy phoned her and told her that Fritzel was now the
mascot of Allied Forces Headquarters and that his picture was in several of the English papers, she almost fainted, and when she had

recovered she yelled into the phone, "*Was! Ist er bei Alexander?*" (What? Is he with Alexander?)

One of my problems during this tense period of waiting was Parri. He was getting restless in his hide-out in Lucerne; he wanted to go back to Italy to resume his underground work. Day after day I had talked with him by telephone and urged him to be patient, but I realized how hard it was for him to follow my advice. For a man who had been fighting Fascism practically all his life, it was not easy to sit by idly during the crucial days of Fascism's death struggle. He felt like a bird in a gilded cage, he told me. He wanted to be in at the kill; he wanted to be fighting with the Italian partisans whom he had had so great a share in organizing. I had the feeling that my persuasive powers had been exhausted, and that Parri would slip away some night for Milan. I discussed this problem with Lemnitzer and Airey and between us we hit upon the idea of sending Parri to Allied headquarters in Italy to work out plans to coordinate the activities of the partisans with those of our advancing forces and to facilitate the orderly occupation of North Italy.

It so happened that General Cadorna, the military chief of the partisans, came from Northern Italy to Switzerland for a few days' consultation. We decided that General Cadorna should also go south with Parri, and Allied Forces Headquarters, on March 25th, approved our recommendations and sent a plane to the field we were using at Annecy, near Geneva, to pick them up. Both went, but Parri with reluctance and only after I had again given him my word to get him back to North Italy before the day of liberation.

Up to this time we had been successful in keeping Parri's whereabouts a mystery. In fact, most people believed, including his closest friends, that he was still in the jail at Verona, and the Italian partisan leaders kept urging me to do something to try to rescue him. One day they sent to me as their emissary Wally Toscanini Castelbarco, daughter of Maestro Arturo Toscanini and a charming lady. Late in 1943 she had escaped from North Italy to Switzerland, since the Fascists were threatening to take her as a hostage in order to bring pressure on her father, a consistent and vigorous opponent of Fascism and all its works. During her stay in Switzerland she had worked unceasingly on behalf of the Italian anti-Fascist movement. The very day she came to see me to beg me to do something to rescue Parri, he was in the next room. It was hard for me to keep a straight face as I assured my eloquent and persuasive visitor that I was doing everything I could to save her friend. Later, when the war was over I had quite a time of it explaining my deception.

Exactly a week after we had seen Wolff, on March 26th, Captain Zimmer came from Italy into Switzerland with a message from him. Wolff had telephoned to Zimmer in Milan from Kesselring's headquarters on the Western Front. Technical difficulties, far great than he had anticipated, had beset his trip. Kesselring was naturally a very busy man, trying to plug up the gaping holes at the front, and he had been so much on the move that Wolff had had a hard time finding him. In guarded language Wolff had let Zimmer know that he hoped to complete his program and return in two or three days. But he asked Zimmer to please find out from me whether the delay would be fatal, and if the "gentlemen" would go away in anger. "Try to keep the door open," Wolff urged Zimmer.

Two days later, on the twenty-eighth, Parilli turned up at the border with a message from Wolff's headquarters. Wolff would be back in Italy the following day.

In another two days—it was now March 30th, Good Friday—Zimmer came over the border at Chiasso and put in calls to Waibel and Husmann, who were holding the fort in Lugano over the weekend. Now the information was firm. Wolff had returned. He was in Fasano. Kesselring had consented to give his support to Wolff's plan and had told him to tell this to Vietinghoff. Wolff was about to see Vietinghoff. If all went as expected, he would come to Ascona on Monday, April 2nd, and would try to bring with him Vietinghoff, or one of his staff officers, and Ambassador Rahn. The three components of the German occupation of Italy would all be represented.

Lemnitzer and Airey were relieved. By April 2nd it would be a full two weeks that they had waited for Wolff to come back, but now the wait seemed justified. They wired the news to AFHQ, Caserta. They were impressed and so were we by Wolff's free-lancing, in the light of his responsibilities and the emergency situation of the moment, and by his apparent immunity and the obvious complicity of the most important members of his staff in this surrender venture behind Hitler's back. It was clear Wolff was in earnest. If Vietinghoff went along with the proposal and communications could be maintained, the surrender might be in our pockets in no time. We all gathered in Ascona the night before Easter Sunday to wait for Wolff.

On Monday, April 2nd, the day we hoped to see Wolff, no one came but Baron Parilli accompanied by Waibel and Husmann, who had met him at the border. He had been at Wolff's headquarters ever since Friday, and Wolff had sent him to tell us the whole story.

Himmler had phoned Wolff early on Easter Sunday morning. He had found out that Wolff had moved his family south of the Brenner Pass into an area which was under his own command. Himmler had moved them back into Austria, and had said, "This was imprudent of you, and I have taken the liberty of correcting the situation. Your wife and your children are now under my protection." This meant that Himmler was in a position to arrest and murder Wolff's wife and children if he chose to do so. Any man would hesitate to take action when facing such a threat.

Himmler then added that he was warning Wolff not to leave Italy; i.e., not to go to Switzerland. Wolff was too depressed to talk. The best he saw for himself was a funeral at state expense, like Rommel's. This was why Wolff had not dared to come to see us.

We fell on Parilli with our questions. How did Himmler get into the act? Who told him what Wolff was doing? How much does he know? What about Hitler? What about Kesselring and Vietinghoff? What about the surrender?

Then the Baron went back to the beginning. Wolff, traveling by car, had finally reached Kesselring's command post near Bad Nauheim on March 23rd. He had been attacked by low-flying bombers a number of times en route. That day the Americans had crossed the Rhine at Oppenheim, a bare fifteen kilometers away, and their continued advance was about to cut Germany in two. All hell had broken loose. While Kesselring was keeping a handful of field telephones hot with orders to his hard-pressed armies, Wolff was trying to tell him what he had done, describing his contacts to the Allies in Switzerland (but omitting his meeting with the Allied military advisers in Ascona). He asked Kesselring not only if he would approve Wolff's surrender attempt in Italy through Vietinghoff but if he would join in by surrendering in the West.

This Kesselring said he could not do. He was defending German soil and he was bound to continue even if he died himself in the fighting. He said he personally owed everything to the Führer, his rank, his appointment, his decorations. To this he added that he hardly knew the generals commanding the corps and divisions under him. Moreover, he had a couple of well-armed SS divisions behind him which he was certain would take action against him if he undertook anything against the Führer's orders. But he would counsel Vietinghoff to go ahead. "I regret that I myself am not in Italy now," he said.

A few hours later, when Kesselring had a chance to talk to Wolff at greater length, he told him that at Hitler's headquarters the Führer's closest advisers were still talking about miracle weapons, about a final desperation weapon (*Verzweiflungswaffe*), but it was all a delusion, he felt—one of Hitler's hallucinations. Kesselring wished Wolff luck. Wolff had succeeded, or so he thought, in his first objective, getting Kesselring's consent for a surrender in Italy.

Unfortunately, just at that moment, when Wolff was ready to return to Italy, Himmler, who had learned of his presence in Germany, summoned him to Berlin. He obeyed. In Berlin he saw both Himmler and Kaltenbrunner. Parilli knew little about this episode except that Wolff had managed to hold his own. He had returned to Fasano on the twenty-ninth, exhausted but in good spirits.

He immediately tried to reach Vietinghoff to tell him of Kesselring's consent to a general surrender in Italy. Unfortunately, Vietinghoff was absent on an inspection of the front and wouldn't return until the thirty-first. Wolff made an appointment to see him on Easter Sunday in the late afternoon.

The phone call from Himmler threatening his family had brought Wolff up sharply against the fact he had been evading ever since he had made his first moves in our direction. He could not charm Himmler and the whole SS over to his side. Kaltenbrunner and his other enemies in the SS, whose own personal plans he was spoiling, would think nothing of getting him out of the way and they had the advantage of being in Berlin, where they could make Wolff look like a traitor to Himmler and Hitler. Wolff saw that if he took a false step at this time he could be liquidated and then the whole surrender project would collapse. His death would serve neither the Allies nor the German people. He had to be careful for a few days at least.

Parilli had finished his account. We were all sitting around the table in the villa by the lake, Lemnitzer, Airey, Gaevernitz, Husmann, Waibel and I. For a moment no one said a word. Finally Lemnitzer said very quietly, "It's not half as bad as it looks."

If he meant it, he was more optimistic than the rest of us. He and Airey had waited in Switzerland two weeks in vain. Wolff had not sent a single word through Parilli about what might happen next. All we

could do now was send a message back to Wolff reaffirming our continued interest in a surrender and suggesting to him the best means of
communicating with us rapidly in case a surrender should suddenly, despite all the setbacks, become a reality.

We jointly composed a message which we had Baron Parilli memo-
rize and repeat back to us until he had it letter-perfect. The essence of it
was that parliamentarians could at any time come to Switzerland or be
sent straight to the Allied lines. In the Allied lines the password they
should use was to be "Nuremberg." We reminded Wolff of his promises: to limit action against the partisans, to avoid any willful destruction of North Italy, to protect Allied and other prisoners and hostages.

The Baron left for Lugano, where he intended to spend the night, returning to Italy the next day. We cabled Caserta that there seemed no
purpose in having Lemnitzer and Airey delay their departure. A plane
was sent up to fetch them and they were back at General Alexander's
Caserta headquarters by April 4th.

What had happened during Wolff's visit to Berlin we were able to
learn only later. Wolff, I think, did not wish to have us know of the
episode at the time and so he had told Parilli little about it. It was, as
we later saw in retrospect, the beginning of the counter-conspiracy on
the part of Himmler and Kaltenbrunner which came close to wrecking
Sunrise.

Wolff, while visiting Kesselring's headquarters on March 23rd, received Himmler's order to come to Berlin. He complied; possibly he
thought he saw an opportunity to put his cards on the table and win
Himmler over to his plan. Before he left Kesselring's command post, he
gave General Westphal, Kesselring's Chief of Staff, a package of American cigarettes he had with him, a rarity at that time. The little gesture
had a special meaning. Wolff said to Westphal. "If things get bad
enough here, I can open the door to the West for you."

He was then driven to Berlin, frequently being forced off the autobahn onto side roads to evade enemy planes which were strafing any obvious moving targets. In Berlin he headed for the Reichs-Chancellery. It
was around 11:30 a.m. The session with Himmler was supposed to take
place in a small bungalow on the grounds of the Chancellery, occupied
by Fegelein, the brother-in-law of Hitler's mistress, Eva Braun. Since
1943, when Wolff assumed his command in Italy, Fegelein had been
holding Wolff's old job of liaison officer between Himmler and Hitler.

Soon Himmler turned up followed by Kaltenbrunner. Himmler told Wolff they knew he had seen Dulles and Gaevernitz in Switzerland on March 8th. They were displeased with Wolff for having made this contact without getting Himmler's permission beforehand and without having first been briefed by the professional intelligence officers of the foreign section of the RSHA (*Amt VI*), such as Schellenberg himself, the chief, and his subordinates in the Swiss and Italian sections. Wolff was somewhat relieved to hear that the complaint against him, or at least the form in which Himmler put it, seemed to stem from the professional jealousy of the intelligence experts in the RSHA, whose expertise he had by-passed and ignored, and probably not from any suspicion of treason or double-dealing.

As the discussion progressed, without going beyond this rather bureaucratic issue, Wolff became ever more certain that Himmler and Kaltenbrunner did not know of his visit to Switzerland on March 19th, when he had seen Gaevernitz and me and the Allied military advisers in Ascona. This would have been much more incriminating and difficult to explain away. Had Kaltenbrunner's agents slipped up there? It was also possible, Wolff surmised, that Kaltenbrunner really knew little except what Harster had reported to him about Wolff's contacts with the Allies in Switzerland. Himmler next told Wolff that he wanted him to go with Kaltenbrunner to a meeting the next day at an evacuation center in northern Bavaria, where some of Schellenberg's intelligence specialists would be present to discuss the whole matter further.

Wolff now thought that the whole affair of getting him to Berlin had been staged by Kaltenbrunner, who, in all likelihood, wanted to take any peace initiative out of Wolff's hands and put it in his own. The real issue of bringing the top Nazi command face to face with the need for taking positive steps to stop the war was simply being avoided. No one had the courage even to mention it, or, as was abundantly clear in the weeks to come, each of them—Himmler and Kaltenbrunner—had his secret ambitions and plans to work through private channels toward this end, hoping at the same time to achieve his own salvation thereby.

Wolff then made a proposal which, though he could not have foreseen it at the time, was to stand him in good stead, indeed to save his life, on a later occasion. At the moment it was merely a sincere and courageous idea that came to him, prompted no doubt by the devious shilly-shallying of his shortsighted and self-serving compatriots. He suggested that all of them in the room should go to see Hitler and inform him that Wolff had established contact with Dulles and through him to the American government. Wolff was ready, he said, to try to convince Hitler, if the others would stand behind him, that this contact with the Americans should be followed up for the purpose of arranging a German capitulation in Italy at the earliest possible date.

The reaction of both Himmler and Kaltenbrunner was immediate and unequivocal. They didn't want to do it. It was a bad time. Hitler was in a very irritable mood. Especially any talk about peace feelers at the moment would be likely to set him off in a rage because Ribbentrop's recent awkward overtures to the Allies in Stockholm, which had been rejected, had soured him on the whole subject.

Himmler had other business to attend to and left the group. Kaltenbrunner then took Wolff to his villa near the Wannsee where the two men had lunch, avoiding in their conversation the subject of Italy entirely. Wolff had the feeling now that Kaltenbrunner was not yet ready to move against him, at least not with any intention of actually removing Wolff from the scene by force, as Wolff had feared when Kaltenbrunner had invited him to Innsbruck after his first trip to Switzerland. Rather he seemed professionally piqued and disgruntled because Wolff, as an amateur, had achieved something which Kaltenbrunner had so far failed to do despite his massive intelligence organization and the large funds at his disposal.

The next day Kaltenbrunner drove Wolff to the evacuation center, which was in a castle near Hof in Bavaria, Burg Rudolphstein. There was an accident on the way because of Kaltenbrunner's reckless driving; the car turned over but Wolff fortunately was not hurt and Kaltenbrunner unfortunately survived. To Wolff's surprise, Harster was waiting for him at the center. He had, as he told Wolff, been ordered up from Verona. The reason given him for the summons was "inadequate reporting." He had been questioned during the day by the *Amt VI* specialists working at the castle. He knew little and had apparently told less. If Wolff had fears that Harster, in his difficult position in Verona, was siding with Kaltenbrunner and his forces in the plot, he could now be assured that this was not so.

The next morning—it was by now March 26th—the official full-dress discussions took place. The chair was taken by Schellenberg's Swiss-Italian specialist, Steimle, who also had an assistant present. Steimle had neither the rank to speak in any but a polite and deferential manner to Wolff nor the authority to engage Wolff in the typical complexities of intelligence operations, since this was not Wolff's line of business. Wolff kept the conversation close to the problems of exchanges of prisoners and the exploration of channels useful for peace feelers, both well outside Steimle's jurisdiction and interest. Steimle wanted to talk about émigrés, enemy intelligence services and the like—matters close to his heart.

If it had been Himmler's or Kaltenbrunner's intention to try by this means to squeeze or trick out of Wolff the details of his recent activities, they apparently had little success, according to the account of the meeting available to us. Kaltenbrunner said little. The upshot of the talk was a rather mild admonition to Wolff to keep away from the Americans. Kaltenbrunner closed the session by saying, "These contacts you think you have we can get, any time, as well." Steimle carefully put his many papers and notes back in his folder and closed it, and then the group went to lunch.

After lunch, Kaltenbrunner and Wolff drove back to Berlin. Harster was to return to Verona by car. That evening in Berlin, Wolff phoned Himmler that he had returned and was ready to report to him. Himmler was angry because Wolff had got back so late. Hitler had just ordered Himmler to leave at once for Hungary to stiffen the German resistance there. He had to catch the night train for Vienna and had no time to see Wolff. His orders to Wolff were to keep the door open to me, but not to go to Switzerland again himself.

It was after Himmler's return from Hungary that he had called Wolff in Fasano and told him he had taken Wolff's family under his protection and had forbidden him any visits to Switzerland. Kaltenbrunner had undoubtedly reported to Himmler Wolff's evasiveness at the meeting in Bavaria. It seems likely that both Kaltenbrunner and Himmler now suspected Wolff was up to far more than he had admitted.

9

The Odds Grow Longer

Over the Easter weekend, while we were waiting in Ascona, a British commando unit broke out of the Allied battle line in Italy, which had been static for three months, and on April 1st surprised the German 162nd Division in the area of Lake Comacchio on the Adriatic coast, taking over nine hundred prisoners. On April 5th, the day after Lemnitzer and Airey had arrived back at Caserta, units of General Truscott's Fifth Army, including a Japanese-American combat team, advanced northward out of the western end of the line on the Mediterranean coast and within a few days had captured Massa and the town of Carrara, famed for the great marble quarries which had supplied Michelangelo in his day.

Were these just probes or diversionary attacks? The rumble of the guns, reasonably inactive since the previous December, shook our hopes for a quick surrender. It is one thing to negotiate and discuss while the guns are quiet, while the situation is in stalemate. It is quite another to try to separate armies locked in active combat. By April 9th, there was no longer any question of what was happening. The spring offensive had started.

On that day Parilli turned up in Switzerland again. He had been gone a week. Captain Zimmer had preceded him into Switzerland the day before to announce his arrival to Waibel and Husmann. Wolff wanted to be certain I was going to be available because the Baron was bringing an important document for me.

Gaevernitz and I talked to Parilli at my apartment in Bern. Before he showed us the papers he had with him, he told us what had happened during the intervening days. Wolff had had a busy week. If we had thought he was backing down because of Himmler's threat, we were wrong. Wolff apparently had recovered from the blow.

First of all, Mussolini had just found out about the release of Parri and Usmiani and he was furious. The fact that he had learned of the release almost a month after it happened showed how cut off he was from events happening right under his nose. Somehow the news of the dramatic release had leaked out and appeared in the Italian press, and it was in this way Mussolini had found out about it. He called in Ambassador Rahn, who had decided, at Wolff's suggestion, to foist off on the frustrated dictator the story that Wolff hoped to get the German Colonel Wuensche in exchange for Parri. Rahn succeeded in selling this now rather shopworn pretext to the Duce. Since he hadn't heard it before, it calmed him for the moment, but there was the possibility that he would complain to Hitler, which would draw renewed attention to Wolff in Berlin. For this reason, Wolff begged me once again to please arrange for the release of some high-level prisoner held by the Allies in order to restore Wolff in the eyes of the people who had become suspicious because of the Parri episode.

More important, Wolff had met with General Vietinghoff three times, on Easter Sunday, and then again on the fifth and the seventh of April. Parilli had been present at the meeting with Vietinghoff on the seventh, also General Roettiger, who had been Kesselring's Chief of Staff and remained in that post under Vietinghoff. This get-together was disguised as a social occasion. Wolff invited the two generals and Parilli to tea at his headquarters. Wolff wanted Parilli to hear with his own ears what Vietinghoff had to say and to report it to us. It was a risky thing for Wolff to do. He was, after all, introducing to the German High Command in Italy an Italian civilian who was working with the Americans in Switzerland and was about to go pay them a visit. It would not be hard for Wolff's opponents to make this single act look like treason on his part. And the charge would have been justified. While Parilli was drinking his tea, word came through for Vietinghoff that the Allies were storming the area of Lake Comacchio. On the telephone Vietinghoff ordered reinforcements of five thousand troops to be dispatched to Comacchio at once, a piece of intelligence which Parilli overheard and reported to us and which we wired at once to Alexander's headquarters.

But the main issue was what would Vietinghoff himself do? Would he stop the fighting? He had received Parilli most cordially. It was not easy for us to imagine the German General having tea with the little Baron while German troops were facing the opening bombardment of the Allied spring offensive. The contrast between the two men was startling: Parilli, a short little wiry bald man, who smoked cigarettes incessantly when he got excited and waved his hands around vehemently; Vietinghoff, a stiff broad-shouldered man, with a long straight nose, hair parted in the middle in the style of the previous century, clipped mustache, high well-polished riding boots, unexcitable, a man of few words—in short, the traditional picture of the German militarist. All he needed was a spiked helmet to look as if he had just come from a council of war with Hindenburg or Ludendorff.

Vietinghoff and Roettiger were both well aware of what Wolff had been doing in Switzerland. There was no need to discuss that. Moreover, Vietinghoff and Roettiger were in full agreement that the time had come to put a stop to any further useless slaughter. But Vietinghoff did not want to go down in history as a traitor to his country or to the traditions of his family and his caste. While he was willing to surrender, there was the question of doing so under honorable military terms. He was ready to sign an unconditional surrender if the Allies would accept the points of honor he wished to have observed. They were these: the Germans would stand at attention when the Allies arrived to accept the surrender; the Germans would not be interned in England or America and would only temporarily be held in Italy and, while there, would be allowed to do some useful work of reconstruction on roads and railways rather than be put behind barbed wire; after the situation had stabilized, the Germans would be returned to Germany still in possession of their belts and bayonets as evidence that they had made an orderly surrender.

I asked Parilli for Wolff's written messages, since they likely would contain in explicit language Vietinghoff's proposals. When he handed them to me, he told me that Wolff had summoned Colonel Dollmann to his office to type them out. He obviously was not going to entrust them to his secretaries. So Dollmann, the SS Colonel, Himmler's confidant in Italy, became a part-time typist in the cause.

The first of the messages was actually from Vietinghoff himself. In Vietinghoff's own words some of the points of honor sounded a lot stronger than they did when Parilli described them, especially one Parilli had not mentioned at all, which requested "the maintenance of a modest contingent of Army Group C [Vietinghoff's command] as a future instrument of order inside Germany." This, Parilli now explained, really represented a wish rather than a demand, but as we studied it we realized that things were getting rather far away from the Casablanca formula of unconditional surrender, so far that Field Marshal Alexander could clearly not accept the terms. It seemed that what Vietinghoff really wanted in order to save his military honor was the right to return his troops to Germany more or less intact after going through the formality of laying down their arms. Lastly, what Vietinghoff, Roettiger and Wolff all wanted was that a draft of the capitulation be sent them through our channels so that they could study it.

The other messages were from Wolff. In great detail he outlined what he was doing to prevent the execution of the scorched-earth policy in Italy. Among other things he pointed out that he could not guarantee what might happen in port areas like Genoa, because the naval units were not under Wolff or Vietinghoff but under the Naval Command in Berlin. He closed by saying he hoped that the German command in Italy would soon be completely cut off from the High Command in Germany. He was certain that once this was so, Vietinghoff would feel free to act on his own initiative, and he begged us "to try to do something to meet the points of military honor that Vietinghoff has raised." If we could only partially satisfy them, North Italy, as he had promised, could be delivered to us on a silver platter in another week. Realizing that speed would now be of the essence and looking perhaps somewhat optimistically toward a successful outcome of the Vietinghoff proposal, Wolff also referred to an earlier suggestion that we place our own radio operator at some central point under his command in Italy so that we could remain in touch on an hourly basis during the rapidly changing military situation.

I immediately radioed a report of the Vietinghoff proposals to AFHQ at Caserta (and to Washington and London). I was not surprised when a rather curt answer came back from Caserta the very next day, April 10th, which said that the terms of the capitulation would be handed to the German parliamentarians when they arrived at Allied headquarters in accordance with the usage of war. They could not be shown them beforehand. Only one visit by German envoys was needed, and they should therefore be officers with complete authority to act in the name of their commander. Not a word about the points of honor. Alexander's silence on this made it clear that there was to be no face-saving for the Germans, but it also wisely obviated any premature discussion on the issue. With this message, Parilli and Zimmer returned to Italy.

We were not so discouraged by the way things stood at this moment as we had been a week before, when Himmler's threat to Wolff had seemed to paralyze Wolff himself and everything he had set in motion. He had talked Kesselring into supporting him, and then he had gone to Vietinghoff and done his best to persuade him. The new stumbling block seemed to be Vietinghoff and his points of honor.

In order to try to overcome the difficulties with the reluctant Vietinghoff, Gaevernitz suggested that he would be quite willing to go himself to the German General's headquarters and try to talk him out of his scruples. Gaevernitz had had a good deal of experience talking to German generals. He knew their mentality and what lay behind it—their code and their prejudices and preconceptions—exceedingly well. He was an American but German was his native language. He knew and understood the Allied position perfectly, had Wolff's confidence and had been present at almost all the Sunrise parleys from the beginning. His plan was to go, possibly accompanied by Waibel, straight to Vietinghoff in order to dissuade him from insisting on his points of honor. Gaevernitz felt that he could rely on Wolff to protect him during this mission, although it was a daring venture to go as an American citizen into the enemy camp while the war was on and the Germans were fighting hard against the Allied onslaught.

Field Marshal Alexander's headquarters at Caserta turned down the proposition. They admired Gaevernitz's gameness, but felt it was too risky. Moreover, they did not trust the sincerity of the Germans. They had begun to feel that perhaps the main intention of the Germans in Sunrise had been, after all, to drive a wedge between the Allies and the Russians. We did not agree with them in this, but there was no point in having a debate by wireless at that particular moment.

Our hopes, in fact, for a successful outcome for Sunrise still remained high enough for us to pursue the idea of placing a radio operator with Wolff in Italy. If Sunrise was revived, an operator would be an absolute necessity. Even if it wasn't, we might get some very useful military intelligence from him. The problem was to find a man who could and would take the job.

A short time before, anticipating a radio link in North Italy as a serious possibility, I had asked our OSS base at Lyon headed by Henry Hyde to look for German-speaking operators. During the winter our people had been assembling and training Europeans of various nationalities with the idea of parachuting them into Germany with radio equipment as agents behind the lines for observing and sending out intelligence on German troop movements, civilian resistance and the like. From this pool of trained men, our base recommended a man to us who seemed to fill the bill and was ready to face practically any danger. The operator Henry Hyde sent us was a Czech about twenty-six years old by the name of Vaclav Hradecky. He was a short, stocky, black-haired, rather uncommunicative fellow. We immediately dubbed him "Little Wally." He knew German almost perfectly and had been trained in radio at one of our bases in Southern Italy. The adventures he had survived in six years of war showed that he could take care of himself in almost any situation. He was arrested by the Germans in 1939 in Prague where he had been a student at the Charles University, one of the oldest in the world. He was deported to the concentration camp of Dachau, where he was forced to do punitive labor, was starved, beaten and mistreated—at the hands of the SS who ran the camp. After six months Wally escaped. Few people ever escaped from Dachau and those who did usually didn't get very far. Wally, however, managed to live underground in Germany for three years. He posed as a laborer, worked in factories and at the same time made contact with the Czech resistance and passed them intelligence on what he observed in Germany. He was finally caught in a raid in a small town in Bavaria and, lacking proper identification, was arrested and sent to a PW camp. He had managed to convince the Germans that he was an escaped military prisoner, not a former concentration-camp inmate (which would have meant death for him). He escaped from the PW camp and made his way into Switzerland. From Switzerland he went into France as soon as the Germans cleared out and there made contact with the OSS.

After a few talks with Wally, I decided he was the man for our job. I gave him his instructions and didn't cut any corners. I told him he was to be turned over to an SS officer at the Italian-Swiss border and he didn't bat an eyelash. Considering the treatment he had suffered from the SS, this confirmed my impression of his courage. Wolff had proposed that our operator work out of a room in Zimmer's office in Milan rather than at Wolff's headquarters in Fasano, which would be too dangerous for everybody concerned. I therefore explained to Wally that he would be hidden in the house of the SS officer who was meeting him at the border, that he couldn't leave the place and that he was to transmit the messages the SS officer gave him and to listen for our signals to him. He was to give our incoming messages to the SS officer. I gave him no clue whatever of the reason for his going or the operation in which he was to play such a vital part. He asked me no questions.

On the thirteenth of April, Zimmer phoned from the border and Wally was driven down to meet him. He had with him a suitcase radio, his code pads and signal plan, a change of underwear and socks and an enormous supply of cigarettes. Zimmer drove him to Milan and installed him in a house on the Via Cimarosa on the top floor so that he could drape an aerial out over the roof. The building was the headquarters of SS counterespionage for Piedmont. It was in an area almost entirely requisitioned by the SS, but nobody had access to Wally's room except Zimmer and Parilli. On April 14th Wally's first signal was picked up in Caserta. He was in business and we, in Bern, had an essential tool for our work: independent and secure communications with General Wolff.

Just at this time I was called to Paris. General Donovan was there and wanted to see me. He particularly wanted to hear about Sunrise in all its detail. I decided to take Gaevernitz with me so that he also could give his firsthand impressions of Wolff and the other participants.

The day before we left, one of our Austrian contacts called in and reported that the SS intelligence chief in Austria had come to Switzerland and was anxious to see me. This was Wilhelm Hoettl, one of Kaltenbrunner's top SS operatives. Hoettl's name had been mentioned some months before as a potential visitor to us by an Austrian agent who had come to Switzerland with peace messages for us from Kaltenbrunner. We had by this time been well warned by Wolff of Kaltenbrunner's displeasure with our independent surrender proposals and of his attempt to thwart them. We assumed Hoettl's request to see us now must represent a direct attempt by Kaltenbrunner to cut across the lines established by Wolff, since he had been unable to stop him in any other way. I had no desire to see Hoettl and I was in any case leaving the country. I felt, however, that it would be interesting to hear what Kaltenbrunner wanted to tell us. I, therefore, asked one of my aides who specialized in Austrian matters but who had no inkling of the Sunrise affair to go to Zurich to see Hoettl. Within our own office, knowledge of Sunrise was restricted to two other officers besides Gaevernitz and me. One of these, Captain Tracy Barnes, was to meet with any envoy of Wolff's who might come to Switzerland during my absence.

The news of another event of far different significance also reached us before we left for Paris. President Roosevelt had died suddenly at Warm Springs, Georgia, on the morning of April 12th. President Truman had been sworn into office on the same day. In neutral Switzerland as we left, as well as in liberated France when we arrived in Paris, there was a feeling of inestimable loss at the death of this great man who had brought the strength of America into the conflict against Hitlerism in Europe. His death, with victory in sight but not yet achieved, cast a pall over us all as we discussed the Sunrise operation with Bill Donovan, who had personally been so close to Roosevelt. Roosevelt's faith in Donovan had been the moving spirit behind the undertaking on which we were engaged and behind the organization entrusted with the task of carrying it on to completion.

Gaevernitz and I gave Donovan and Russell Forgan a detailed account of Sunrise. Forgan was one of Donovan's chief aides and head of the Paris Mission of OSS, an old friend of mine who had been of constant help to our Bern operations. We made our account as objective as we could, outlining our hopes and fears. We underplayed its prospects of success because at that moment Vietinghoff's points of honor and the fact that Wolff himself could not hope to achieve a surrender without Vietinghoff's cooperation did not allow for any optimism. But Donovan was enthusiastic. It was just the kind of operation he liked to see us fight through to the end. He wanted us to try everything possible to bring it off. Forgan had helpful guidance for us. Both men saw the larger picture. They knew that Vietinghoff had almost as many divisions facing the Allied armies in Italy as Kesselring had on the Western Front. The Western Front was getting all the news coverage. The folks at home wanted to read about our armies overrunning the enemy's homeland, and consequently the Italian campaign was confined to the inside pages. But much American and British blood would be shed on Italian soil if the German armies continued to fight in the Alpine mountains because the German High Command in Italy was unwilling to quit a battle which they couldn't possibly win and which no longer served any military purpose whatever. As we might have it within our grasp to put a stop to the war in Italy, we must try everything to accomplish it.

Donovan with knowledge of the Washington background told us what was then known about developments since the Soviets had been informed of Sunrise. As already stated, I had first heard about the Soviet reaction from Lemnitzer and Airey at Annemasse on their arrival about a month before. But all we had learned then was that the Soviets had been told of the operation and were insisting that Russian generals should come to Switzerland to take part in any discussions with the Germans. Later Stalin, it now appeared, had sent an accusatory message to Roosevelt. The burden of it was that we were making a separate peace with the Germans behind Stalin's back. Roosevelt had believed in the good faith of Stalin and Molotov at Teheran and at Yalta. Then suddenly the masks had fallen. The Soviet attitude toward Sunrise had given President Roosevelt his first nasty jolt in his experience with the Soviets. A message which the President sent before his death on April 12th—probably his very last—was a note to Stalin regarding Sunrise, and referring to it as "the Bern incident." Now it was President Truman who inherited the issue.

Donovan's news surprised and disturbed me. He assured me, however, of his conviction that if the surrender was forthcoming the United States and Britain would not let any complaint of the Soviets get in the way of it. We were acting in good faith. If American and Allied lives could be saved by an unconditional surrender of the German armies in Italy, we were to go ahead.

As I thought over the Soviet attitude, I began to see what was probably troubling the Soviet leaders. If we were successful in getting a quick German surrender, Allied troops would be the first to occupy Trieste, the key to the Adriatic. If we failed and the Germans, still fighting, fell back in a tight defensive knot west of Venice under the shadow of the Alps, then Communist forces, either Soviet troops coming across Hungary or Tito's followers reaching up out of Yugoslavia, supported by the pro-Communist partisans, would be in Trieste and possibly west of there before we arrived.* Hence, there was an impelling reason for us to achieve the surrender. In this regard, it is well to remember that while zones of Allied and Soviet occupation in Germany, including Berlin, and in Austria had been fixed by earlier agreement between the Allies and the Soviet

---

* According to Rahn, the German Intelligence Service at about this time intercepted a communication between Stalin and Tito in which Stalin urged Tito to prepare to move his forces across Northern Italy as far as the French border. Rahn theorized that a junction of these forces with Communist partisans in France would have created a Soviet-controlled belt across Southern and Western Europe which would become the base for the eventual Communization of both France and Italy. (Silvia Bertoldi, I Tedeschi in Italia [Milan, 1964], p. 186.)

government, this was not so in Northern Italy, since Italy was treated as an ally; thus, prior occupation of this area by Communist-dominated forces might well determine the zones of postwar influence, or even occupation.

It wasn't until well after the end of the war, of course, that I learned the full details of this disagreement between Russia and the Allies, which, as we will see later, became such a serious threat at a crucial stage of Operation Sunrise. The chronology of what Admiral Leahy has called "our first acrimonious altercation with the Russians since they joined the Allied cause" was the following:*

March 9, 1945—Field Marshal Alexander notified the Combined Chiefs of Staff of his intention to send two general officers (Lemnitzer and Airey) to Switzerland to look into the German surrender proposals. On March 11, 1945, it was decided by the American and the British governments that each would inform the Soviets of what was developing. Ambassador Harriman, after informing Soviet Foreign Minister Molotov, was told by Molotov on the next day, March 12th, that the Soviet government did not object to the talks but wished to send three Soviet officers to Switzerland to take part in them.

March 13th—Major General Deane, Chief of the U.S. Military Mission in Russia and Ambassador Harriman's adviser on military matters, referred Molotov's request for Soviet participation to Washington, suggesting, however, that it be disapproved because he though it would only delay the proceedings and would set an unfortunate precedent. He pointed out that we did not participate in local German surrenders on the Russian front.

March 15th—The State Department wired Ambassador Harriman asking that Molotov be informed that Soviet representatives would be welcomed at Field Marshal Alexander's headquarters when the surrender became an actuality; the talks in Switzerland were only exploratory. Moreover, since the German proposal involved a surrender on an Anglo-American front, only the Americans and the British could be responsible for the negotiations.

---

* This account is largely from the following sources: Fleet Admiral William D. Leahy, *I Was There* (New York: McGraw-Hill, 1950); Winston Churchill, *Triumph and Tragedy* (Boston: Houghton Mifflin, 1953); John R. Deane, *The Strange Alliance* (New York: Viking, 1947); James F. Byrnes, *Speaking Frankly* (New York: Harper, 1947); Herbert Feis, *Churchill, Roosevelt, Stalin* (Princeton: Princeton University Press, 1957).

March 16th—The above implied refusal to allow Soviet representatives to join in the discussions in Switzerland seems to be what started the controversy. Molotov passed a peremptory note to Harriman. It declared that since the United States refused to allow Soviet participation in the discussions, which was to the Soviets "unexpected and incomprehensible," the Soviets insisted the negotiations with the Germans be broken off.

March 21st—The top American diplomatic and military advisers (Ambassador Harriman, Admiral Leahy, Secretary of State Stettinius and Secretary of War Stimson) having all agreed that we should not accede to Russian pressure in the matter, the Soviet government was simply informed that discussions had taken place with General Wolff on March 19th, but that nothing specific had come of them.

March 23rd—In reply to the above, Molotov now sent a note to both the British and the American governments accusing them of negotiating with the Germans "behind the back of the Soviet government which is bearing the brunt of the war against Germany." This insulting accusation which seemed to threaten the whole fabric of the Anglo-American-Soviet effort was naturally brought to the attention of both Prime Minister Churchill and President Roosevelt. At the same time, Molotov also announced that he would not personally attend the conference at San Francisco which was to set up the framework of the United Nations. This was an obvious expression of Soviet displeasure with the recent unilateral action of the Anglo-Americans, and it disturbed the leaders on both sides of the Atlantic. As Admiral Leahy writes: "An open break between Russia and her Anglo-Saxon allies would be the only miracle that would prevent the speedy collapse of the German armies" (p. 333). Prime Minister Churchill decided it was fitting for President Roosevelt to draft and submit the joint Anglo-American answer to the latest Russian insult.

March 24th—President Roosevelt cabled a personal message to Marshal Stalin in which he assumed that there had been a misunderstanding, but politely and firmly maintained that he could not agree to suspending investigations of the possibility of a surrender that would save American lives, especially since there were no "political implications whatever and no violation of our agreed principle of unconditional surrender."

April 3rd—Stalin answered Roosevelt's message of March 23rd in an alarming and inflammatory letter. It is clear from this letter that he drew upon information which Soviet intelligence had gathered about our discussions in Switzerland, much of it incorrect and probably purposely distorted, and it may have been the need to assemble and sift this information which caused him to delay as long as he did in answering Roosevelt. Among other items in Stalin's long piece there is a claim that the Germans had agreed "to open the front to the Anglo-American troops and let them move to the east while the British and Americans promised in exchange to ease the armistice terms for the Germans." This seemed to corroborate my theory that what worried the Russians most was that we might get into Trieste and Venezia Giulia before they did.

April 5th—President Roosevelt answered Stalin's accusing letter. This note was drafted first by General Marshall and Admiral Leahy and is quoted in full by Churchill (*op. cit.,* p. 447). The tenor of the note was that there had been discussions but no negotiations and that Stalin had been misinformed, possibly by German sources. It was hinted that the purpose of the Germans may, in fact, have been to create dissension between the Anglo-Americans and the Soviets, a thought which had remained in the minds of the top leadership in Washington throughout the Sunrise Operation. The message closed with a strong paragraph which Churchill surmises was added by President Roosevelt himself to the draft:

> Frankly, I cannot avoid a feeling of bitter resentment toward your informers, whoever they are, for such vile misrepresentations of my actions of those of my trusted subordinates.

(Regarding this message, former Secretary of State James F. Byrnes recently wrote me that Roosevelt's original answer to Stalin was even more strongly worded than this and that he had modified it because, in the meantime, he had received a note from Stalin on a different subject which was couched in very friendly language. Mr. Byrnes also quotes President Roosevelt as saying to him at the time that he did not understand this technique of the Soviets.)

April 6th—Because Stalin had commented, among the other insinuations in his letter to Roosevelt of April 3rd, that he "could not understand the silence of the British, although it is known that the initiative for this whole affair belongs to them," Churchill wrote a long message to Stalin reviewing the developments of Sunrise and pointing out that an American agency (referring to the OSS) had been handling the contacts.

April 7th—Stalin replied to President Roosevelt's reproachful letter of April 5th, backing down somewhat from his accusations of bad
faith against the Anglo-Americans but belaboring the point with many
arguments that the Soviets should have been invited to the discussions,
which apparently was a point that rankled throughout. He could not
omit in this note, however, numerous recriminations concerning earlier acts of the Allies in which he implied that there had been bad faith
and he also defended the excellent information-gathering capabilities
of his informants; i.e., the Soviet Intelligence Service, on which President Roosevelt had cast some aspersions. He also sent a somewhat
apologetic note to Churchill on the same day—or, as the Prime Minister put it, "as near as they can get to an apology."

April 12th—On the morning of this day, which was the day President Roosevelt died, he wrote a message to Stalin thanking him "for
your frank explanation of the Soviet point of view of the Bern incident,
which now appears to have faded into the past without having accomplished any useful purpose."

We came away from the Paris meeting with Donovan with a renewed
determination to throw the book at Vietinghoff or try to get his subordinate generals to quit, even if he wouldn't. We left General Donovan's
room late and went off up the dim corridors of the Ritz. As I was looking
for the room assigned to me, a stranger came up to me and asked a question. It wouldn't have seemed unusual to the outsider, but it threw me for
a moment. I have to explain that in the OSS we all had code numbers assigned us which we used in secret communications. If the messages were
intercepted, at least the identity of the persons mentioned therein could
not become known. Since we had occasion to use these numbers practically every day in incoming and outgoing messages, they became attached
to us in our minds very much like a name. I was 110, and had been 110
day in and day out for two and a half years. What the stranger asked me
as we met in the shadowy corridor after midnight was, "I beg of you,
where is 110?" Since my mind was echoing the thoughts Donovan had
just left with us, the question caught me off guard. I was just about to say
"You're talking to him. I'm 110" when I suddenly woke up to the reality
of the situation. He was lost in the badly lighted corridors of the hotel and
was looking for his room, which happened to be 110.

We got back to Switzerland on the fifteenth of April late at night
and found many reports waiting for us. The one from my assistant

who had talked to Hoettl showed that Kaltenbrunner was playing a cagey game. Hoettl, Kaltenbrunner's emissary, claimed he wanted to help the Western Allies by doing everything possible to prevent the establishment of the Alpine mountain redoubt. He had hinted at a desire of the Austrian group among the Nazi leadership (this no doubt included Kaltenbrunner) to make some kind of separate settlement with the Allies. Whatever its meaning, Hoettl's representations to us seemed of little moment compared to the disturbing news from the Sunrise front itself.

Zimmer had come to Lugano that same day, where he had met with Waibel and Husmann and my representative, Captain Barnes. Zimmer reported that he and Wolff had gone to see Vietinghoff at his headquarters three days before and had been given a very cold reception. Vietinghoff related that a British major, whose name he never learned, had turned up at the intelligence section of the Ligurian Corps in Genoa, one of the Italian Fascist units attached to the German armies. The "major" wore civilian clothes and claimed to have been sent by Field Marshal Alexander with a verbal message which he asked the intelligence office of the Ligurian Corps to pass on to Vietinghoff.

The message said that Vietinghoff was on the wrong track negotiating with American representatives in Switzerland; that he should follow a "British line" and negotiate directly with the British, who, after all, were Europeans and were keenly interested in the future of Europe and better acquainted with European conditions. He asked the intelligence officer to relay the message to Vietinghoff as promptly as possible and said that he would return within a few hours for a reply. The man was never seen again.

When Vietinghoff received the message, he became very upset. He was deeply disturbed that the news of his and Wolff's contacts with American representatives in Switzerland was obviously no longer a top secret, and was being bandied about apparently as a subject of contention between the British and the Americans. He now began to fear for his life, as he knew that his actions from the German point of view amounted to nothing less than high treason.

To cover himself he decided to report the entire Sunrise project to General Jodl, the Chief of the Operations Staff of the German Armed Forces at Hitler's headquarters in Germany. It took the combined persuasive powers of Wolff, General Roettiger and Ambassador Rahn to talk Vietinghoff out of doing this. Even so, the net result of this mischievous incident was to make the cautious and self-righteous Vietinghoff even more difficult than he had been before.

We immediately cabled a report of this incident to Allied headquarters at Caserta and received the reply that the British had never sent any such man. To this day the affair remains a mystery. One explanation we later considered was that it could have been a disruptive operation mounted by Soviet intelligence. It seemed calculated not only to frighten off Vietinghoff, which it came close to accomplishing, but also to create at misunderstanding between the American and the British Allies.

Wolff himself was apparently undismayed by this disturbance of the rapport he had established with Vietinghoff. He took the occasion of President's Roosevelt's death to write me a long personal letter which he sent via Zimmer, undoubtedly one of the most unusual documents I have received during many years of unusual experiences with unusual people. This was the Commander of the SS writing a letter of condolence on the death of the President of the United States while Germany and the United States were at war. He wrote it by hand on his official stationery but deleted the three lines at the top of the page that spelled out in engraved letters all his weighty titles. Under them he had written "Personal." I quote the opening section of it, translated.

> HONORED MR. D:
>
> On the occasion of the passing of the President with whom you were so close and whose loss must have been painful to you in equal measure as a man and as a member of the government, I would like to express to you my sincere and deeply felt sympathy. . . . Although at the moment I have no idea what effect this change of Presidents might have on the effort to seek some understanding between the warring parties, I want to assure you in this painful moment that I remain now, as before, convinced that a prompt cessation of hostilities is possible. . . .

Although I appreciated Wolff's thoughtfulness in sending me this letter, I could not dispel the idea that he might be worried about the attitude of a new administration toward our dealings with him, and even about whether I would remain in my job. As already mentioned, the rumor that I was "the personal representative of President Roosevelt" was current gossip in Switzerland and repeated in the files of German intelligence (as I discovered after the war). This undoubtedly accounted for Wolff's having used the words "with whom you were so close" in his letter.

The remainder of Zimmer's report was a mixture of good and bad. The good news was that General Roettiger was now fully supporting Wolff's attempt to arrange a surrender, as was General von Pohl, the Commander of the Luftwaffe in Italy, whom Dollmann had brought together with Wolff the previous September. Roettiger, who as Vietinghoff's Chief of Staff was not in a command position, could only keep working on Vietinghoff, but Pohl, who had now been brought into the Sunrise conspiracy, had fifty thousand men under his command, airmen and ground personnel. Wolff had, according to Zimmer, also talked to the German Army commanders in Italy under Vietinghoff and felt sure that they were with him regardless of what Vietinghoff might do. Zimmer also passed along a verbal message from Wolff, which ran like this: "I beg you to do everything possible that the Allies do not make useless sacrifices in an intensified offensive. I take full responsibility and guarantee that during the coming week all will be surrendered."

The bad news was that Himmler had been after Wolff again. On April 14th, Himmler had telephoned from Berlin ordering Wolff to report to him in Berlin at once. Wolff had succeeded in putting Himmler off by claiming that his presence was absolutely necessary in Italy. Local unrest was growing. Mussolini was beginning to lose his head as the Allied advance succeeded in breaking through the German lines south of Bologna and was threatening to order his inactive Fascist troops into the line. Only Wolff could keep order in these ticklish circumstances. Himmler was persuaded for the moment. Then Wolff sat down and wrote Himmler a letter. Playing on the idea which he had long since abandoned himself but which he knew would alone appeal to the wishful hallucinations of the top Nazis in Berlin, he declared that he was pursuing important negotiations with the Allies with a view to separating the Anglo-Americans from the Soviets. At length he pointed out to Himmler how he, Wolff, had been right on all the previous occasions when he had advised Himmler, and he begged him to take his advice now. Germany's western defenses were falling, as Wolff had told Himmler they would. Further fighting in the south would only kill off more Germans to no advantage. Wolff was seeking honorable terms with the Allies. He closed his letter by inviting Himmler to come down and join him in his attempt to make peace. (If Himmler had accepted his invitation, Wolff, we learned later, planned to arrest him on arrival.)

Wolff sent his letter to Himmler via a trusted SS courier who flew to Berlin on the fourteenth. On the same day Himmler telephoned twice to Wolff, who had purposely absented himself from his headquarters until his letter could reach Himmler.

As already noted, we knew that Himmler's strangle hold on Wolff was his power to bring harm to Wolff's family. At the moment, therefore, while more and more generals subordinate to the vacillating Vietinghoff were evidently beginning to share Wolff's sentiments, everything seemed to hang on the outcome of the personal battle between Wolff and Himmler. Because without Wolff, the moving force in the whole operation, it seemed to us there would be no surrender, not now at least.

We waited two days for word. On the seventeenth, Baron Parilli arrived in Switzerland. The plot was thickening, as was evidenced by the fact that Parilli was now afraid to travel openly in Italy and had driven up from Milan to the border disguised as a priest. I didn't see him in his disguise. He was wearing ordinary business clothes when he talked to me in Bern, and I had a little difficulty imagining this *bon vivant* and incessant cigarette smoker in cassock and robe. The day before, Wolff's adjutant, Major Wenner, had summoned Parilli to Fasano and had given him some startling messages and papers from Wolff for us. Wenner told him that the courier carrying Wolff's letter had reached Berlin and had seen Himmler the night of the fifteenth. Himmler had telephoned Wolff immediately after reading the letter. He hadn't discussed the contents of it. He had said to Wolff, "I didn't ask for a report. I want to talk to you personally." After thoroughly considering the matter, Wolff gave in and set out by plane for Berlin on the sixteenth, flying via Prague to avoid the densest battle areas. He still had to fly through some areas where at times the fighting in the air was violent. Berlin was, moreover, by then partly surrounded by Soviet troops. But these were only the dangers of war. The other dangers Wolff had to face were even more sinister.

Parilli had not seen Wolff before he left and Wenner was not very talkative. The verbal message he relayed to Parilli from Wolff for me was: "I am going to Berlin because I believe that by making this dangerous trip there may be a chance of accomplishing something for the entire German people. I shall be back in Italy in a day or two." The question we asked ourselves was whether he would ever be back. To us the chances seemed slim indeed.

I did not learn until some time later that Parilli had a piece of paper in his pocket from Wolff. It was a kind of personal testament of Wolff's addressed to me. Parilli had decided to hold it for a while just in case Wolff did come back, which neither he nor I felt was very likely. If, however,

Wolff did return, this document, the Baron felt, might sound a little awkward. These were the contents of the testament which Parilli handed me a little later:

> In case I should lose my command . . . and the action with which I have associated myself should not succeed, I request that the German people and the German troops in Italy should not suffer the consequences.
>
> If, after my death, my honor be assailed, I request Mr. Dulles to rehabilitate my name, publicizing my true, humane intentions; to make known that I acted not out of egotism or betrayal, but solely out of the conviction and hope of saving, as far as possible, the German people.
>
> After my death, I ask Mr. Dulles, in the name of the ideas for which I shall have fallen, to try to obtain for the German and Italian troops honorable terms of surrender.
>
> I request Mr. Dulles to protect, after my death, if this is possible, my two families, in order that they not be destroyed.

Before Wolff left, he had made arrangements for the SS chief in Milan, Rauff, to remain in close touch with Cardinal Schuster of Milan, the purpose being to avoid clashes wherever possible between the retreating Germans and the Italian populace and the partisans.

Parilli had one other piece of news. The Gauleiter of the Tyrol, Franz Hofer, had also been won over, so Wolff thought, for the surrender plan. Hofer, a party appointee, had absolute political power in the region of Austria and South Tyrol, backing on Wolff's territory, in which a part of the mountain redoubt was to be located. Hofer had, in addition, told Wolff that when he was in Berlin on April 12th he had talked to both Hitler and Himmler and had learned that neither of them planned to go to the redoubt. They were going to stay in Berlin, Hitler madly planning new offensives against the Soviet onslaught.

Whatever was to happen next, Wolff had, as usual, made the necessary arrangements to keep us well informed. He had ordered Wenner, at Fasano, to take any messages that came in from Berlin to Milan. From there Zimmer was to carry them to the border, where Parilli would bring them to us. Or if this was not possible, Little Wally, in his SS attic in Milan, could radio them to us.

In the meantime, Wally was trying to make himself useful. On the eighteenth of April we received a message from him in which he reported that Mussolini was coming to Milan that evening and would stay at the Palazzo Governo for three or four days. He gave an accurate description of the location of the building, and suggested we dive-bomb it, being careful to avoid his own quarters which were only about three hundred meters to the southeast. However, the Allied Air Force had other business at the time besides bombing Mussolini, and Wally was too important for us to take such chances just for the sake of burying the futile dictator under a pile of rocks.

10

Face to Face with Hitler

The battle of the Argenta Gap east of Bologna had begun in earnest on April 18th. The British Eighth Army had broken through the German defenses; the heavy artillery of the Polish Corps was now close enough to Bologna to reach the enemy positions defending it. The Germans were fighting back and suffering heavy losses from the combined assaults. Hitler's insane stubbornness and Vietinghoff's delay over his points of honor cost thousands of casualties in the next two weeks.

Although neither we nor Wolff knew at the time, Vietinghoff had sent an urgent plea to the Führer's headquarters on April 14th. It was of purely military nature—not a word about surrender. He told Hitler that it would be impossible to maintain his position and asked permission to withdraw to the line of the Po River.

As we know from documents which came into our hands after the war, General Jodl, the Chief of Staff at Hitler's headquarters, answered him abruptly on April 17th: "All further proposals for a change in the present strategy will be discontinued. I wish to point out particularly that under no circumstances must troops or commanders be allowed to waver or adopt a defeatist attitude, as a result of such ideas apparently held at your headquarters. . . ." This sounded like a clear reference to the rumors of peacemaking which had reached Berlin from Italy. "The Führer expects . . . the utmost steadfastness in the fulfillment of your present mission, to defend every inch of the North Italian area entrusted to your command. I desire to point out the serious consequences for all those higher commanders . . . who do not carry out the Führer's orders to the last word."*

The threat was clear. Vietinghoff could not have failed to appreciate the implications of this order. No doubt the likely results of disobedience would be court-martial and execution.

During the night of April 18th and the morning and afternoon of the nineteenth, several messages came in from Zimmer. They had been sent to him by Wenner in Fasano. The first two messages Zimmer telephoned to us from the Swiss border. We were told (1) that Wolff had reached Berlin safely on the night of the sixteenth; (2) that Wolff was having a final conference with Hitler on the afternoon of the eighteenth and would return to Italy directly thereafter. Wolff had spoken on the telephone from Berlin with Wenner and we knew, therefore, that he was still alive. I wondered, however, if he was still a free man. The third and last message reached us via Little Wally's circuit, signed by Zimmer. It stated that Parilli would meet Wolff at Fasano on the morning of the twentieth and that we might expect some decision regarding the surrender by the twenty-first. But it did not say that Wolff had actually left Berlin. We were inclined to be doubtful about it. Himmler might have been playing cat-and-mouse with Wolff's co-conspirators and subordinates in Italy. Or, if Wolff was really on his way back, what kind of deals had he made with Himmler and Hitler to get out of the lion's den alive? What had happened to his promise to deliver the German forces in Italy to us on a silver platter?

We kept Washington and Caserta informed of the latest developments and stood by. We waited all day on the twentieth but there were no phone calls from the border, no signals from Little Wally. There was a message from General Lemnitzer at Caserta which presumably reflected the thinking of Field Marshal Alexander. After my talk with Donovan in Paris and his revelations concerning Soviet opposition to Sunrise, I had cabled Lemnitzer my theory of the reasons for the Soviet attempt to stop Sunrise. They desired to get their hands on Trieste and North Italy before the Allies could occupy the area. I also had re-emphasized my conviction that Soviet opposition should not deter us from going ahead with the surrender if the Germans were ready. Donovan had left me with the impression that this had been President Roosevelt's position just before his death. But I did not know where President Truman stood on the issue.

* *The Italian Campaign, op. cit.,* p. 45.

Caserta's reply to the cable seemed to support my views. While Lemnitzer did not mention the Soviet problem, the impression was that Alexander seemed as anxious as ever for the Nazi surrender. Lemnitzer's message closed with the word that the Eighth Army was breaking out of the Argenta Gap and the fall of Bologna was imminent.

Troops of the Fifth and Eighth Armies entered Bologna at dawn on Saturday, the twenty-first. I arrived at my office hoping that something further might have come in during the night from Little Wally about Wolff's return. Instead, I found a message from Washington waiting for me, Urgent—Top Secret. It was brief, to the point:

WASHINGTON

Dated: 20 April 1945

1. BY LETTER TODAY JCS [Joint Chiefs of Staff] DIRECT THAT OSS BREAK OFF ALL CONTACT WITH GERMAN EMISSARIES AT ONCE. DULLES IS THERE- FORE INSTRUCTED TO DISCONTINUE IMMEDIATELY ALL SUCH TACTS.

2. LETTER ALSO STATES CCS [Combined Chiefs of Staff] HAVE AP- PROVED MESSAGE TO ALEXANDER STATING THAT IT IS CLEAR TO THEM THAT GERMAN COMMANDER-IN-CHIEF ITALY DOES NOT INTEND TO SURRENDER HIS FORCES AT THIS TIME ON ACCEPTABLE TERMS. MESSAGE CONTINUES: AC- CORDINGLY, ESPECIALLY IN VIEW OF COMPLICATIONS WHICH HAVE ARISEN WITH RUSSIANS, THE US AND BRITISH GOVERNMENTS HAVE DECIDED OSS SHOULD BREAK OFF CONTACTS; THAT JCS ARE SO INSTRUCTING OSS; THAT WHOLE MATTER IS TO BE REGARDED AS CLOSED AND THAT RUSSIANS BE IN- FORMED THROUGH ARCHER AND DEANE [Allied Military Representa- tives—Moscow].

This was all Washington gave me at that time about the reason for the reversal of their previous position.* It was true that negotiations had dragged on interminably; that Wolff had disappeared into Hitler's bunker and might, at the very moment, be his captive. President Roo- sevelt had died and it was too much to expect that President Truman

---

* President Truman writes in his memoirs: "At Churchill's urging, in order to avoid further friction with the Russians . . . the Allied commander in Italy was instructed to drop the talks . . . and the OSS in Switzerland to cease contact with the Germans." (Harry S. Truman, *Years of Decision* [New York: Double- day, 1958], pp. 200, 201.) Churchill, however, makes no mention in his mem- oirs that this was his decision.

could have grasped the significance of Sunrise. He had been in office only eight days. There were too many other pressing problems, other battle fronts. Very possibly our Joint Chiefs felt that there was little to be gained then by pressing the Italian surrender issue with the Soviets.

In any event, it was useless for me, sitting there in Bern, to indulge in speculations. The question was how should the orders be carried out? For the moment, I had lost contact with Wolff. Parilli and Zimmer were in Italy, and I did not want to use our radio link with Wally to inform them of what was about to happen. To send such a message through Little Wally might have been signing his death warrant. Possibly SS men were looking over his shoulder as he deciphered our messages. Certainly I was justified in holding up word to Wolff until I could get Wally out of the clutches of the SS.

So the first thing I did was to send a radio message to Wally asking him to come from Milan to the Swiss-Italian frontier for consultation. To give a plausible excuse I added that we were not picking up his signals satisfactorily and wanted to see if we could improve the transmission.

In view of the strict wording of my orders, I then wired Washington that I faced certain practical problems they might not have considered. One was Wally's safety; the other was how to handle Parilli. He was not a "German emissary" but an Italian intermediary. He would doubtless soon be on his way up to Switzerland to see me and to report on his meeting with Wolff, if Wolff was actually returning from Berlin. I had no way of intercepting Parilli en route. Moreover, he might be in possession of vital intelligence. And then there was the problem of what to tell Waibel. The basic success of our mission in the past had depended on his friendly cooperation, and he had been instrumental in the smooth working of the complicated Sunrise operation. He certainly deserved to be informed as tactfully as possible of my new orders.

These were realistic considerations, and I was, at the same time, hoping that by getting approval to handle the termination diplomatically, I could perhaps keep the door open ever so slightly until we knew what had happened to Wolff in Berlin. Washington's answer to this was that they appreciated my problems but that orders were orders and I would have to solve them in such a way as to comply with the strict directions from the Joint and Combined Chiefs of Staff.

On Sunday, the twenty-second, there was no word from Parilli. If Wolff had returned safely from Berlin and Parilli was to see him on the twentieth, as we had been informed by Wally, it was unusual that the Baron had not gone immediately to the Swiss border to give us the story. Was it possible that our fears for Wolff had become a reality? If so, the Joint Chiefs of Staff had timed their orders precisely.

Gaevernitz and I spent a very gloomy Sunday together in Bern. In addition to my other troubles, I was beginning to develop a severe pain in the knee. I knew it was the gout, with which I had had many years of experience. Mental strain is as likely to bring it on as the more widely advertised cause of overindulgence.

That night our code clerks called from the office. There was a message in from Wally. Since it was by then difficult for me to maneuver, the clerk brought the decoded text over to my apartment in the Herrengasse. Wally reported that Allied bombing of Vietinghoff's headquarters at Recoaro had wrecked the place, three dead, fifteen wounded. The headquarters was being shifted at once. I turned in for the night wondering what effect this would have on Vietinghoff.

The first piece of business I had set myself for Monday morning was to inform Waibel how things stood. I was not looking forward to it, but it had to be done. As I was planning my moves, the phone rang.

It was Waibel. Parilli, at the Swiss-Italian border at Chiasso, had just called him; he had astounding news.

General Wolff, his adjutant, Major Wenner, and one of Vietinghoff's high staff officers, Lieutenant Colonel Viktor von Schweinitz, were on their way to Switzerland. They were coming to surrender.

Parilli's message added these important facts: Schweinitz had full powers to sign for Vietinghoff and he would bring them to me. Wolff and Schweinitz were ready to go to Caserta immediately to arrange for the capitulation of all German forces, Wehrmacht and SS, in North Italy. They proposed an immediate meeting with me in Lucerne to arrange the details of the trip to Allied headquarters. And I was under the strictest military orders to have no dealings with them!

To say that I was in a predicament would put it mildly. Treating with the Germans now would be a clear violation of instructions. Yet I was convinced that the Joint Chiefs would never have directed breaking off contact if it had been known in Washington and London that the German envoys were already on their way to surrender.

I radioed this news to Alexander in Caserta and to Washington and asked for new instructions. I confirmed that until I had their reply I would have no dealings with the envoys other than to examine the documents empowering them to act, and to get precise information about their powers and their intentions.

Then I told Waibel that my hands were tied. He offered to see the Germans until I had new instructions. Both of us were convinced that I would get new orders when my messages were received. It was unthinkable that the Allies would refuse to go ahead with the surrender when envoys were in Switzerland ready to sign. Major Waibel also offered to house the German envoys in his well-isolated villa overlooking the Lake of Lucerne.

Alexander reacted immediately. He cabled back that AFHQ was requesting a reconsideration of the entire matter by the Combined Chiefs of Staff, so that we could at least ascertain whether the intentions of the German envoys were serious and the scope of their powers. Meanwhile, he hoped I could parry for time and endeavor to keep Wolff, Schweinitz and Wenner in Switzerland until a final decision came from Washington and London.

Washington's answer to my messages was equivocal. I was to avoid any action which could be construed as a continuation of Sunrise. If, however, the Swiss, in talking to the Germans, were acting on their own and not as my intermediaries, then any information which the Swiss wished to pass to me about the affair could be transmitted to headquarters.

Then the two Swiss, Waibel and Husmann, went off to the frontier to meet the German envoys and see that they got safely to Lucerne. As one can see, they had a delicate task and I had to leave it to Waibel's discretion how best to divulge the Allied position to Wolff. If Waibel told the Germans bluntly that I would not see them, I feared the envoys might turn around and go back to Italy. Then any possibility of a quick surrender would have been lost.

Waibel handled the matter with great tact. He told Wolff at the border that there had been some difficulties, that the delays and Wolff's visit to Hitler had made Washington and London skeptical. However, Waibel told Wolff, he had better come to Lucerne to see what could be done. So much Waibel felt he had to say. He did not want to bring Wolff along under false pretenses. Wolff did not hesitate for a moment. That evening Waibel and Husmann reached Lucerne with Wolff, Wenner and Schweinitz and they settled them in Waibel's house.

Shortly after their arrival, Gaevernitz and I reached Lucerne. Even if I could not meet the emissaries, I decided it would be well to be nearby, in spite of the difficulty of moving from Bern with an acute attack of the gout. This was not the kind of business to be settled by telephone. I directed Captain Tracy Barnes to remain in Bern and to relay any incoming messages to me in Lucerne. Waibel, in turn, was willing to carry messages back and forth between the Germans at his villa and Gaevernitz and me, by now established at the Hotel Schweizerhof in Lucerne. That night I had the good news that Wally was safely back in Switzerland.

The following day, the twenty-fourth, I informed the Germans through Waibel that I had to refuse to see them. In the same way I explained to them that Wolff's trip to Hitler had naturally made us believe that further negotiations were useless, and that the instructions to me had come under the influence of this visit and without any knowledge that Wolff was prepared to carry through with the surrender. I urged them to be patient. They consented to stay a day or two and sent me Schweinitz's full powers, which I radioed to Caserta and Washington. In translation, they read:

> THE COMMANDER-IN-CHIEF, SOUTHWEST, AND
> COMMANDER-IN-CHIEF OF ARMY GROUP "C"
>
> HEADQUARTERS, 22 April 1945
> Lieutenant Colonel in the General Staff von Schweinitz has been authorized by me to conduct negotiations within the frame of the instructions given by me and to make binding commitments on my behalf.
>
> [sgd.] V. VIETINGHOFF

I was naturally worried by the phrase "within the frame of the instructions, etc.," and I asked Schweinitz to send me his interpretation of it through Waibel. It appeared that while Schweinitz had been instructed to try to negotiate on Vietinghoff's points of honor—somewhat watered down from the earlier version—he was not bound by the wording of his authorization to hold to them strictly. As regards the surrender of the German SS troops, Wolff, by virtue of his position as Supreme SS Commander in Italy, had full authority to act.

From Parilli I then learned that originally General Roettiger, Vietinghoff's Chief of Staff, had expected to come as envoy, but had at the last moment been unable to leave his post in view of the critical military situation. Schweinitz had been sent in his stead because he spoke English fluently. Before the war he had been an Exchange Officer in England with the Royal Inniskilling Fusiliers, and was obviously thought to be just the right man to go to Alexander's headquarters. At the moment, according to Parilli, he was whiling away the time reading English books in Waibel's library. Parilli also learned that Schweinitz on his mother's side was descended from a famous American who had signed the Declaration of Independence. Parilli did not get the name straight, but I later learned that it was our first Chief Justice, John Jay. More to the point was the fact that before leaving Fasano Wolff had sent Dollmann to see Kesselring. It was a last attempt of Wolff's to try to get Kesselring to join him in a common action—the surrender in the West at the same time as in North Italy.

Then the waiting began. Would the Combined Chiefs change their minds? Would pressure from the Russians still hold them back, despite the apparent optimistic turn of events in Italy? Would the Germans quit and walk out on us before we got an answer? All day on the twenty-fourth there was no word. I was by then in such pain with the gout that Gaevernitz on his own decided to do something about it. He located a Swiss doctor and, somewhat against my will, had him come to look at me. They went out in the corridor and Gaevernitz had a chat with him out there. I didn't find out what passed between them until much later. Gaevernitz insisted the doctor give me something to kill the pain. The doctor told him that he could give me morphine but first he had to ascertain whether I had any allergies; if so, my reaction to the morphine might be serious. Gaevernitz, who did not consult me and had no idea whether I had any allergies or not, assured the doctor he had known me all his life and I definitely had no allergies. It was the first time I had ever had morphine, and the relief from the pain made it possible for me to tackle Sunrise again.

I then got hold of Parilli and asked him to tell us what had happened during Wolff's visit to Berlin and during that silent weekend after Wolff returned from Berlin to Italy. Waibel and Husmann soon joined us in my room. All three had already heard various episodes of Wolff's recent adventures from Wolff himself, and, gathered around my bedside, they each contributed to the tale which is recounted below. I have put it in chronological order, which is not the way I heard it. I have also taken the liberty of adding certain details which Wolff later gave to Gaevernitz after the war was over, to make the story complete.

One of Wolff's main reasons for giving in to Himmler's demand that he come to Berlin was his fear that if he refused he would be replaced in Italy by some fanatical SS commander who would stick it out to the bitter end and carry out the destruction in Italy which Wolff had so far worked to prevent. In going, he knew that he was taking heavy risks and had less than a fifty-fifty chance of ever returning. There were the physical dangers of the trip itself and the even greater dangers of the inquisition to which he would be subjected in Berlin. On April 15th he flew from his headquarters in Italy, to Munich and early the following morning to Prague at close to the treetop level most of the way to avoid interception by Allied planes which were constantly overhead. From Prague he flew to an airfield just outside Berlin, and there he was met by Professor Gebhardt, one of Hitler's personal physicians and a close associate of Himmler, who had sent him down to pick up Wolff. Gebhardt took him to Berlin where rooms had been reserved at the Adlon. Wolff was so exhausted that he slept through all the air raids in his fourth-floor room instead of going down to the shelter. Actually the Adlon had been bombed and part of it burnt out the week before. The next day, April 17th, Gebhardt drove Wolff to his clinic at Hohenlychen, about a hundred kilometers north of Berlin, where Himmler was waiting for him. Wolff saw at once that Himmler was even more indecisive and nervous than when he had seen him on his last visit in March.

As Himmler began to press Wolff, building up to what looked like an accusation of treason, Wolff produced and asked Himmler to read a letter he was carrying written and signed by Ambassador Rahn. The letter, addressed to Hitler, subtly indicated that the contacts to the Allies which had been established—Rahn did not say by whom—had been useful in achieving an objective Hitler had sought; namely, the holding up, to some extent, of the Allied offensive in Italy. (This was made up of out of whole cloth solely for the purpose of calming Hitler.)

The letter, in fact, was really a trick cooked up by Rahn for Wolff's protection in case Wolff was ordered to Berlin. Since Rahn, as both Himmler and Kaltenbrunner well knew, then had Hitler's ear and his trust, a message from Rahn via Wolff to Hitler could not safely be sidetracked. If Himmler or Kaltenbrunner had tried to get Wolff out of the way and Rahn had later called Hitler and learned that his message had not been delivered, Himmler and Kaltenbrunner would have had to answer to Hitler for the disappearance of Wolff. The letter seems to have had a pacifying effect on Himmler. Anyway, after reading it, he returned it to Wolff without comment.

During the afternoon Kaltenbrunner appeared and, as Wolff expected, revealed himself as the primary antagonist to what Wolff was trying to accomplish. He presented the evidence of Wolff's treason to Himmler as though Himmler were the judge, but it was all too evident that Kaltenbrunner was merely trying to corner Wolff and no longer felt that the vacillating Himmler was of real importance in the case. Kaltenbrunner had a file of papers with him. Presumably it contained all the information Kaltenbrunner had gathered through his informants in Italy and Switzerland about Wolff's actions. Some of it apparently was perilously close to the truth, but Kaltenbrunner's bumbling agents had somehow never quite got the whole story straight, nor had they got their hands on the most incriminating evidence of Wolff's contact with the Allies. One report claimed that the German armies in Italy would surrender in five days; another that Wolff had met with Cardinal Schuster for the purpose of arranging a surrender. Wolff swore he had not met with Schuster, and that he had already told them all there was to tell about his contact to me during his previous visit to Berlin. He then showed to Kaltenbrunner Rahn's trick letter to Hitler. This did not lesson Kaltenbrunner's vindictiveness; on the contrary, but if he had thought he was going to trap Wolff or get an admission from him, he had been mistaken.

The argument went on for hours, through the afternoon until midnight. Finally, Wolff decided it was time to put an end to the confrontation. He said he now wanted to go to Berlin to see Hitler. He insisted that both Kaltenbrunner and Himmler accompany him so that he could account to Hitler in their presence for what he had done in Switzerland and why he had done it. Himmler begged off, possibly because at this point he was himself very vulnerable. He had already become deeply engaged in his Swedish negotiations with Count Bernadotte, and probably did not know how widely it was suspected or known. As an excuse, he told Wolff he was out of favor with the Führer since the armies under his command in East Germany had suffered such great losses. He suggested that Kaltenbrunner and Wolff go without him.

So Kaltenbrunner and Wolff went off in a chauffeur-driven SS car to Berlin and arrived there at about three in the morning. They couldn't talk en route because the chauffeur would have overheard them. They parked in front of the Chancellery on the Wilhelmstrasse below which Hitler's bunker was situated. Before they entered the bunker, Wolff, according to his story, took advantage of the only moment he would have alone with Kaltenbrunner. He told Kaltenbrunner that if Kaltenbrunner started accusing him of secret negotiations in front of Hitler or showed Hitler his agents' reports, Wolff would inform Hitler that he had already given an account of his contacts with me to both Himmler and Kaltenbrunner during his previous visit to Berlin on March 24th, and that they had both asked him at the time not to bring Hitler into the picture. If Wolff was going to the gallows, he would see to it that Kaltenbrunner would swing next to him.

Kaltenbrunner, according to Wolff, turned pale. He normally had a flushed vein-swollen complexion, resulting no doubt from the fact that he was a heavy brandy drinker. Then they went into the bunker. They waited in the anteroom outside Hitler's private apartment, which was several stories below ground. The place was infested with guards. One of the major personalities in evidence, scurrying in and out of the various offices on that floor, was SS-Gruppenführer Fegelein. A few days later Fegelein was shot on Hitler's orders allegedly for trying to escape from Berlin.

Suddenly Hitler stepped out of his private quarters to cross the hall to another room where a military briefing was to take place. He seemed surprised to see Wolff but greeted him cordially and asked him to wait until the briefing was over. Fegelein and Kaltenbrunner took part in the briefing and Wolff was left alone cooling his heels in the anteroom.

Shortly after 4:00 a.m., Fegelein called Wolff into the briefing room. Kaltenbrunner had remained inside. All the others who had attended the briefing had left. Fegelein and Kaltenbrunner were silent throughout the conversation which now took place between Wolff and Hitler. Wolff later attempted to recall and reconstruct for us in detail the course of this crucial talk with Hitler. The accuracy of his report of an event which happened in an atmosphere charged with suspicion, the rivalry of deadly enemies and the threat of death cannot, of course, he vouched for. All the other participants or witnesses are dead.

Hitler seemed not unfriendly, but disturbingly critical. He called Wolff's approach to the Allies, which he had heard about from Kaltenbrunner, a "colossal disregard of authority," but he did not accuse Wolff of having acted behind his back. If anything upset him, it was that Wolff had engaged in a political move of vital consequence to the whole Reich when he was only acquainted with one front and was, therefore, not in a position to understand how his independent actions might interfere with Hitler's over-all plans.

Hitler then waited for Wolff to explain, and Wolff launched into a long and detailed review of his work in Italy. He cleverly placed great emphasis on the meeting he had had with Hitler on February 6th, when, with Ribbentrop also present, Hitler had more or less given the nod—at least he hadn't said no—to explorations of contacts to the Western Allies. He explained his not having informed Berlin before he went to see Mr. Dulles on March 8th by claiming that in entering into this contact on his own, without the official backing of Hitler, he was giving Hitler the possibility of disowning and discarding him if the whole thing went wrong, i.e., Hitler would not lose face. He concluded by saying that his undertaking had succeeded. He was happy to be able to tell Hitler that he had opened a channel for him that led directly to the President of the United States and to Prime Minister Churchill—if he wanted to use it.

Wolff did not mention the meetings in Ascona with the Allied military advisers. He was convinced by now that Kaltenbrunner and Himmler, and therefore Hitler, knew only of the March 8th meeting in Zurich. Hitler watched him closely, apparently waiting for him to waver or to avoid his penetrating glance. Wolff held firm, looked his Führer in the eye and seems to have succeeded in giving an impression of frankness and honesty, because after Wolff finished Hitler told him that he understood and accepted Wolff's presentation. He then asked Wolff what he thought the terms of a surrender would be. Wolff replied that unconditional surrender could not be avoided. There might, he thought, exist the possibility of some mitigation, but in general things would depend on the Germans demonstrating good will and respect for the country and the people of Italy.

Hitler then broke off the interview by saying he had to get some sleep, and he asked Wolff to come back around five in the afternoon. In the interval he would consider Wolff's action.

Wolff seemed to have survived the first round. The old charm, so it seemed, the blue-eyed openness and frankness, that had helped him arrive in high places years before, even in the SS ranks, had worked again. He was not through yet. But he had seen that Hitler was by now a mental as well as a physical wreck, and realized that it may have been simply his good luck that the presentation he had made, which was after all full of holes, had just possibly harmonized with some passing obsession in Hitler's mind. Kaltenbrunner had said nothing. Hitler's acceptance of Wolff's explanations had dimmed the hopes Kaltenbrunner may have had to rid himself of Wolff's competition as a peacemaker.

Hitler, who, according to Wolff, had always carried himself in stiff military posture, was now bent, shaky and flabby, his features sunken. He dragged his body around heavily and slowly. His right hand trembled constantly; he seemed to have trouble with his equilibrium and after walking only a few steps would appear to lose his balance and have to sit down. His eyes were bloodshot. For years his vision had been so bad that all memoranda addressed to him were printed on a special typewriter equipped with letters three times the normal size that he could read without glasses, which he felt were unbecoming to a dictator. At times his mouth dripped saliva, which he was unaware of. When he spoke, however, he seemed to be able to regain temporarily the ruthless energy for which he had so long been known. He would suddenly become animated, in contrast to the picture of general physical decay he presented. In such moments his famous memory for names, facts and figures seemed as good as ever.

Wolff, who was utterly exhausted, returned to the Hotel Adlon, where he slept during the morning. It was now April 18th.

On his way back to the bunker in the afternoon, so Wolff told us years later, he passed the bank where various securities belonging to him and his wife were deposited and for a moment considered going in and picking up the securities and withdrawing all his money from his Berlin bank account. He stood outside the bank trying to make up his mind. Finally he walked away, having decided that it was improper to concern himself with his private affairs at a moment when the life and fate of armies and nations were at stake.

Waiting for his next appointment with Hitler, Wolff noted that the atmosphere in the bunker offices was desperate and frightened, though everybody was trying to put up a courageous front. Everyone except Hitler knew there were no more miracles to be expected. Everyone knew the Russians would seal off Berlin in a matter of days—everyone except Hitler, who was still planning military actions to stop them. Wolff learned that Hitler in all probability was not going to the mountain redoubt but would stay in Berlin, though many members of his staff were still hopeful of escaping somehow to southern Germany. There was little talk of a redoubt, as such, or of a last stand in the Alps—only of avoiding the danger from the East, Russian captivity.*

While Wolff waited, there was an air raid. Sitting down deep in the bunker, he could feel the concussion shake the earth and wondered if he was ever going to get out of Berlin, even if Hitler let him go. About the time the air raid was over, Hitler appeared and invited Wolff to join him in a walk along the terrace in front of his office upstairs. He had his overcoat brought to him, Kaltenbrunner and Fegelein appeared from somewhere and the three men accompanied Hitler up and down the terrace. There was an odor of scorched timber in the air. The Chancellery itself had been considerably damaged and most of the park had been torn up by bombs, but there was still a good usable path on the terrace.

Hitler told Wolff that he had considered the matter he had presented to him in the morning in the light of his over-all plans for the future. After dismissing the stubborn General Guderian, he explained, he had finally found the right chief for his General Staff in General Krebs,** who understood his thoughts and was able to put them into effect.

---

* There are a number of accounts of these last days in the bunker of the Reichs-Chancellery (Trevor-Roper, Boldt, General Warlimont). One of the stories about this period, which I have never seen printed anywhere, was told me by a German general who visited the bunker two days after Wolff's visit (April 20th) to give Hitler a military briefing. In a room in the bunker set apart for smoking (Hitler detested tobacco and wouldn't let anyone smoke in his presence) the general found Fegelein, Martin Bormann and General Burgdorf, Hitler's military adjutant, with a large quantity of emptied and still unopened wine bottles, their faces flushed, their jackets open. (Burgdorf, incidentally, was the man Hitler had sent down to Rommel the October before with the poison ampule which Burgdorf persuaded Rommel to take at the Führer's request.) Now Burgdorf invited the visiting general to join the drinking party with these words: "In a couple of weeks the whole stinking mess will be over. In the meantime we might as well drunk up all the booze the old man has in his cellar." *(In einigen Wochen ist der ganze Dreck hier vorbei. Nun wollen wir dem Alten wenigstens noch vorher den Keller aussaufen.)*

** Hitler had appointed this last of his military chiefs on March 28th, some twenty days before. Krebs was typical of the toadying Nazi hacks with whom Hitler surrounded himself during the last months. Guderian had been dismissed after many violent disagreements with Hitler over strategy.

In the East, Hitler said, an anti-tank system against the powerful armored masses of Russian tanks had now been established, with lines of anti-aircraft and anti-tank guns up to seven kilometers deep in various well-chosen positions, so that in the last three days the Russians had lost an average of two hundred and fifty tanks per day. Not even the mighty Russian armored force could stand to be bled in such a manner over an extended period of time, and attrition in the Russian armies and consequent crippling of their attack could be expected soon.

He had decided upon using the following general plan of warfare from now on. Three large strongholds should be established inside Germany: one in the center, under his command, in the capital city of Berlin; one to the north, in Schleswig-Holstein, Denmark and Norway; and one in the south, including the Alpine stronghold. He was intentionally withdrawing from the wide open areas between Schleswig-Holstein and Berlin, and between Berlin and the Alps, and had issued orders that the German troops should retire to whichever of the strongholds was nearer. Soon, doubtless, the Russians and the Anglo-Americans would meet somewhere in these open areas, and if he was any judge of the Russians, they would never stop at the line agreed upon at Yalta.

The Americans, however, could not under any circumstances put up with this. They would therefore be forced to push the Russians back by force of arms—here Hitler stopped and fixed Wolff with a piercing glance—and that would be the point at which he, Hitler, would participate in the final war on one side or the other. He claimed he could hold out in Berlin against East and West for at least six weeks, possibly even eight weeks, and for this reason he told Wolff that he must hold out in Italy that long. In the meantime Hitler expected the conflict would come about between the Western Allies and Russia, and then Hitler would decide which side he would join.

Wolff replied to Hitler, "My Führer, isn't it clear which side you would take in such a conflict?" Hitler looked at Wolff and, after deliberating briefly, said, "I will decide in favor of the side which offers me the most. Or the side which establishes contact with me first."

It was apparent that Hitler's mind under the stress of events was filled from moment to moment with utterly contradictory thoughts which he voiced as they came to him without further reflection. A few moments later he said with a sudden otherworldly and unnatural calmness, "You know, my private ambition ever since the beginning of the war has been to withdraw and to observe the development of the German people from a distance, and to have my influence on it. I shall soon turn my power over to the most competent of my associates."

Wolff tried to bring the conversation back to practical realities by referring to the overwhelming strength of the Allies and the losses Germany was suffering every day.

To this Hitler replied, "That is of no concern at all. I have just detailed to you the further course of events, and I will await them calmly. Don't lose your nerve, man. I need my nerves for other things; I cannot allow myself to be softened by these reports. For the man who is to make the final decision must not let himself be moved by the misery and the horror that the war brings to every individual on the front and in the homeland. So do what I say. Fly back, and give my regards to Vietinghoff."

Then came a series of instructions, culminating in the order to hold fast and defend. Hitler added that should this fateful battle of the German people under his leadership not bring success, the German people would have forfeited their right to existence. The greater, stronger race from the East would then have proved itself biologically superior, and there would be nothing left but to go down heroically. He concluded: "Go back to Italy; maintain your contacts with the Americans, but see that you get better terms. Stall a bit, because to capitulate unconditionally on the basis of such vague promises would be preposterous. Before we come to an agreement with the Americans, we've got to get much better conditions."

One of the orderlies then came and told Hitler it was time for the evening briefing. It was five minutes to six.

Before Hitler left, he expressed his appreciation for the conscientious manner in which Wolff had acted and repeated his greetings to Vietinghoff. After Hitler had gone, Kaltenbrunner took Wolff aside and made the following farewell remarks to him: "Be sure no important civilian prisoners in your area fall into Allied hands. As the Allies approach, liquidate them."

In the meantime, Wolff's plane had been brought to Berlin's main airport at Tempelhof. He flew at dusk to Munich and at dawn of the next day, April 19th, from Munich to Bergamo in Northern Italy; from there he went by car to his headquarters in Fasano.

On the following day, April 20th, Parilli, who had been waiting with Zimmer in Milan, was summoned to Fasano to hear Wolff's story about his trip and to get instructions on what was to happen next. Wenner and Dollmann were also at the session. When they were all gathered together, Wolff called for a bottle of champagne and they drank to Wolff's lucky stars—to the fact, as Wolff put it, "that his head was still attached to his shoulders." Parilli noticed soon, however, that Wolff was in a strange mood. He had never seen him quite like this before. It was not only that he was exhausted from the physical and emotional strain of the trip to Berlin; he also seemed to have been somewhat infected by the paralysis of the Berlin bunker atmosphere, or perhaps a deep-set conflict of loyalties had been awakened, despite Hitler's confused and senseless plans. Hitler had after all extracted a kind of promise from Wolff, and Wolff had Hitler to thank, in a sense, that neither Himmler nor Kaltenbrunner had been able to eliminate him.

In any case, and Parilli could not quite explain it, Wolff after returning from Berlin seemed unwilling to act on Sunrise. At best, he sounded as if he were trying to find some compromise between Hitler's request that he hold out and the promises that had been made to us to deliver the surrender of Italy as soon as possible. He succeeded in finding a number of excuses for not acting, some of which sounded a little specious. He made much of the fact that there was obviously a traitor among those who knew about Sunrise or Kaltenbrunner would not have had so much information, even though most of it was garbled. The first thing, Wolff asserted, was to find out who this traitor was. Next, he pointed out that Vietinghoff had, after all, been unwilling to talk unconditional surrender, only surrender if his points of honor were observed, and Wolff saw no way of bringing Vietinghoff around. He suggested as a compromise that he try perhaps to induce Vietinghoff to pull his troops back ten kilometers a day with only a nominal show of resistance, thus relinquishing the territory to the Allies but without doing so in an act of surrender.

What mostly depressed Parilli was hearing Wolff parrot the same line many German generals had been mouthing, Kesselring and the others. With the encirclement or the fall of Berlin, with the death of Hitler, with the Italian front completely cut off from the Reich, then Wolff would feel he had complete freedom of action. He told Parilli that he could not let himself go to Switzerland—not for the time being—or let any of his officers go. But he wanted Parilli to go and to see me and explain his position. "Assure Dulles," he said, "that I have not changed my mind but that under the circumstances I cannot negotiate at the moment. I consider this tragic but I have no other course now. Tell him I will resume contact with him as promptly as possible in order to carry out the original plan."

Parilli returned to Milan with Zimmer and Dollmann. They talked over the situation and Parilli, sensing that the whole undertaking was about to collapse, decided he could not transmit any such message to me. It would mean the end of any possibility of surrender. He did not know, of course, that I had received orders at that very time to break off for quite another reason. What he did know was that in and around Milan the partisans were beginning to stir. There were signs of an uprising. If Wolff just sat on his hands and a conflict between the Germans and the Italians came to a head, the very thing that had prompted Parilli to act in the first place—the attempt to save North Italy from destruction—would be utterly frustrated. He decided to go back to Wolff and tell him that he could not bring me the message Wolff had given him and to plead with him to take action.

So Parilli returned to Fasano alone on the twenty-second. Wolff had ordered Zimmer to stay at his post in Milan and Dollmann had other business. When Parilli reached Fasano, Wolff was not there. Wenner told Parilli that Wolff had gone to see Vietinghoff. A crucial meeting was in session at Vietinghoff's headquarters. According to Wenner, the purpose was to name plenipotentiaries and to draw up the written authorization for the surrender of the Wehrmacht forces to the Allies.

Parilli was dumbfounded but delighted by this turn of events. The meeting had been called not by Wolff but by Rahn, who had stepped back into the picture during Wolff's absence in Berlin. This was fortunate at a time when Wolff was at his lowest point and had momentarily lost his initiative. Rahn, together with Roettiger, had succeeded in stiffening Vietinghoff's backbone. Rahn had invited to the meeting Gauleiter Hofer, who, in his blustering fashion, declared that if Hitler should show up in his territory he would arrest him. The atmosphere of this meeting evidently revived Wolff and helped him throw off the spell cast in Berlin. The next day, the twenty-third, Wolff and the other emissaries left for Switzerland. On the same day Vietinghoff, in the face of the Allied advance, began to move the headquarters of Army Group C to Bolzano in the South Tyrol. Before

Wolff left for Switzerland, he decided to move his headquarters to Bolzano also.*

Waibel, Husmann and Parilli, in relating to Gaevernitz and me the account of Wolff's adventures in Berlin and his confrontation with Hitler, brought us up to date on these crucial developments, about which we had been completely in the dark. It helped to dispel doubts raised by Wolff's secret visit to Berlin about his ability to resist the pressures of Himmler and Hitler.

It was now April 24th and we were still awaiting word from Washington or Caserta. At least we knew how Wolff had survived the ordeal.

---

* I no longer recall when we learned of it, but sometime before the events described in this chapter Wolff had managed to get his family moved back to a safe place in the South Tyrol and out of the grip of Himmler.

11

The Sun Rises

Two more days passed and there were still no new instructions from Washington or Caserta. Time was running out. Every few hours the impatient German envoys at Waibel's villa would inquire whether we had had any word. Probably never in all history had plenipotentiaries, desiring to surrender a great army, received so strange a reception.

I had sent strong messages to Washington and Caserta. I knew that Field Marshal Alexander and General Lemnitzer were working on both Washington and London. There was nothing to do but wait.

After inflicting a crushing defeat on the Germans south of the Po and around Bologna, the American Fifth and the British Eighth armies were beginning to push the enemy northward. We were fearful that any day a signal from Berlin would order the beginning of the destruction of the great industrial and power plants of North Italy as well as the port installations of Genoa. We realized that as the front became more and more fluid, it would be increasingly difficult to put through a surrender for the entire Italian front. The lines of communication between the various German fighting units were becoming precarious.

While we were waiting, a message came through for General Wolff from Himmler. It had had a circuitous route to travel. Sent from Berlin to Wolff's headquarters at Fasano, in Italy, it was then relayed from there to Guido Zimmer, at Milan, who brought it to the Swiss-Italian frontier and telephoned it to Waibel, who passed it to me. For an intelligence officer it is not an unpleasant sensation to be able to read your antagonist's message before it reaches the addressee. Himmler's message was dated April 23, 1945, and read:

"It is more essential than ever that the Italian front holds and remains intact. No negotiations of any kind should be undertaken." (*Es kommt jetzt mehr denn je darauf an, dass die italienische Front hält und intakt bleibt. Es dürfen nicht die geringsten Verhandlungen gepflogen werden.*)*

This last sentence contained an ominous threat for the Germans concerned with Sunrise. We were keenly interested to hear of Wolff's reaction to it. Waibel, as he handed the message to him, observed him closely. Without comment, Wolff passed it to his aide, Wenner, and to Schweinitz. They looked at him questioningly. Wolff, Waibel told me, shrugged his shoulders. "What Himmler has to say now makes no difference," he commented.

On the afternoon of April 25th, Wolff sent word to me that he felt he should return immediately to Italy. He had already been gone several days, and he could not tell what might be happening in his absence. If he was away too long, Himmler might come to North Italy and try to take control of Wolff's forces; Vietinghoff might change his mind, and there was also the unpredictable Duce, although we had discussed his ability to make firm decisions.

News had just come to us from Milan that Mussolini was there and had been holding frantic conferences. It would be important to thwart any desperate last-minute steps Mussolini and the Neo-Fascists might take to prevent an orderly surrender. Wolff also pointed out that North Italy was now in such a turbulent state that if he did not return soon to his headquarters he might find the road there cut off by the partisans. They were rising for the kill all over Piedmont and Lombardy.

I was reluctant to see him go although I felt he would best be able to keep order and avert ruthless violence and destruction in North Italy if he was there in person. Wolff proposed that Schweinitz should remain on for a short time in Lucerne with Major Wenner, and Wolff gave Wenner full powers in writing to represent him—if the word should come through from Washington for the German envoys to go to Caserta to sign the surrender.

---

* At this time Himmler was making contact on his own with the Allies through the Swedish Count Bernadotte for the purpose of negotiating a surrender. Naturally, he wanted no competition from Wolff.

His authorization for Wenner was simply worded with no qualifying phrases. It read:

25 April 1945

I hereby authorize my Chief Adjutant, SS Major Wenner, to negotiate on my behalf and to make binding commitments on my behalf.

[sgd.] WOLFF

Before leaving Lucerne, Wolff wrote out and gave us a longhand memorandum giving the locations, in various Tyrolean castles and hideouts, of priceless Italian art objects, which, as Wolff had told us in Zurich, he had shipped northward for their protection at the time of the battle for Florence. Wolff's idea was that before plundering bands started their work as the Germans retreated, we should send Army detachments to these spots to save the art treasures.

On the evening of April 25th, Wolff took the train south for the Italian frontier, accompanied by Husmann, and Gaevernitz and I returned to Bern as the best point from which to operate our communications network. As the battle fronts in Central Europe were disintegrating, Switzerland became a focal point for news.

Schweinitz, who had powers to act for Vietinghoff, and Wenner, with Wolff's proxy, remained behind in Lucerne as Waibel's guests. They were increasingly restless and in an understandably dubious frame of mind regarding our intentions. Were they refugees or parliamentarians? Neither Gaevernitz nor I had seen them or General Wolff since the receipt of Washington's "stop" order.

Wolff crossed the Swiss-Italian border in the late evening of April 25th. He promised to send a report to Husmann, who intended to wait on the Swiss side of the border. He then proceeded to the SS command post at Cernobbio on the southwestern shore of the Lake of Como only a few miles away. This was located in the requisitioned Villa Locatelli, which belonged to the manufacturer of Italian cheese. Here Wolff immediately got in touch by telephone with his headquarters at Fasano and with SS headquarters at Milan.

At this time both the German military and the SS staffs were in the process of moving to Bolzano in the South Tyrol. Wolff's calls caught some of his people in Fasano before they left, some in Bolzano after they arrived, and missed others. He sent a courier to the border around midnight with a situation report for Husmann. In it he expressed fears

about the possibility of his getting out of Cernobbio because the partisans were moving up in force to seal off the Swiss border area. He also
reported that Mussolini had had a three-hour conference with Cardinal
Schuster in Milan on the twenty-fifth to discuss an armistice between
the partisans and the Fascist forces. Last of all, Wolff wanted to know
what was happening in Lucerne. Had we heard from Washington?

After that, there was nothing but silence. Early the next day Husmann, who had waited near the border all night, still had no further
word from Wolff. He called Waibel to say that Wolff must be in serious
trouble. There was also no word from Washington, London or Caserta.
In all our negotiations since February 28th this was really our lowest
point. We had been discouraged and frustrated before, but now we felt
that the whole undertaking was about to end in hopeless confusion.
Waibel told me he felt compelled to tell Schweinitz and Wenner, who
were still awaiting news in his house at Lucerne, that the border would
be in chaotic condition in no time and probably impassable. Since there
was no word for them from us, they might wish to return to their military units while it was still possible.

They decided to hold out a little longer, but Schweinitz began to talk
about showing his authorization as a surrender envoy to representatives
of the press if something didn't happen soon. The world would find out,
he said, how they had been led down the garden path and who was now
responsible for the continuation of unnecessary slaughter in Italy.
Waibel calmed him down for the moment.

In the early hours of April 26th, Waibel learned through one of his
own Swiss intelligence agents that the Villa Locatelli, where Wolff was
spending the night, had been completely surrounded by partisans and
that there was great danger they might storm the villa and kill Wolff and
the other SS officers staying there with him. Waibel decided to go down
immediately to the Swiss-Italian frontier to see what might be done to
save Wolff as well as Sunrise. When Gaevernitz heard this—it was a little later in the morning—he came into my office and asked permission
to join Waibel at the border. He had an idea that we might effectively
use one of my men in Lugano, a former newspaperman by the name of
Don Jones, who had nothing to do with Sunrise but was deeply involved
in our operations with the Italian anti-Fascist partisan elements in the
border area and was well known to them as "Scotti." Possibly he might
be able to save Wolff from his partisan friends. I told Gaevernitz that
under the strict orders I had received I could not get in touch with Wolff,

but there was no ban on getting information about him. Gaevernitz listened silently for a moment. Then he said that since the whole affair seemed to have come to an end, he would like to go on a little trip for a few days. I noticed a twinkle in his eye, and as he told me later, he noticed one in mine. I realized, of course, what he was going to do, and that he intended to do it on his own responsibility.

So, as I surmised, Waibel and Gaevernitz went off to try to save the life of the SS General Karl Wolff, who might well be in the hands of our allies the Italian partisans. They in turn might well be on the point of having their joyful moment of vengeance against the German enemy and occupier.

Early in the morning of the following day, April 27th, I was awakened in Bern by the telephone. It was Gaevernitz calling from Lugano. Wolff, after a total disappearance in the partisan-controlled area near Como, had again entered Switzerland and gone on to Lugano with Gaevernitz and Waibel, where they had sat up most of the night in a small hotel room discussing what was to be done next. There was no time for Gaevernitz to tell me the details of the story of Wolff's rescue. That would have to wait.

There were new and urgent problems. Wolff had proposed going to Milan and issuing a surrender proclamation over the German-controlled radio. Gaevernitz and Waibel were against the idea after what they had seen of partisan activity at the border. They doubted that Wolff could reach Milan or that the radio station would still be in German hands by the time he got there, if he ever did. Gaevernitz felt that the proclamation, even if it got on the air, would not be very effective. Certain individual commanders might heed it, but without the cooperation of Vietinghoff, Army Group C would probably disregard it. Furthermore, the advancing Allies would not know what it meant and would certainly not cease firing, and then there would be recriminations on both sides.

Gaevernitz had proposed instead that Wolff cross Switzerland to the Austrian frontier and go from there to his new headquarters at Bolzano. The partisans were not yet strong in the area and the German forces were still in full control. Bolzano was now Army as well as SS headquarters, and it might be possible from there to make a last attempt at getting all concerned to arrange an orderly surrender instead of continuing the fighting in the difficult mountain terrain of the southern Alps. Wolff had accepted the idea. He was, in fact, already on his way to Bolzano. Before he left, however, he had performed one service that justified his being rescued, whatever else happened next.

The partisan uprising in Northern Italy was in full swing, and the German SS and the Fascists were their main targets. Wolff had written out an order to Colonel Rauff, in charge of the SS in Milan, to avoid any clashes between the SS and the partisans at all costs. If there was no alternative, the SS was to surrender to the partisans.

A young Italian priest had turned up at the border anxious to do what he could to prevent unnecessary bloodshed at the last moment. He was Giovanni Barbareschi, a daring man, known to us, who had undertaken dangerous missions in the past as courier between the Papal Nuncio in Switzerland and Cardinal Schuster in Milan. He was willing to carry Wolff's order to Rauff in Milan. He got there—and, as we later learned, the order was obeyed.

The account of Wolff's adventures, from April 25th to 26th, while he was surrounded by the partisans in the Villa Locatelli at Cernobbio is really a story within a story, and I was not able to get all the pieces and put them together until after the surrender was over. There was Gaevernitz's account, there was Scotti's account, there was Wolff's account; and of parallel interest was the account of the events which were transpiring in Milan, many of them of historic significance and only partly known to Wolff himself at the time.

My man in Lugano, Scotti, as I explained, was not privy to the Sunrise operation and knew nothing whatever of our relations with Wolff. He had been supporting the anti-German partisan bands in North Italy—guiding them, and setting up communications to them—ever since he had joined me in 1943. He had been one of the prime actors in the Campione revolution I described earlier and had organized the partisan training center in this Italian enclave after the Fascists were turned out. He was well known to the partisans and highly respected by them. He also had extremely good working relations with Swiss police and military intelligence in the Ticino, the Italian-Swiss canton in which are located several of the towns I have been mentioning in this account: Lugano, Ascona, Chiasso, and so on. At the time he had an able co-worker. Captain E. Q. Daddario, a young Italian-American, who had headed an OSS detachment in Italy and had been transferred a short time before to Lugano.*

---

* At present writing, Daddario is a distinguished member of the House of Representatives and represents the 1st District of Connecticut in the United States Congress.

Gaevernitz was well aware of the fact that in accompanying Waibel to the border to see what could be done about Wolff he had to act with great discretion and without disclosing any official connection with my office. Also, he could not readily involve Scotti in whatever he was going to undertake since Scotti was an American official. The orders from Washington forbidding contact with the German emissaries therefore applied to Scotti too. Gaevernitz knew that Scotti and Daddario would probably be in evidence in the area around Chiasso, as the Italian side of the border was mostly unguarded by now and it was a comparatively simple matter for the partisans to go up to the border and report what was going on to Scotti in person. Gaevernitz fully intended to keep away from Scotti, to duck if he saw him, to avoid involving him in any way with Wolff.

Imagine Gaevernitz's surprise, then, when at the railroad station at Chiasso, as he and Waibel alighted from the train late in the afternoon of April 26th, Daddario and Scotti came up to him smiling, and Scotti said, "I have been waiting for you. I understand you want to liberate General Wolff." The explanation was simple. Waibel had phoned his intelligence chief in the Ticino earlier in the day instructing him to try to find out about Wolff, and the chief had told this to Scotti and also that Waibel and Gaevernitz were coming down.

Waibel informed Scotti that there was considerable Swiss interest in rescuing Wolff. He said that the Swiss had done many favors for Scotti, often closing one and sometimes two eyes to his not so legal activities at the border. Now he, Waibel, wanted a favor in return—the rescue of Wolff.

Scotti agreed enthusiastically and immediately went to work to carry out the job. It was the kind of operation he loved. Gaevernitz, however, felt he had to persuade Daddario, who wanted to go along, not to accompany him. Things were touchy enough without having an American Army officer liberating an SS general. At least Scotti was a civilian.

By ten o'clock in the evening Scotti had organized his expedition. First of all, an aide of Waibel's tried to reach Wolff's villa at Cernobbio by phone and, to his amazement, discovered it was still possible. The partisans had neglected to cut the telephone lines! Wolff was told that a convoy was shortly going to try to get through to him. "Don't shoot us when we come," Wolff was admonished.

Soon after ten, the rescue party crossed the border into Italy and disappeared into the darkness. The convoy consisted of three cars. The organizers had tried in gathering the party together to prepare for every eventuality. The group consisted of a makeshift international truce team whose various members could presumably pacify any hostile interference. There were three Swiss, all from the Ticino border areas, one of them the Ticino intelligence chief's chauffeur. All of them were well known to the partisans as well as to the Germans in the border area, since they had worked on and off in arranging various exchanges of sick, wounded or captured persons during the last months. There were also two SS officials from the now dissolved German border post who could deal with any trouble caused by wandering and suspicious German soldiers in the area that had to be crossed. In addition, Scotti had rounded up an assorted group of armed partisans who happened to be at the border at the moment. The first car, in which the Germans were installed, was decorated with white flags, and the headlights of the second car, in which Scotti and the three Swiss rode, kept the white flags in their beams. The armed partisans brought up the rear in the third car. The plan was to go to Como, where the partisans had already taken over and where, since Scotti knew the officials the partisans had installed, he intended to get papers that would allow the convoy to pass through the lines to the Cernobbio area where fighting was still going on.

Shortly after the cavalcade left Chiasso for Como, it was greeted with rifle fire from the partisans. Scotti jumped out of the car and stood in the headlights, trusting that as the partisans saw him they would recognize him and stop firing. It worked. An old friend of his, who was in charge of the trigger-happy squad, rushed out of the darkness and flung himself into the arms of *l'amico Scotti*, and that ended the firing. From there to Como there was no difficulty. The Prefect was a friend of Scotti's, and issued the necessary papers to pass through the lines. After minor adventures including more rifle fire directed at them and an occasional hand grenade, the party reached the Villa Locatelli, where the German officers in the lead car succeeded in passing the cortège through the German guards. There they found General Wolff in full SS uniform. This would not have been a good introduction to the partisans. Scotti told him to put on civilian clothes, and to hurry. Wolff ceremoniously offered the rescue party some real Scotch whiskey and Lucky Strikes, which he claimed had been captured by Rommel in North Africa. He quickly changed his clothes, and off they started. Each partisan band they encountered on the return trip required prolonged negotiations and much argument and showing of papers. Wolff was kept out of sight in the back of the second car. Strangely enough, no search was initiated. Finally, the little cavalcade made its way safely to the Swiss frontier, arriving around two-thirty in the morning.

In the meantime, Waibel and Gaevernitz had been waiting in the restaurant of the Chiasso railroad station. The small, dimly lit place seemed more like a Mexican tavern during the days of the gold rush than one of those prim eating places one finds at the larger stations of the Swiss Federal Railways. Characters of doubtful appearance with distraught looks on their faces, the riffraff in the wake of war and revolution, kept rushing into the station restaurant, most of them trying to get away from the destruction of war into peaceful Switzerland.

Some were no doubt agents of the various intelligence services operating across the Swiss-Italian frontier. Others were members of the Italian partisans, down from their hiding places in the mountains enjoying setting foot on Swiss territory for the first time in years. Some had relatives or close friends in the Ticino, and had come across the border to get food or to engage in black-market currency operations. There were also a few newspapermen representing Swiss and foreign papers, looking for stories, to whom Gaevernitz gave a wide berth. To Waibel and Gaevernitz, at this moment they were more sinister than the smugglers. Nothing would have done more harm to our surrender project than the slightest premature press publicity.

Fortunately the station slowly emptied as the night progressed. Gaevernitz and Waibel left and went to the border control post, less than a mile away, where the highway crosses from Switzerland into Italy. Several times the noise of a car was heard across the border and then faded out again in the distance.

Finally, after an hour or so of waiting, they saw the two bright headlights of a car approaching the border post from the other side. It was Scotti and his party. To avoid unauthorized talking with Wolff, Gaevernitz sat in a parked car at the corner of the customs house, planning to disappear quietly once he was sure that Wolff was safely on Swiss soil. But when Scotti's car drove up, Wolff got out and was told by someone that Gaevernitz was present. Wolff thereupon came directly over to him, shook hands and expressed his fervent thanks. "I will never forget what you have done for me," he said. At this point, Gaevernitz, orders or no orders, began to talk to Wolff.

The party—Gaevernitz, Waibel and Wolff—moved on to Lugano to get away from the border and to decide what Wolff was to do next. There in the room of a small Lugano hotel, while they waited for the dawn, Wolff told Gaevernitz and Waibel of the events of the previous twenty-four hours.

Wolff had been in continuous touch with Rauff, the SS chief in Milan, by phone. Rauff reported that the center of the city was held by the SS while the suburbs were controlled by the partisans. On some streets, one side was held by the SS, the other by the partisans. Men of both sides were stationed at doorways and windows, with their guns at the ready, but no shots had yet been fired. Wolff ordered Rauff to draw the SS away from the windows and doorways and forbid them to fire. Once the first blood was spilled, everything would get out of control. He also ordered him to release all political prisoners at once. Rauff had then tried to send an armored car to Cernobbio to pick Wolff up, but it could not get through the partisan bands. Cardinal Schuster, who learned from Rauff of Wolff's predicament, had sent a car toward Cernobbio with a priest and an SS officer, who happened to be a relative of the former chief of German Intelligence, Canaris. This probe also failed, and the car turned around and went back to Milan.

One of the reasons the Cardinal was so anxious to get Wolff to Milan was that he thought he had all the parties lined up for the signing of a local peace or armistice, or whatever the word for it might be. This was to involve chiefly the Italian Fascists, the partisans and the Germans in the Milan area. The Cardinal, who had played a prominent role in attempts to make peace between the Germans and their Italian Fascist allies and the Italian partisans ever since the previous autumn, was especially anxious to act because of Mussolini's disturbing presence in Milan. Mussolini was now talking of last-ditch battles at the head of his Fascist supporters and was apparently anxious—like his mentor, Adolf Hitler—to go down at the head of his troops, his broken empire leveled to the ground. For this reason the Cardinal invited Mussolini himself to attend a meeting to discuss a truce on April 25th.

Actually, Wolff knew only a small part of the complex events which had been taking place in Milan; what he knew came from Rauff's phone calls and from an unexpected visitor to Cernobbio. The visitor was Marshal Graziani, Mussolini's Armed Forces Minister, who was theoretically still more or less in command of the four Fascist divisions who were supposed to fight alongside the Germans but so far had not done so.* Graziani, who was consulting with his subordinate generals near Como, heard that Wolff was nearby in the Villa Locatelli at Cernobbio. On his own, without consulting Mussolini, who was by now moving northward in a German convoy, he went to see Wolff early on the twenty-sixth. In the course of the morning he prepared and signed a document which he gave Wolff and which Wolff later gave to Gaevernitz. In it, Graziani handed over to Wolff the power to surrender the Italian Fascist forces along with everything else that was to be surrendered. Graziani obviously knew something about Sunrise. The document read as follows:

MINISTRY OF THE ARMED FORCES
MILITARY SECRETARIAT
April 26, 1945/XXIII

Herewith I, Marshal of Italy Rodolfo Graziani, in my capacity as Italian Minister of War, extend to General of the Waffen-SS Karl Wolff, the highest SS and police leader and fully empowered general of the German Armed Forces in Italy, the following powers: to conduct negotiations on my behalf and, with the same conditions as for the German Armed Forces in Italy, to enter into agreements binding me with respect to all regular troops of the Italian Army, Navy and Air Force as well as of the military Fascist units.

MARSHAL OF ITALY
[sgd.] RODOLFO GRAZIANI

After Wolff was safely in Switzerland, he noted at the bottom of the Graziani document: "I hereby delegate the above authorization to my Chief Adjutant, Major Wenner."

With a flip of the wrist, so to speak, the Italian armies were added to the German forces Major Wenner was already empowered to surrender.

* Describing the "Fall of Italian Fascism," F. W. Deakin, in his book *The Brutal Friendship* (New York: Harper, 1963), p. 772, recounts Graziani's bitterness at Wolff's earlier failure to keep him advised of the surrender negotiations. Wolff replied that it was a "sad necessity" and that if Mussolini had been informed "the secret would have been nil." Here again, even as between putative allies, "great secrecy was necessary."

A few days later Graziani personally surrendered to Captain Daddario, who took him to Milan where he was locked up with the other Fascist prisoners of war.

Various witnesses to the meeting which Mussolini attended in the Cardinal's palace on April 25th disagree on exactly what happened there but most agree about the one key incident which broke up the meeting.* Mussolini at the beginning of the meeting had told the Cardinal that he planned to go up to the Valtellina (one of the northernmost mountainous sections of Italy just below eastern Switzerland) to lead a final stand against the Allies with his most loyal adherents. The Cardinal, seeing Mussolini's confused mental state, evidently did not take this statement too seriously. Soon after, General Cadorna and other representatives of the partisan forces who had also been invited by the Cardinal arrived, and a plan was discussed for an armistice which called for the partisans laying down their arms if the Fascist forces also did so. In the middle of this discussion Graziani appeared on the scene and reported that he had just learned of German plans for a surrender to the Allies on which the Italians had not been consulted at all.

This surprised and angered Mussolini, although some historians find it difficult to believe that Mussolini could have known nothing all this time about Wolff and Sunrise. Mussolini is supposed to have said, "They [the Germans] have always treated us like servants and at the end they have betrayed me." He then stamped out of the meeting followed by his Fascist aides. There was some talk of his coming back in an hour. He never returned. He drove to the Prefecture of Milan where he had an office. Here he said somewhat inappropriately to a lower-ranking German officer in the escort assigned to him, who could not have understood what he was talking about, "Your General Wolff has betrayed us." He then left in a column of ten cars for Como and the lake region. The rest, Mussolini's end, is history. During the confusion of the next days his German escort dwindled, and roaming partisans recognizing Mussolini as he sat in a stalled car, took him out and held him in a small farmhouse in the hills above Lake Como. He was shot nearby along with his mistress, Claretta Petacci, by a Communist from Milan, Walter Audisio, who claimed to have orders to execute him.

On April 26th, two days before Mussolini's execution, Scotti advised me that the Prefect of Como was trying to persuade Mussolini to

* Ibid., pp. 806 ff.

surrender to the Americans in Switzerland. The Prefect, in fact, sent a message to Scotti to sound out the possibilities, and Scotti informed me of this development.

At first glance Mussolini looked like a tempting hostage to have in one's hand but the operation was more tempting than wise or practical. I did not wish to be responsible for bringing the Fascist dictator into Switzerland. Once he was there physically, the Swiss might have been obliged to give him at least temporary asylum under their procedures regarding political refugees, and they would have had an embarrassing case on their hands for which I would have borne a measure of responsibility. I refused to have anything to do with getting him into Switzerland. I sent back word to Scotti to keep clear of Mussolini. Later I heard that Mussolini himself had rejected the idea of seeking refuge in Switzerland.

12

The Surrender Is Signed—
But Not Delivered

Shortly after I arrived at my office on the morning of April 27th, three signals came in, all marked TRIPLE PRIORITY—an emergency communications designation which requires that the message take precedence over absolutely everything else on the line.

All previous "stop" signals were reversed. The Combined Chiefs of Staff were instructing Field Marshal Alexander to make arrangements for the German envoys to come immediately to Caserta to sign a surrender. There were to be no conferences or discussions in Switzerland. The Russians had been invited to send a representative to Caserta. A plane was being sent up that very day from Caserta to Annecy, near Geneva, to fetch the surrender team. It was suggested that both Gaevernitz and Waibel accompany the envoys if possible.

Then the messages began to fly and the phones to ring. Since at this very moment Waibel was driving Wolff to the Austrian border, I contacted Waibel's office urging that he be intercepted en route and given the news. I then informed Washington and Caserta of our situation, told them that with luck we would stop Wolff before it was too late. I proposed, however, that even though we might induce Wolff himself to go to Caserta if we reached him in time, it was probably better to let him continue on to his headquarters at Bolzano. He would be essential to keep the generals in line there; Wenner and Schweinitz could do the signing in Caserta. I then phoned Gaevernitz at the villa in Ascona, where he had gone after leaving Wolff. I told him to come to Bern immediately to be ready to fly with the Germans to Caserta. At first he couldn't believe it.

Before noon Waibel phoned that our message had reached him when he arrived with Wolff at the Austrian-Swiss border. Wolff was delighted with the turn of events but had decided to continue on to Bolzano. He felt he would be more needed there than at the signing in Caserta, where Wenner already had the authority to represent him. Wolff had two suggestions, both regarding the ever-present problem of communications, now more important than ever. One was to leave Zimmer at Buchs to function on the Austrian-Swiss frontier as he had done at Chiasso on the Italian-Swiss frontier. The other was to send Little Wally to Bolzano, right into German SS headquarters, where Wolff would set up the same secret arrangement for him as in Milan. Wally had been waiting in Bern for further orders since returning from Milan, and Wolff knew him to be a capable and courageous fellow. From Bolzano, Wally could establish a radio link to Caserta, and AFHQ could have direct communications to Wolff and through him to the German Army. By this means the detailed execution of the armistice, once the surrender was signed, could be worked out. I immediately wired this suggestion to Washington and Caserta. Schweinitz and Wenner had also been informed and were taking the next train from Lucerne to Bern.

By then the plane from Caserta had landed in Annecy and the pilot was in touch with me. I informed him that the two envoys and Gaevernitz would be ready to fly with him the next morning, April 28th, a Saturday. In the meantime, I had extended to Waibel Field Marshal Alexander's thoughtful and diplomatic invitation to be present at the ceremonies in Caserta.

With Gaevernitz I saw Schweinitz and Wenner at my home in Bern early that evening. As there were to be no negotiations in Switzerland, my job was to get them on their way to Caserta, and our talks were largely concerned with the arrangements for the trip, and to prepare them for the tasks ahead, after their long and disillusioning delay. The three of them left shortly for Geneva. The next morning we arranged for their passage into France and to Annecy, from where they were to fly to Caserta. Providence, as I had felt when Wolff was rescued, was with us after all. If the cables from Washington had arrived a few hours later, Wolff would have returned to Bolzano under the impression that the deal was off and consequently might not have been able to keep the generals in line to support the surrender. Also Schweinitz and Wenner might well have lost patience and gone home.

On the morning the party left for Caserta, approval came in for Wally to go to his dangerous post at Bolzano. Before the afternoon was over, Little Wally, with his radio kit, his change of underwear and the usual large supply of cigarettes, was on the way to his new post of duty and danger accompanied as far as the Swiss border by Captain Tracy Barnes. Zimmer took him over the border into Austria at Feldkirch and waited with Wally until an SS car driven by one of Wolff's men drove up. In the car, Wally changed into an SS uniform which Wolff had provided for him, another ironical touch when one recalls Wally's days at Dachau. When he reached Bolzano, he was taken up to a small room on the third floor of the immense stone Palace of the Duke of Pistoia, which had been taken over by Wolff as a communications center in 1944 and had now become his final headquarters in Italy. Wally set up his antenna and was in radio contact with OSS Caserta by noon of the twenty-ninth and ready to perform his vital service in keeping communications open during the next crucial days, when the surrender was to be signed.

Since secrecy was still the order of the day and I was too well advertised as President Roosevelt's personal representative, I did not go to Caserta for the signing. My presence at the surrender ceremony might well have been discovered by the press and have blown the security of the operation we had so carefully preserved up to this point. It was still, and should for the time being remain, a "secret surrender." Furthermore, it was to be a military surrender conducted by military representatives on both sides, reflecting the total military victory of the Allies.

Gaevernitz, at Field Marshal Alexander's request, joined the German envoys and acted as interpreter throughout the proceedings at Caserta on the twenty-eighth and twenty-ninth of April, 1945. He wrote for me a full account of these days. As the reader will see from the account, Gaevernitz's functions were much more important than those of an interpreter, though he had no other officially announced duties. In fact, he exercised unique influence on the German envoys, and his skill in dealing with them was of vital importance particularly in persuading Schweinitz to interpret liberally the oral instructions he had received from his principal, General Vietinghoff. If Gaevernitz had not been on the spot acting as an experienced negotiator, serious trouble might have developed and the surrender might never have been signed. This is Gaevernitz's story of those two crucial days:

"At noon on April 28th, Field Marshal Alexander's plane, a comfortably fitted C-47, took off from Annecy. Major Hanley of General Lemnitzer's staff, who had come up with the plane from Caserta to act as escort for our party, was the only one of the three American officers from Caserta on board who even knew the nature of our mission.

"The plane flew by the majestic beauty of Mont Blanc and winged its way over Nice and Corsica with the blue Mediterranean between. For the first two hours of the trip the German emissaries brooded or slept. But in the last stretch of the journey they began to talk and ask questions.

"They were concerned with questions of protocol. Would they shake hands with the Allied officers upon their arrival? Would they be treated as parliamentarians and, according to the usages of war, be blindfolded so that they should not see anything of military importance behind the Allied lines? Would they be interned if the parleys broke down?

"Our plane arrived at the Marcianese airfield near Caserta about 3 p.m. Generals Lemnitzer and Airey were waiting for us at the field. A few weeks before they had faced similar problems of protocol at our secret meetings at Ascona. I managed to leave the plane first and presented the recurring question of handshaking to the generals. They decided there would be none, but asked me to introduce the Germans to them by their true names, and vice versa. The formalities over, the two parties having bowed and nodded curtly as the introductions were made, the two Germans were driven off in one car and the Allied generals and I followed in another.

"The Allied headquarters of the Mediterranean theater was located in a great castle which had formerly belonged to the kings of Naples. Behind the castle cascades of water tumbled down a hill feeding into a series of terraced pools and fountains decorated with baroque statuary, surrounded by eighteenth-century English gardens.

"It was shortly after three o'clock in the afternoon when our two cars reached a compound on top of this hill completely fenced in by barbed wire. This camp, which had been evacuated for the occasion, was situated at a spot offering one of the most glorious views in Italy. The hill with its pine trees overlooked the magnificent Bay of Naples, the white houses on the blue shores of the Mediterranean, and several distant islands off the coast. But for the German 'tourists,' who were not there for aesthetic reasons, the glorious view had been blocked off. Large sheets of canvas were fastened from tree to tree. This was done to prevent the Germans from recognizing the exact location of the camp and obtaining any detailed knowledge about the site of Allied headquarters. After all, the war was still being waged and bombs were falling.

"To maintain absolute secrecy during the talks which were to take place shortly, the camp was also heavily guarded. So strict were the orders to keep everyone out that our own party was at first denied entrance. The MP's insisted that no one was to be admitted to the camp, according to special instructions from General Airey. 'I *am* General Airey,' insisted the General. At first the guards were not impressed. They replied that anyone could say that. It took several telephone calls before General Airey was at last able to enter the camp which had been set up under his special instructions.

"The camp was composed of a number of Quonset huts and bungalows. The Germans were given a small bungalow by themselves and I was put up in another one. There were other, larger temporary buildings, one containing a mess hall and an attractively furnished living room. In another there was a conference room where the discussions were to take place.

"A first informal talk between Generals Lemnitzer and Airey and the German emissaries went off well, while we all sipped the traditional British cup of afternoon tea. Airey tried to impress upon the two Germans that they were there to accept unconditional surrender rather than to negotiate any kind of agreement. We then left the two Germans on the hill and drove on to General Airey's villa. When we arrived, I asked him if there were any microphones installed in his room and he assured me that there were not. I continued, 'I want to be quite sure because I intend to tell you something you might not want recorded.' Then I told him that I had violated the instructions of the Combined Chiefs of Staff, had liberated Wolff and sent him through Switzerland and Austria to Bolzano. I was relieved but not surprised when he said, 'Don't you worry about that.'

"The first official meeting took place at six o'clock in the evening. In addition to Generals Lemnitzer and Airey a small number of the highest-ranking Allied officers in the Mediterranean theater were present, but at this first meeting there were no Russian representatives. The Allied officers were seated on one side of a long table which almost completely filled the conference room, and the two Germans were seated on the other side.

"Lieutenant General W. D. Morgan, Chief of Staff to Field Marshal Alexander, who presided, presented the rather voluminous document containing the terms of surrender, and asked me to translate his comments into German. He informed the emissaries that another, more important meeting would be held at nine o'clock the same evening, at which time they would have an opportunity to raise questions and ask for explanations. Thus, they would have three hours to study the document. General Morgan also informed the two Germans that one or more Russian representatives would be present at the nine o'clock meeting.

"Immediately following this first meeting, the German emissaries went to their quarters and began to study the documents. When they set out on their trip, they still entertained some illusions about the meaning of the word 'unconditional.' The powers which Vietinghoff had conferred upon Schweinitz were couched in rather elastic terms. Although he had the right to sign in Vietinghoff's name, these powers had been curtailed by the equivocal addition 'within the frame of the instructions given by me.' The instructions given verbally by Vietinghoff to Schweinitz referred in particular to the German commander's wish to spare his army from internment in Allied prison camps. He wished to obtain from the Allied Military Chiefs an agreement under which the armies he commanded would be demobilized in Northern Italy and the men sent home to Germany as soon as possible. Another concession the German emissaries were instructed to request was permission for officers to keep their side arms.

"Now, after the first meeting, it seemed unlikely that the Allies would make any such concessions. The surrender document was written in the sober and imperative style of the victor. It was a deep shock for the two Germans.

"The second meeting started promptly at nine o'clock in the evening. This time a Russian Major General A. P. Kislenko,* representing the Russian General Staff, together with his interpreter, Lieutenant Uraevsky, were present.

"The German emissaries were given an opportunity to raise any objections, and they made a strong plea for demobilization of the German armies on the spot without internment in prison camps. They also reiterated their request that German officers be permitted to retain their side arms, which they claimed was necessary to maintain discipline until the surrender was completed.

* Major General Aleksey Pavlovich Kislenko was an officer of the Soviet Military Intelligence (GRU) and apparently a Japanese expert since he had served in Japan before World War II and was for five years after the war one of the Soviet members of the Allied Control Council for Japan.

"The terms of the surrender agreement provided that the Germans would not be permitted any motor transport after they had put down their arms. The emissaries pointed out that this was not feasible because it would take two or three weeks to carry out the surrender in its entirety and in the meantime the German troops had to be supplied with food.

"Another point for argument was the naval craft in the ports. Schweinitz pointed out that these vessels were not under the control of the Army Group but under the orders of the German Navy. Therefore, he could guarantee the surrender of the ports only, but not of the craft.

"An important objection the Germans made concerned the ports of Trieste and Pola. They explained that they could make no commitments regarding these famous ports, the latter of which had once served as naval base for the Austro-Hungarian empire. Recently, Trieste, Pola and all the territory east of the Isonzo River had been taken from the German command in Italy and was now under the command of General Löhr, the German commander in the Balkans. He was not connected with General Wolff's surrender negotiations. The British admiral attending the meeting was visibly disappointed at the vanishing prospects of raising the Union Jack at Pola and obtaining the surrender of German naval craft.

"The Allied commanders listened to the Germans' observations and made concessions on some of the minor points. They agreed to the continued use of German military motor transport. They conceded that the German officers could retain their hand weapons until the surrender operations had been completed. However, on the main German requests concerning the demobilization of the German troops and their quick return to Germany, the Allies remained adamant.

"Thus, when the meeting broke up, the Germans, chiefly Schweinitz, were unhappy. At their request I accompanied them back to their headquarters, as they wished to discuss further the terms of the surrender and, in particular, the terms of the radio report which they intended to send to German headquarters at Bolzano. Our discussion lasted throughout most of the night.

"It was soon clear that Major Wenner, the representative of the SS, had in his own mind capitulated and appeared to be under instructions to sign the surrender agreement in whatever form it might be presented. Schweinitz, however, speaking for the Wehrmacht, felt he could not back down on the issue of internment. He claimed he wanted to spare the German soldiers a long sequestration in Allied prison camps on foreign soil.

Again and again he referred to the verbal instructions which he had received in this regard from his Commander-in-Chief, and which he said prevented him from accepting the surrender terms as presented.

"At last I put forth an argument that seemed to make some impression: 'Don't you realize,' I said, 'that every sentence which we speak may cost the lives of hundreds of soldiers? While we are arguing here, every minute may mean further destruction, further air raids on German cities, further death.'

"At this point Schweinitz weakened. But he still insisted that his chief, Vietinghoff, should be informed regarding the surrender terms and be asked to give his final consent to the signing of the surrender document. Jointly we completed the draft of a telegram to be sent to his chief at once. It was then four o'clock in the morning.

"I felt that considerable progress had been made. With the draft of the telegram in my pocket, I drove in the early dawn alongside the cascades of the Royal Park, which reflected the waning moonlight, to General Lemnitzer's office in the huge building of the Royal Palace.

"I found him still at work at his desk. He was greatly encouraged when I showed him the draft of the message and ordered it to be encoded at once. As Wally, our OSS radio operator, had not yet taken up his post at Wolff's headquarters in Bolzano, the message was sent to our office in Bern, Switzerland, from which point we requested that it be taken by courier to Vietinghoff's headquarters at Bolzano. This lengthy method of transmission made it unlikely that an answer would be received before two or three days at the earliest.

"We then caught a few hours' sleep. Another informal meeting between Generals Lemnitzer and Airey, the German emissaries and myself took place early in the morning. This meeting was opened by Airey with the statement that there would be no time to wait for Vietinghoff's reply. He insisted that the surrender be signed that very day so that the emissaries could leave the same afternoon and try to reach Bolzano the following day. It was then that the long debate of the previous night bore fruit, as Schweinitz now agreed to sign without his chief's renewed consent.

"Thereupon the many arrangements necessary for carrying out the surrender were discussed and determined. To make a fighting army put down its arms is in many respects as painstaking a task as to mobilize it. Most important of all is to fix the precise hour when hostilities are to cease, and to see to it that orders reach the front line units in time and are carried out. Nothing would be worse than to have one side stop fighting while the other continued. To bar any misunderstanding and to synchronize action, it was decided to fix the time for surrender according to Greenwich mean time.

"Almost equally important was the establishment of radio communications between Allied military headquarters and those of the enemy. A code, as well as radio wave lengths for the transmission of messages between the two armies, was given to the Germans to take back to their headquarters.*

"The day and time of the surrender was set for May 2nd at twelve noon, Greenwich time, which was 2 p.m. local time. It was now April 29th and we assumed it would require approximately twenty-four hours for the emissaries to return to their headquarters. Thus, forty-eight hours would remain for the surrender orders to be issued and reach the German military units in the field. We realized that to meet this deadline—seventy-two hours hence—matters had to be rushed. It was of vital importance that the party carrying the surrender agreement should leave Caserta by plane not later than 3 p.m. the same day in order to land at the Swiss-French border before darkness. There was not even time to retype the surrender agreement, which covered some thirty pages, in order to incorporate the changes to which the Allied commanders had agreed. At General Lemnitzer's suggestion, I inserted the changes by hand while the General looked over my shoulder to make certain the wording was correct.

"At two o'clock in the afternoon everything was ready for signature. For this purpose a third and final official meeting between the Allied commanders and the German emissaries took place in the solemn setting of the Royal Summer Palace. A former ballroom had been turned into an office for General Morgan. This huge room was decorated with a large strategic map of the Po Valley, and a second map which showed the whole region of the Mediterranean, the old and recent battle grounds to which peace was to come once more through the action to be performed in this room.

* Later, however, this code, which had been carefully prepared for communications between the two armies, was burned at German headquarters by the German chief signal officer at a moment when he feared that the surrender plot had been prematurely discovered and that he might be shot for high treason if the code was found in his possession.

"Although the signing of the first German surrender of World War II was still top secret, it nevertheless was staged in the glaring light of modern publicity. To record this historic event, a small group of British and American newspaper and radio reporters, drawn by lot, had been flown in from Rome; movie cameras and floodlights had been installed. Upon their arrival, the newsmen had been pledged to absolute secrecy until the official announcement of the surrender was made, which could not be until it went into effect on May 2nd. This complete news blackout was faithfully observed by the reporters.

"At this point I suggested to General Airey that the names of the German emissaries be withheld altogether, as I feared they might be killed as traitors by the Nazi underground, which at that time was expected to operate throughout defeated Germany.

"The Germans, who had no inkling of the publicity arrangements, were shocked when they entered the room flooded by the blinding glare of the eight huge klieg lights, saw the microphones and heard the grinding sound of the movie cameras.

"American, British and Russian officers stood at one side of the room. Altogether there were eleven high-ranking American and British generals and admirals, one Russian general and his interpreter, three Allied senior officers, a small group of Allied newspaper and radio reporters and myself.

"A long, polished conference table had been placed near the center of the room. General Morgan stood alone at one end of the table. The two Germans were led to the other end.

"General Morgan, standing behind his chair, opened the proceedings with the following question:

" 'I understand that you are prepared and empowered to sign the terms of a surrender agreement. Is that correct?' I translated.

"Schweinitz answered, '*Ja*.'

"The General then turned toward Wenner and repeated the question. The SS representative replied, '*Jawohl*.'

"General Morgan went on, 'I have been empowered to sign this agreement on behalf of the Supreme Allied Commander, the terms to take effect by noon May 2nd, Greenwich mean time. I now ask you to sign and I shall sign after you.'

"At this moment the representative of the German Army sprang a surprise. Schweinitz, once more plagued by doubts about the extent of his powers, interjected in German, 'May I repeat, before signing, the point I made during the preliminary talks; namely, that I personally am going beyond my powers. I presume that my Commander-in-Chief, General von Vietinghoff, will accept, but I cannot be entirely responsible.'

"I translated the words slowly and carefully into English. General Lemnitzer and I exchanged some doubtful looks while a flutter went through the audience. It was possible that this declaration would render the signature of the German Army officer worthless in the eyes of the Allies. General Morgan, though, seemed to have no such doubts. He said in a firm voice, 'I accept.'

"After having mentioned once more that the terms were to enter into force at noon, Greenwich mean time, on May 2nd, General Morgan again asked the German emissaries to sign.

"Before the beginning of the ceremony, pens and inkpots on the table had been carefully checked. Some reporters, who had already set their eyes on the pens which would become splendid souvenirs of historical value, were rather disappointed when another souvenir hunter, one of the junior officers serving as secretary to the meeting, handed his personal fountain pen to the Germans for their signatures. Thereupon both German emissaries signed the five copies of the agreement, and thereafter General Morgan affixed his signature.

"It was 2:17 p.m. when General Morgan closed the proceedings. The Germans were led out of the room and the floodlights faded. The room seemed suddenly dark and barren, like a stage after the play is over.

"The document had been signed.* Now one of the last difficult jobs was still ahead. The fact that they had surrendered had to be made known to the German armies through their top military commanders. This meant that the emissaries with their surrender document again had

---

* There was little if any recent precedent for the drafting of an unconditional surrender. The text of this one had been composed more or less out of whole cloth by General Lemnitzer and his staff and then shown to Field Marshal Alexander for his approval. This is all the more interesting because this text, it is reported, was used as the basis for the surrender document hastily drawn up for the over-all German surrender at Rheims a week later. That this was an "unconditional" surrender was amply set forth in the opening paragraph:

"1. The German Commander-in-Chief Southwest hereby surrenders *unconditionally* all the forces under his command or control on land, at sea, and in the air and places himself and these forces *unconditionally* at the disposal of the Supreme Allied Commander, Mediterranean Theatre of Operations."

to be passed secretly via France, neutral Switzerland and German-controlled Austria to German headquarters at Bolzano. The last part of the journey had to be made through territory patrolled by Gestapo agents and threatened by partisan bands.

"When our party left Marcianese airfield near Caserta at 3 p.m., twenty-four hours had gone by since our arrival. Thanks to the resourcefulness of Generals Lemnitzer and Airey, the job had been done with amazing efficiency and speed.

"We landed at Annecy at 7:15 p.m. French time, which corresponded to 6:15 p.m. Swiss time. We had hopes of catching the last train from Geneva to Bern shortly before 8 p.m. if there were no difficulties getting over the border into Switzerland. It was, I suppose, too much to expect; when the big things go well, then the little things often rise to plague one. Our OSS base at Annemasse, right near the French-Swiss border, had not yet received the message from Caserta informing them of our progress at Caserta and of the time of our expected arrival at Annecy. We had, it seemed, outflown our radio. Hence, no arrangements had been made to get us to and across the border into Switzerland.

"To make things even more complicated, Major Waibel, who had usually arranged these delicate border crossings into and out of Switzerland in a quiet and masterly manner, had in the meantime received permission from his superiors to join us in Caserta. Not realizing that he would be too late to be present at the signing of the surrender, an event to which he had contributed so much, he had left Switzerland in a special plane Lemnitzer had sent up to fetch him some hours before our return. We had probably passed him in the air flying in the opposite direction, and he was in all likelihood just arriving in Caserta when we needed his help badly at the Swiss-French border in Annemasse.

"Since there was nothing else to be done, I went up to the frontier post myself, hoping to persuade the Swiss frontier guards to let the two Germans in. My story was that they had left Switzerland only the day before for a short visit to France, intending to return to Switzerland as soon as their business was done. I unfortunately could not tell them that these two men had sealed the fate of almost a million German and Italian soldiers and at the same time had protected Switzerland against intrusion from the south by a disorganized horde of defeated German armies.

"The Swiss officials seemed obliging. 'What are their names?' they asked innocently. To my great embarrassment I had forgotten the assumed names they had used at the border when leaving, and was afraid that they also had forgotten them. In any case, I couldn't run outside where they were waiting and ask them. I answered I would show them that my companions had only left Switzerland on the previous day on a temporary absence if we could go over their records. They somewhat naïvely acceded to this proposal, and together we went down the list of names in their ledgers. After a quick perusal I spotted the two names they had used. When I then intimated that officers of the Swiss General Staff were particularly interested in the journey of these two gentlemen and had arranged for their exit out of Switzerland the previous day, the Swiss frontier guards softened and agreed to let our emissaries re-enter the country.

"The series of mishaps had only started. In Geneva the last train for Bern had just pulled out of the station when we arrived. The OSS representative in Geneva, who also had not yet been informed of our arrival, was out for the evening. It was not possible to hire a car because gasoline was severely rationed. So for a while all we could do was wait impatiently among the slow-moving Sunday crowd of peaceful Swiss bourgeois at the outdoor restaurant of the Geneva railroad station, with the surrender documents of such immense urgency in our pockets. I called the house of the OSS man every fifteen minutes, hoping he had come home. Eventually he did, around nine o'clock, after another wasted hour, and provided us with a car in which we left for Bern." This ends Gaevernitz's report.

To return to my story, early on the morning of April 29th, General Lemnitzer had cabled the text of the surrender terms to me in Bern. Lemnitzer was convinced that Schweinitz and Wenner would sign the agreement before the day was over. With the military situation in Italy becoming more chaotic every hour, and now that we were about to achieve what we had been striving for since the end of February, he strongly felt that not a minute should be lost in preparing the ground for the actual cessation of hostilities. For the immediate implementation of the surrender, the German command, headquartered in Bolzano, had to have the document its representatives were about to sign at the earliest possible moment. Any delay in its transmission to them meant more needless casualties on both sides.

Since contact had not yet been established with Little Wally's radio at Bolzano, Lemnitzer suggested that we seek some means of getting a courier to Vietinghoff there. I assigned this courier mission to Captain

Barnes and gave him a copy of the surrender terms as we had received them. He left immediately for Lucerne to make contact with one of Major Waibel's men, a captain in the Swiss Army. The two of them would drive to Buchs at the Austrian border, find Zimmer there, and give him the papers to carry over the border and somehow deliver to Bolzano. So I thought.

Barnes was young and daring, and Waibel's man was the same. He had a Swiss friend who owned a private plane. Barnes was a trained parachutist. Earlier in the war he had made a number of successful jumps on dangerous missions for the OSS. So the two men cooked up the idea, without consulting me, of calling on the owner of the plane for assistance. Their plan was to fly Barnes from Zurich over the Alps to Bolzano, and Barnes would parachute in, the surrender terms in his pocket. Barnes would somehow make his way on foot to the German High Command and deliver the papers.

It was a brilliant, if dangerous, idea. There is no use suggesting all the things that could have happened to Barnes before he reached General Vietinghoff. I have always been thankful that the weather turned so impossibly bad by noon that flying was out of the question. While Barnes was waiting for the heavens to clear, two more messages came in from Caserta. Radio contact had been established with Wally. The surrender terms had been wired to him directly and he had acknowledged their receipt. The other message informed me that the surrender had been signed and that the emissaries and Gaevernitz were on their way back to Switzerland.

Gaevernitz and the two German emissaries reached my house in Bern just before midnight, April 29th. Three more exhausted men I have rarely seen.

I produced one of the last bottles of our waning supply of Scotch; hot coffee was brewed, sandwiches were made and the surrender party thawed out before a great open fire. The tricky weather in Switzerland had turned against us. It was cold and there was even a threat of snow in the air. I gave them a pep talk, as I knew the German emissaries had a rough and perilous trip ahead of them. It would take at least twelve hours' hard motoring, even under the best of conditions, to get by car from Bern to Bolzano, and then there were only two days left to meet the May 2nd deadline fixed for the surrender.

They could not tarry long, and soon after one o'clock in the morning they were off, still accompanied by Gaevernitz, for the frontier at Buchs.

The car was now loaded with blankets and pillows so that they could get some sleep during the ride.

I went to bed hoping that the surrender would now go through without further obstacles. Experience should have taught me this was too much to expect.

Before seven in the morning the telephone rang. Gaevernitz was on the other end of the wire calling from Buchs. The envoys had arrived at the frontier, but they were blocked. The Swiss government, by formal action, had hermetically closed the Swiss frontier. No one could enter or leave without special permission. Ordinary visas were of no use, and even the special facilities enjoyed by the Swiss intelligence officers under Waibel's command were ineffective. Only direct action by the Swiss government could help us out.

There was no time to be lost. Immediately I called the Acting Minister for Foreign Affairs, Walter Stucki, at his home. Up to this point I had not disclosed to any member of the Swiss government what I was doing, nor to the best of my knowledge had Waibel. But now the time had come to put the cards on the table. I told Stucki I must see him immediately. He replied he would meet me at the Foreign Office as soon as I could get there.

I knew that Stucki was a man of action and courage. He had represented the Swiss government with rare distinction in many diplomatic posts and was always chosen for tasks of particular difficulty. He had returned from his post at Vichy, where he had rendered distinguished services, so that when the time came, in the summer of 1944, for the Germans to withdraw and the French to take over in Pétain's ill-fated capital, Stucki had arranged a peaceful transfer.

In a few sentences I sketched the problem to Stucki. Two German envoys with the signed surrender of the German armies in North Italy were waiting at the Swiss frontier. If they passed quickly and safely to the German headquarters in Italy, the war in North Italy would be over—without further destruction and bloodshed. Guerrilla warfare in the mountains surrounding Switzerland would be avoided. The Swiss might be spared the flooding onto their territory of many thousands of desperate Germans and Fascists, who might try to pass through Switzerland on the way to Germany or to find refuge and internment in a neutral country rather than become prisoners of war. It was no time for formal consultations.

Stucki got the point immediately. Within a few minutes the orders were dispatched to the frontier to let Schweinitz and Wenner cross.

Wolff had sent a car from Bolzano which was waiting for them on the Austrian side of the border. He had also sent a message for them of the greatest importance for the successful conclusion of our whole venture. Hofer, Gauleiter of the Tyrol, who had been present at the decisive meeting with Vietinghoff on April 22nd and had at that time declared himself a supporter of the surrender, had switched and was now siding with Kaltenbrunner against Wolff. Together Kaltenbrunner and Hofer were trying to stop the surrender from going through. They had reported the independent actions of Wolff and Vietinghoff to Kesselring. They were aware that the envoys were going to return to Bolzano via Austria with the surrender documents and had signaled the Gestapo to arrest them when they passed through Innsbruck, as they would normally do on the way to Bolzano. For this reason Wolff told the envoys to take the longer southern route over Reschenscheideck Pass to avoid Innsbruck, even though the longer route was in some places still covered with snow. The only car Wolff had been able to procure for them was far from robust, but nevertheless they slipped through Hofer's trap and arrived in Bolzano with the surrender documents late that night.

On the morning of that same day we had our own independent confirmation of the fact that Kaltenbrunner was desperately doing everything he could to make some kind of peace deal with us and for this reason, no doubt, would not stop at arresting Wolff's envoys. This was confirmed by my assistant for Austrian affairs, who had seen the questionable Hoettl, Kaltenbrunner's Austrian intelligence chief, a few weeks before. He reported to me that Hoettl had just contacted him in Zurich, having come into Switzerland apparently on forged papers. Hoettl reported that Kaltenbrunner was now in Austria and wished to come to the Swiss border to discuss the whole matter. According to Hoettl, he had reached on Kaltenbrunner's behalf not only General Vietinghoff but also Field Marshal Kesselring on the Western Front, Generals Rendulic and Löhr of the Balkan and Adriatic commands, Gauleiter Hofer of Tyrol and all the other *Gauleiters* of Austria. Wolff was not even mentioned by Hoettl. It was rather obvious that Hoettl and Kaltenbrunner were trying to invalidate Vietinghoff's surrender. It was also clear that Hoettl, whose previous messages had always played on American military fears of a redoubt, was again humming this tune. He was promising to deliver to us the whole of Austria, including the redoubt. Kaltenbrunner was himself an Austrian, and one of the most wanted men on the list of war criminals. It is difficult to conceive, then as now, how he could have imagined that the Allies would deal with him, would believe his transparent lies and claims or would entertain the idea of a separate surrender with Austria, which for some years had been an integral part of the Greater German Reich.

Little Wally's messages in the first twenty-four hours he was in business in Bolzano contained a new cause for alarm. Early on the thirtieth he radioed out that the night before American bombers had attacked Bolzano, some of the bombs falling about fifty meters away from the building being used as headquarters by Wolff. Wally informed us that some of the SS were mad and that his own life would be in danger if the bombing was repeated and if, as a result of the bombing, he was discovered. We wired Caserta requesting that the Air Force he instructed to skip this target, and so informed Wally. The next night, however, the same thing happened, but the bombs this time fell wide of the building. Throughout the bombings Wally stayed at his post.

13

The Climax

The last days of April, 1945, were momentous ones in the annals of history. On April 28th, the day before the German envoys signed the surrender document at Caserta, Mussolini was shot near the shores of Lake Como. His body and that of his mistress, Claretta Petacci, were taken to Milan and hung from the girders of an unfinished building in the Piazza Loreto, at the site of a reprisal shooting of partisan hostages by Fascist units the year before.

Less than forty-eight hours later, on April 30th, Adolf Hitler shot himself in his Berlin bunker. The public announcement of Hitler's death was delayed until the night of the following day, May 1st, and, as we shall see, this delay played an almost fatal role in the closing events of Operation Sunrise. The official announcement of the Führer's death stated that he had fallen at the head of his troops, which was untrue.

On April 30th, while Colonel von Schweinitz and Major Wenner, the German envoys, with the signed surrender documents, were driving from the Swiss border over the snow-covered passes of the Tyrolean Alps, certain other actors in the drama of the surrender were gathered at Bolzano, where the last act was yet to be played. They included General Vietinghoff, who had moved his headquarters there, and his staff, General Wolff and Little Wally.

The next day, May 1st, we received no messages until evening. Then Field Marshal Alexander sent an urgent personal message via Wally to General Vietinghoff, which Caserta repeated to me in Bern. Alexander had to know immediately whether Vietinghoff intended to carry out the provisions of the surrender which fixed the cease-fire to take effect at 2:00 p.m. local time the following day. Otherwise, he could not issue the necessary orders to the Allied forces in time to stop the fighting; without them the whole surrender would be in jeopardy.

Later that night Caserta received a radio message signed by Wolff thanking the Field Marshal for his message and saying that a decision would follow within an hour. What kind of decision? There was no mention of Vietinghoff and no further word for us in Bern that night.

Early the next morning, May 2nd, the day for the surrender, a message came to Caserta from Bolzano sent by Wolff. It contained the startling news that Vietinghoff had been relieved of his command by Kesselring. However, it also reported that the commanding generals of the Tenth and Fourteenth German armies, Herr and Lemelsen, which comprised Army Group C under Vietinghoff, and Luftwaffe General von Pohl and Wolff himself had issued orders to their respective commands to cease hostilities at the stipulated time of 2:00 p.m. As soon as this had happened, according to Wolff's message, an order had been issued by Kesselring for the arrest of all the surrendering generals. For this reason Wolff requested Alexander to drop Allied paratroopers to protect those who were carrying out the surrender in the Bolzano area. This all sounded very grim. A surrender that had to be enforced by Allied intervention might well turn into a continuation of hostilities.

Was that uncertain and indecisive character Kesselring, routed militarily on German soil, going to frustrate a surrender in Italy at the last moment? The news of Hitler's death had just been heard all over Europe. In earlier months, Kesselring had said he would surrender once Hitler was dead. The Fifth Army had taken Verona and was moving toward Austria and Trieste. The German garrisons in Genoa, Milan and Venice had capitulated. The idea that military honor was still involved was fantastic unless one was to assume that Hitler's private lunacies had now infected his generals. Cowardice and fear of the SS could no longer explain this stubbornness of hopeless loyalties.

These were our thoughts as we waited out the last hours in Bern on the sunny morning of May 2nd, the red geraniums blooming in the window boxes on the well-kept and orderly streets of the federal capital as the farmers' carts rumbled over the cobblestones on market day.

Lunchtime passed and there was no news. Sitting there in our office in Bern, Gaevernitz and I had the radio turned on and let it run continuously. There were no messages from Caserta and there was no news on the radio. We tried, of course, to attend to other work and there was plenty of it, but, keeping one ear cocked for news bulletins, we didn't really get much work done.

At last, shortly before five in the afternoon Swiss time, the news broke. It was perhaps the final irony that after two months of intense activity under conditions of great stress and secrecy, Gaevernitz and I, two of the engineers of the operation, learned the same way as the rest of the world that the surrender had gone through and hostilities had ceased—over the radio. The news flash was not very elaborate; the Germans in Italy had surrendered. That was about it. But since this was a period of frequent rumors, was it really true? Could we believe it? A few minutes later our fears were finally put to rest. We picked up Field Marshal Alexander's official announcement of the surrender and not long thereafter the BBC's broadcast from London giving in full detail Churchill's statement to the House of Commons on the surrender, which I quoted in Chapter 1.

With a tremendous sigh of relief and joy we stood up and all but danced around the room. In short order some bottles of champagne were produced and we invited all our Bern staff to join us in a toast to the peace that had finally been achieved, and at last was no longer secret.

Shortly thereafter we began to receive from Caserta reports on their radio traffic with Bolzano. The intense communications activity at Caserta those last hours, when it had been necessary to keep all the lines open to the commanders at the battle front, had precluded their sending messages to us in Bern, where, after all, we could merely be spectators in those last hours.

From the Caserta relays we saw that it had not been until around noon that day, two hours before the deadline, that Field Marshal Alexander's headquarters had received the message that finally counted. It had been sent by Wolff (through Wally) in Marshal Kesselring's name. It said:

> For the sphere of command of the Commander-in-Chief South-west, I subscribe to both the written and oral conditions of the armistice agreement.

One last hitch, a minor one to be sure, had held up the actual announcement of the surrender, as we saw from further cables Caserta relayed to us. Kesselring, again through Wolff and on Wally's circuit, had requested that although hostilities would cease at the stipulated time, no public announcement should be made for another forty-eight hours. When Alexander's staff officers brought to his attention that the cease-fire order had been radioed to the various components of the German Tenth and Fourteenth armies in the clear—i.e., not in code—so that anyone listening in could easily find out what was going on, Alexander sent word to Wolff and Kesselring that he could delay the announcement of the surrender no longer. Kesselring's reasons for requesting the delay were somewhat similar to the reasons he later gave for having resisted the whole surrender idea.* He wanted time to withdraw German troops stationed farther east in Yugoslavia and Istria so that they would not be forced to surrender to the Yugoslavs or to the Russians.

But we still did not have the inside story of what had been happening in Bolzano the last twenty-four hours before the surrender. To tell the story properly it is necessary to go back a few days.

The turning point for the last phase of Sunrise had been a meeting held at Vietinghoff's headquarters at Recoaro on April 22nd, shortly after Wolff's return from his confrontation with Hitler in Berlin. As we found out later, it had been chiefly General Roettiger and German Ambassador Rahn who, at Recoaro, had persuaded Vietinghoff to send Schweinitz to Caserta as the surrender envoy of the German Wehrmacht. Vietinghoff, however, had insisted that an emissary also go to Kesselring to get his final consent to the surrender. Dollmann was sent on this mission. To this meeting also, for the first time in the long evolution of Sunrise, which had steadily expanded to include more and more conspirators, the Gauleiter of Tyrol, Franz Hofer, had been invited. The sole reason for his presence at this late date was that the theater into which the German command had now been forced to withdraw was under Hofer's civil administration and in a part of the vaunted Alpine redoubt area. The problem of maintaining order to carry out the surrender in the area required Hofer's cooperation. He had already been sounded out by Wolff, who was inclined to trust him and accept his apparent willingness to go along with the surrender plan. Hofer turned out to be, however, a dangerous intriguer, interested solely in protecting his position as leader in the Tyrol. Most of what happened next resulted from his plotting.

* See footnote p. 192.

At the critical meeting with Vietinghoff on April 22nd, Hofer had tried to argue for certain stipulations in the surrender agreement which would have guaranteed political autonomy for the Tyrol with him remaining in charge. He had been talked out of this, or so it was thought. It was obviously not a time for such minor ambitions to get in the way of the surrender. Hofer left the meeting apparently reconciled and with full knowledge of what was to happen next and with a promise of cooperation and secrecy, neither of which he kept.

On April 24th, the day after Wolff arrived with Schweinitz and Wenner in Switzerland, planning to go to Caserta, Dollmann set out for Kesselring's headquarters near Munich. He took with him a German doctor by the name of Niessen, a member of Vietinghoff's staff, who for many years had been Kesselring's private physician. Niessen, in Dollmann's opinion, was the man who probably knew Kesselring's mind better than any other living person.

On the way to Munich, Dollmann and Niessen stopped in Innsbruck, where they were Hofer's guests for dinner. Knowing that Dollmann was on his way to see Kesselring to get his consent for Sunrise, Hofer seized the opportunity to talk to Dollmann about a new plan which had been generating in his mind since he had left the meeting at Vietinghoff's, two days before, where his private ambitions had been shelved. Dollmann soon realized that the headstrong Hofer was wavering in his support of Sunrise. Kaltenbrunner and Hoettl were in Innsbruck, and Hofer was apparently in touch with them. They, too, said Hofer, had a plan to reach the Allies to negotiate for an "Austrian" surrender. Kaltenbrunner, so Hofer said, was coming to see him in a few hours. Wouldn't Dollmann like to stay and talk to him? Dollmann sensed trouble; Kaltenbrunner was the last man he wanted to see at this particular juncture. He got out just in time. He claimed that he would be late for his appointment with Kesselring if he stayed longer. It was apparent to Dollmann that if Kaltenbrunner and Hofer joined forces, they would stop at nothing to thwart Wolff's plans, even at the eleventh hour.

Dollmann's visit to Kesselring took place on April 26th, at Pullach, outside Munich. The American armies were approaching Regensburg at that moment, only fifty miles north of Munich. At Kesselring's headquarters Dollmann learned that the Field Marshal was about to be appointed Commander-in-Chief of all German forces in South Germany and Italy. This meant that Vietinghoff's command in Italy, hitherto subordinate only to Berlin, would now come under Kesselring. If this happened, Kesselring would have to give his specific approval for a surrender of Army Group C, not just his personal moral support. Kesselring, as Dollmann saw when he finally talked to him, had become embittered and sarcastic. The Reich was disintegrating. He had received orders from Berlin to arrest Göring if he showed up in Bavaria. Scores of prominent Nazis in South Germany were trying to reach him and to ask for his protection and advice. Still Kesselring insisted on continuing the struggle, at least as long as the Führer was alive. With his back to the wall, he intended to set an example.*

Dollmann brought Kesselring up to date on Sunrise including the fact that Wolff had just gone to Switzerland with Schweinitz and Wenner, but he did not mention the mission of the emissaries to Caserta to sign the unconditional surrender. He left this last and crucial detail out, on Niessen's advice, assuming that Kesselring guessed as much and would be happy not to be burdened at the moment with the problem this knowledge would create for him, especially if Vietinghoff became his subordinate during the next few days. Instead, Dollmann, according to his own account, asked him this question:

"What will you do, sir, what answer will you give the German people, if at the critical moment they should appeal to your sense of responsibility?"

"You can be sure," answered Kesselring, "that in such a situation I would not hesitate to place everything I have and am at their disposal."

Dollmann was reassured by this vague answer. He thought it meant that Kesselring would support any move that would lead to a cessation of hostilities once he felt free to do so; i.e., once Hitler was out of the way and the generals were on their own. He left Kesselring considerably relieved. But his judgment of Kesselring was not right, as the events of the following days show.

Shortly after Dollmann and Niessen left Kesselring's headquarters on the twenty-sixth, Kesselring called Vietinghoff and requested a personal meeting with him in Innsbruck. How Kesselring found time to leave his command post at the crumbling South German front, I do not

---

*Kesselring later maintained that his prime motive in continuing the fighting had been to give the German soldiers on the Eastern Front the opportunity to move to the West and escape Russian captivity, although he did not say this to Dollmann at the time. (See Field Marshal Albert Kesselring, *Kesselring, A Soldier's Record,* New York, 1954, pp. 331 ff.)

know, but a meeting did take place on the twenty-seventh at Innsbruck, about halfway between Munich and Bolzano, and the site of the meeting was Gauleiter Hofer's private farm. Besides Vietinghoff and Kesselring, Rahn and Hofer were also present.

Hofer does not seem to have said much. He was the minor figure on the scene and was watching the other players, waiting no doubt for certain cards to fall into his hands. The upshot of the conference was that Kesselring held to his original resolve not to agree to any kind of surrender as long as the Führer was alive. He had to assume, he said, that the Führer's claim that the battle for Berlin would bring about a change in the war in Germany's favor was based on a substantial foundation, although he was not familiar with the facts. So long as he, Kesselring, believed this and was bound by his military oath, he could not make any independent settlement. Vietinghoff and Rahn could not shake his stubborn resolve. Rahn tried to hold the door open by suggesting that they were all operating in the dark, since they did not know the outcome of Wolff's trip to Switzerland and what terms the Allies were offering. He proposed that Dollmann go at once to Switzerland to see Dulles and find out how the negotiations stood. Kesselring agreed to this, but it was not much of a concession. It only put off the whole matter and avoided further argument for the moment.

Kesselring returned hurriedly to Munich. Hofer stayed at his post in Innsbruck, where he apparently reported to Kaltenbrunner what had happened. Vietinghoff and Rahn, returning from the meeting, stopped off for a short talk at Merano, a South Tyrolean town north of Bolzano, where Rahn had set up his emergency headquarters after dissolving the German Embassy to Mussolini's republic on the Lake of Garda.

General Roettiger had remained in Bolzano and was staying in touch with Vietinghoff by phone. He learned with dismay of the inconclusive outcome of the meeting with Kesselring and drove up to Merano to join Rahn and Vietinghoff. He may have felt that Rahn would be helpful in any attempt to persuade Vietinghoff to act on his own now that there was no other way out. He took Dollmann with him because he had been informed of Rahn's plan for Dollmann to go into Switzerland.

I should explain at this point that our knowledge of what happened at the session at Merano and others that followed is based on a series of written memoirs which we obtained from three of the participants,

Vietinghoff, Roettiger and Dollmann, and from Wolff himself after the war was over. What happened at Merano can be judged from excerpts from these accounts.

Roettiger wrote: "Vietinghoff was completely disheartened and believed that he would no longer be able to carry out the surrender. I contradicted him. A most spirited discussion followed, in the course of which I had to use very harsh words. Rahn remained neutral."

Dollmann wrote: "The mood of Vietinghoff was pessimistic, irritable, nervous. Thank God that General Roettiger was there. The whole thing would have been impossible without Roettiger. Vietinghoff went on about the honor of a soldier and his loyalty to the Führer, which, however, had not stopped him a few days before from sending his staff officer, Schweinitz, with an authorization to act in arranging a final capitulation in Italy. . . . I heard for the first time in my life a verbal duel without quarter between two top military men, at the end of which Roettiger declared in so many words that honor and loyalty and such talk was not going to convince anybody when it was obvious that the cause of the trouble was a complete lack of personal courage. . . ."

Vietinghoff does not mention that day in his own memoir. He evidently did not care to remember it.

Thus, in the afternoon of April 27th, not many hours after I received word from Washington that the ban on negotiations was lifted, a conference was taking place which threatened to undermine the mission of the German emissaries to Caserta. The man in command, Vietinghoff, who five days before had agreed to send an emissary to sign a surrender, was now on the verge of backing down.

Just as the session ended, word reached the group that Wolff had crossed into Austria and was on his way back to Bolzano. This obviated the need for Dollmann's trip to Switzerland. Instead, all four men, Vietinghoff, Roettiger, Rahn and Dollmann, returned to Bolzano to meet Wolff there. They also felt that had to inform Hofer of Wolff's return. He was reached by phone in Innsbruck and was asked to come to Bolzano that evening.

Wolff arrived in Bolzano just before midnight, April 27th. The full-dress session of the main German conspirators in Sunrise began around two o'clock in the morning of April 28th. Wolff brought his listeners up to date on everything that had happened in Switzerland—the Allied breakoff of negotiations, then the change in Allied instructions and the dispatch of Schweinitz and Wenner to Caserta. Wolff argued that unconditional surrender would be the only terms the Allies would accept. Any special deals, he said, were now out of the question. There might have been some chance earlier if the Germans had not delayed and disagreed among themselves so long. The successful offensive of the Allies—the rout of the German armies which had taken place in the weeks since the first serious possibility of an armistice had been considered—had settled the matter. No one could expect that the victorious Allied Army was now going to let the Germans ask for special terms.

No one, that is, except Hofer. He apparently was deeply disappointed. He claimed this was the first he had heard of "unconditional surrender," and had he known these were the terms he never would have agreed to anything. He now demanded that all military formations in his territory be placed under his control. This demand from the crafty boss of the Tyrol met with vehement opposition from everyone present, even Vietinghoff. Roettiger started a heated argument with Hofer which came to no conclusion, and the meeting broke up in disagreement after daybreak. Hofer left in a huff. The others present had decided there was no further action to take until the emissaries returned from Caserta with the surrender terms. Obviously no one felt inclined to inform Kesselring about their presence there.

It was now the twenty-eighth of April; the emissaries had just arrived at Caserta. On this day the event that all the German Sunrise conspirators had feared took place. Kesselring was appointed by Hitler Commander-in-Chief of all German armies in the south, including Vietinghoff's. It was one of Hitler's last acts and it almost wrecked Sunrise.

Sometime on the twenty-ninth of April, Hofer managed to get in touch with Kesselring. He reported to Kesselring what Wolff had told the conspirators the day before: that the Allied terms were unconditional surrender. Roettiger, who unlike Wolff had never trusted Hofer, was the first to catch wind of what had happened. In a phone conversation he had with Hofer on the twenty-ninth, Hofer shouted at him over the wire, "People are going over my head! I won't have anything more to do with your plans! Why don't you fight instead of negotiating?" Roettiger told Wolff he thought grave danger was in the air. Still Wolff could not believe Hofer had betrayed them. Later that day in another phone conversation, Kesselring warned Roettiger, "Fight—don't think about negotiating."

The ax fell early on the morning of April 30th. Orders arrived in Bolzano from Kesselring relieving Vietinghoff and Roettiger of their commands. They were to report to a secret command post of the Army Group in the Dolomites near Lake Carezza to face a court-martial. A General Schultz, one of the commanders in Germany, was to take Vietinghoff's place and a Major General Wenzel Roettiger's. Wolff, who did not come under Kesselring's command, was reserved for special SS treatment. He was notified that Kesselring had turned over his case to Kaltenbrunner for investigation, since Kaltenbrunner was the highest-ranking SS and Gestapo chief in the area. At this point Wolff finally realized that Hofer had betrayed them.

The man in whose name the surrender had been signed, Vietinghoff, obedient soldier that he was, immediately went off to Lake Carezza as ordered. It almost seemed as though he were glad to be removed from the scene and the responsibility of carrying out his own decision. Roettiger, on the other hand, claimed he had to stay on the spot until Schultz and Wenzel had taken over in order to brief them. This allowed him further time for action. That afternoon both Schultz and Wenzel arrived. The same afternoon Wolff learned that Schweinitz and Wenner with the signed surrender document had returned from Caserta and were at the Swiss-Austrian border. He sent word to them, as I have already related, to avoid Innsbruck, Hofer's headquarters, now that he knew what Hofer was up to. They arrived safely in Bolzano after midnight on May 1st, and in a secret session with Wolff and Roettiger showed them the surrender documents which provided for the capitulation to take place at 2 p.m. local time on May 2nd, then only thirty-six hours away.

Schultz and Wenzel meanwhile had told Wolff they could not issue orders to cease fire without the specific approval of Kesselring and, as Wolff knew, there seemed to be little hope of changing Kesselring's mind now.

Thus things stood in the small hours before dawn on May 1st. Vietinghoff, the commander whom it had been so difficult to persuade and who had never quite thrown his real weight behind the surrender, was gone, in disgrace. The one military mainstay behind the surrender, Roettiger, was supposed to follow him into custody as soon as Schultz and Wenzel were ready to take over their commands, presumably on the day that was about to dawn. These two unknown generals, like most last-minute appointees in the dissolving Reich, no doubt felt that their moment to play a part on the pages of history had come—and that they should use it to rescue the honor of the Army from the betrayers who were pressing for surrender. In any case, they would obey Kesselring and not suffer the same fate as Vietinghoff and Roettiger. Wolff himself, now fully aware of the hostile and vengeful attitude of Hofer and Kaltenbrunner, had to watch out for his personal safety, since Kesselring had "turned over" his case to Kaltenbrunner. In Caserta, Field Marshal Alexander was standing by the terms of the surrender agreement, awaiting confirmation that the Germans would also do so. The Allied soldiers were prepared to stop firing on the Germans. Wolff and Roettiger had done everything they could except use force. As the dawn of May 1st broke, Wolff and Roettiger decided upon a desperate measure—the arrest of Schultz and Wenzel. If they were out of the way, then Wolff and Roettiger would have a free hand to induce the subordinate commanders of Army Group C to pass the cease-fire order to their units. These commanders were General Herr of the Tenth Army, General Lemelsen of the Fourteenth Army and General von Pohl of the Air Force. For weeks Pohl had stood by Wolff and could be relied upon to do so now. The other two were favorable to the surrender plan, but not as staunch in its support as Pohl.

The Army headquarters in Bolzano were in a stronghold tunneled into the rocky side of a mountain a short distance from Wolff's SS headquarters. Schultz and Wenzel, the two new generals, were at work early that morning in the Army headquarters, studying the ragged battle lines of the two armies comprising the army group. Shortly after seven o'clock Roettiger, at the head of a detachment of his military police, surrounded and blocked their offices and courteously but firmly announced that they were under arrest. They were to be detained under guard on the spot for the time being. Schultz and Wenzel, tight-lipped, submitted.

Roettiger then assumed the supreme military authority over Army Group C. He ordered the Chief Signal Officer, General Kempf, to close down all telephone and teletype communications with Germany. Kempf complied. Thus, no one on the outside would know what had happened. No one in Berlin or Munich could send in orders to subordinate commanders.

He next called Generals Herr and Lemelsen and told them of the arrest of Schultz and Wenzel and of his intention to proceed with the surrender. To Roettiger's dismay, both Herr and Lemelsen balked at the fact that their superior officers had been illegally arrested and they refused to go along with the surrender under these conditions. They would not, they told Roettiger, attend a conference of generals Roettiger had called for early that evening. This seemed to be the end for Roettiger. He had committed a gross act of insubordination, punishable by death, and apparently had achieved nothing by it.

Around noon, one of the highest officers on Roettiger's staff, Colonel Moll, rushed into Wolff's office and told him that Roettiger was contemplating shooting himself. Wolff raced over to the command post, talked Roettiger out of his suicidal impulse and proposed they now change their tactics in order to bring Schultz and Wenzel around to their side. To do this, of course, they would have to withdraw the guards, give them their freedom and permit them to take over their commands.

Wolff volunteered to talk to Schultz and Wenzel alone. Now it was a matter of bringing about peace among the German generals in order to secure the larger peace among armies, if that was still possible. Roettiger left Wolff with the two generals. After talking with them at great length, Wolff brought them around. They agreed to go along with the surrender under one condition: Kesselring must approve it. At this point Wolff had Roettiger called in and Roettiger apologized to Schultz and Wenzel for what he had done. There was a general reconciliation. The two officers Roettiger had arrested forgave him and even shook his hand. Now communications were restored with Kesselring's headquarters. Lemelsen and Herr, the two Army commanders, were informed that Schultz and Wenzel had been liberated and were restored to their commands, and they both stated their willingness to attend the general conference which was to take place at six o'clock that evening, May 1st.

Present at the conference were Generals Wolff, Roettiger, Schultz, Wenzel, Herr, Lemelsen, Pohl, and Vice-Admiral Löwisch, the last representing the German Navy; also Moll, Dollmann and some senior staff officers.

Roettiger and Wolff made their appeal to the assembled commanders. They explained that no time was to be lost, for the hostilities were scheduled to end in about twenty hours. Herr and Lemelsen supported Wolff to the extent of attempting to impress on Schultz, who was now the Supreme Commander in the Italian theater, that their armies were in a precarious plight and almost without heavy guns. Neither of them, however, would take independent action without Schultz's approval, even though they went so far as to state emphatically that fighting could no longer be justified. Pohl expressed similar views, but Schultz once more declared that he would not act without Kesselring's approval. However, he did promise to communicate with Kesselring immediately and to submit the matter for Kesselring's decision. That was as far as he was prepared to go.

Time was now running very short. At eight in the evening, Wally picked up the message from Field Marshal Alexander asking for a confirmation of the surrender and the surrender hour, so that he might carry out his side of the agreement. It was then that Wolff instructed Wally to radio back that a final decision would be forthcoming within two hours.

Both Wolff and Schultz tried to telephone Kesselring at his headquarters in Germany but at this crucial moment Kesselring could not be reached. Wolff finally did succeed in getting Kesselring's Chief of Staff, General Westphal, on the line. He now tried a new tack. He told Westphal that, instead of stalling, a new Army Group commander should be appointed immediately who would be willing to assume responsibility for surrender, and that the new commander should be chosen from those generals at Bolzano who were willing to take independent action. Wolff requested that either Roettiger, Herr, Lemelsen, Pohl or he himself be appointed as head of Army Group C for the purpose. To this, Westphal replied that he would submit the matter to Kesselring and would telephone a reply within half an hour. By ten o'clock in the evening, however, no reply had been received from either Kesselring or Westphal.

Wolff was determined that he would keep his promise and give Alexander a reply by ten-thirty. According to Dollmann's account, at about this time, despite the tension and the open conflict between the contending parties, a certain human weakness took precedence over everything else. The group ranged along the conference table had been sitting there arguing for four hours—and everybody was hungry. Accordingly, a gigantic batch of sandwiches was ordered and for a few minutes there was silence while everyone, pro-surrender and anti-surrender, gorged himself. This done, Wolff begged Schultz to try Kesselring on the phone one last time. Then it was ascertained that he was absent on an inspection tour of his remaining fighting troops in the Tyrol, but would return to his headquarters after midnight. Schultz shrugged his shoulders. There was nothing he could do. Without Kesselring he would not move.

A short time before ten-thirty, as the group sat silently facing each other across the table, the break came. General Herr, commander of the Tenth Army, who had obviously been wavering ever since the conference began, suddenly turned to his staff officer and said, "Pass down the order to the Tenth Army to cease fire tomorrow at two in the afternoon." The staff officer left the room. Immediately after, each of the following generals transmitted a similar order: Wolff, Pohl and, last of all, Lemelsen. Wolff then left the room to send the crucial message to Alexander via Wally that the surrender would take place on the basis of the cease-fire of these major units, which comprised the main body of the German fighting force—but without Schultz's or Kesselring's consent.

Just after the message to Alexander was sent at 11 p.m., the news of Hitler's death came over the radio. Wolff hoped that this event would immediately bring Kesselring and Schultz over to the side of the surrender. The oath of allegiance to Hitler was no longer binding. However, there was still no word from Kesselring, and without his word Schultz would not move.

During this time Rahn was seeking another kind of solution to Wolff's problems. Earlier in the evening he had talked to Wolff on the phone from Merano and had learned of the dismissal of Vietinghoff and Roettiger and of Wolff's precarious position. For reasons not entirely clear to me, he immediately set out by car for the Swiss border in hopes of getting in touch with me. I could not, of course, have done much about the situation in Bolzano, although I would have had to inform Alexander that the outlook for a consummation of the surrender was bleak at the moment. In any case, the Swiss border guards refused to let Rahn cross. They did let him put in a phone call to some Swiss official in Bern. Rahn requested permission to telephone Allen Dulles. The official asked him to wait while the matter was deliberated. Rahn waited for two hours. It had suddenly begun to snow, and as the light flakes fell he paced up and down in front of the lowered barrier at the border to keep warm. Then word came; the answer was no, nor would the Swiss authorities permit him to enter. He drove back to Merano, where he kept trying to reach Wolff by phone without success. Finally, in the early morning hours he set out for Bolzano to see what was going on.

May 1st blended into May 2nd in one long night of tension, and gradually the forces opposing the surrender began to close in again. Shortly before midnight an order arrived from Germany for the arrest of General von Pohl. It was issued by Pohl's superior officer, General Dessloch, Commander-in-Chief of the German Sixth Air Fleet. It was not carried out because Major Neubert of Pohl's staff, to whom the order was sent, refused to act. Even more disturbing, orders from Kesselring arrived at 1:15 a.m. directing the arrest of Vietinghoff,* Roettiger, Schweinitz and several of the other officers within the surrender plot. Wolff was not included, as he was not under the command of Kesselring. However, the orders left little doubt that direct action would be taken against all of them, including Wolff. It occurred to Wolff that Schultz himself, who was still sitting in the room with the others, might hold the revolting generals in his headquarters to prevent their further action. Wolff excused himself for a moment on the pretext of going to the lavatory. In the hallway he noticed groups of armed soldiers assembling. He quickly returned to the conference room and signaled for his co-conspirators including Generals Herr and Lemelsen to follow him. They did so. Wolff knew the layout of the tunnels in the shelter, and took the group to a little-used exit. It was unguarded. Once outside, Wolff told them that he was going to return to his own command post in the Palace of the Duke of Pistoia and suggested that they follow suit and go to their separate army headquarters, where they could best defend themselves against any attempt to arrest them and could supervise the execution of the orders they had given their troops to cease fire.

No sooner had Wolff and Dollmann reached the Palace than they learned from some of Wolff's officers that an order had just been given to a Wehrmacht tank unit to surround the Palace. Wolff immediately ordered seven police tanks under his command to draw up within the palace park. He also alerted several units of his mobile guards to defend the grounds of the building. Thus, around two in the morning, preparations were made for a small war among the Germans themselves over the issue of the surrender. All the ironies and conflicts of Sunrise had now come to a head—the SS on the side of the surrender party, the top command of the Army opposing it. It was at this point that Wolff sent his message to Alexander asking for the intervention of Allied parachutists.

Before these contending forces had actually arrived to fight each other, Wolff's telephone rang. It was Kesselring. Kesselring said he had just been informed that orders for surrender had gone out to all German troops on the Italian front. He showered on Wolff the most severe accusations. He knew well, he said, that Wolff had been the driving force in

---

* Vietinghoff's name was included in Kesselring's arrest orders even though he had already gone into custody. Possibly Kesselring was making doubly sure for fear Vietinghoff had not complied with the original order.

the sequence of events which had led up to the issuance of these orders. He accused Wolff and his associates of military insurrection. Wolff again began to plead with him to join forces and give approval to the surrender.

It was a long telephone call. It lasted from two in the morning until four. Wolff pleaded for an end to the senseless fighting. He reminded Kesselring that every hour meant the loss of more lives and the destruction of more German cities. He said that they were all agreed on the hopelessness of Germany's continuing the war, which had already lasted too long, which was already lost.

Frequently the conversation faded out and at times it was completely interrupted. Some of the time it was carried on between General Westphal, Kesselring's Chief of Staff, and Major Wenner, Wolff's adjutant. It is not hard to picture the scene—the distraught, exhausted men in the two headquarters arguing out the last hours of the war.

Wolff reviewed for Kesselring the whole history of Sunrise, point for point, justifying his action at every turn. Knowing Kesselring's fear that a Soviet Europe would be the end result of a German capitulation, he wound up with the following argument (Dollmann, who was standing by during the entire conversation, reported Wolff's words): "And it is not only a military capitulation in order to avoid further destruction and shedding of blood. A cease-fire now will give the Anglo-Americans the possibility of stopping the advance of the Russians into the West, of countering the threat of the Tito forces to take Trieste, and of a Communist uprising which will seek to establish a Soviet republic in Northern Italy. . . .* Since the death of the Führer has released you from your oath of loyalty, I beg you as the highest commander of the entire Alpine area devoutly and with the greatest sense of obedience to give your retroactive sanction to our independent action which our consciences impelled us to take."

At four in the morning of May 2nd the conversation between Wolff and Kesselring ended with Kesselring saying that he would give his final

---

*With this statement Wolff was reading the minds of the Allied commanders. No sooner was the surrender accomplished than Field Marshal Alexander ordered General Bernard Freyberg, in command of the New Zealand Motorized Division, to move as rapidly as possible toward Trieste. They arrived at the same time as Tito's partisans. General Clark then moved the American 91st Division in the same direction in a show of strength. Trieste was saved from Communist takeover. (See Mark Clark, Calculated Risk [New York: Harper, 1950], pp. 443 ff.)

decision within half an hour. Shortly after 4:30 a.m. Schultz telephoned Wolff to say that he had just received a call from Kesselring. Kesselring had given his approval to the surrender. He also withdrew orders for the arrest of Vietinghoff, Roettiger and the others.

When Rahn arrived in Bolzano early in the morning and caught up with events, he felt it to be of the utmost importance that Kesselring also reinstate Vietinghoff in his command, a point which had been over-looked during Schultz's last phone conversation with Kesselring. He rea-soned that the surrender at Caserta had been signed in Vietinghoff's name. If there was any recalcitrance by subordinate German command-ers in carrying out the surrender, they could easily justify it by claiming that Vietinghoff's removal had invalidated the surrender. The Allies might also fear that the surrender arrangements would not be honored if Vietinghoff was in disgrace.

Wolff and the others saw Rahn's point but they had had enough of Kesselring. They suggested that Rahn himself do the telephoning this time, and he did. After some "sour and grudging remarks," as Rahn de-scribed it, Kesselring gave in to Rahn's arguments and reinstated Viet-inghoff, who was to his great surprise hurriedly fetched back to Bolzano from his mountain retreat.

Meanwhile, what were the Allied troops thinking as the fighting was approaching its end in the Alpine foothills of Northern Italy? General Lucien K. Truscott, Jr., then commander of the American Fifth Army, which was in the spearhead of the attack, describes the tension of the troops in a booklet issued later to the officers and men of that army.*

A few Allied military commanders knew that negotiations were in progress and had reached a critical point, but the precise time of actual capitulation, if it should come, was known to no one. "Monday, 30 April," Truscott wrote, "was a day of anxious waiting. Would the Ger-man officers be able to reach Vietinghoff's headquarters without being captured by American troops? Would Vietinghoff and Wolff honor the signature of their representatives? Would the news leak out and upset everything?" Until definite word was received, no intimation of what was in the wind could be given lest carefully laid plans disintegrate in a premature wave of celebration.

* Lucien K. Truscott, Jr., "19 Days from the Apennines to the Alps—the Story of the Po Valley Campaign."

In fact, an Allied major attack was planned, but at the last moment it was held up. It was imperative that it not take place unless the surrender was off. Who could tell? The German commander and his negotiators might, in the meantime, have been arrested; they might be dead. General Truscott dared not trust the telephone or radio to impart word of the impending surrender.

On May 2nd, however, listeners monitoring the German radio had picked up broadcasts to German troops sent in the clear from Bolzano, ordering them to cease firing.

At two o'clock local time in the afternoon of May 2nd, the German soldiers began to lay down their arms. The war in Italy was over.

14

Aftermath

Vietinghoff, restored again to his command after the extraordinary events at Bolzano on the night of May 1st–2nd, picked an appropriate subordinate to work out the complex details of putting the surrender into effect. For this task he chose General Frido von Senger und Etterlin,* Oxford educated, who had masterminded the German defenses of Monte Cassino over a year before. Senger was ordered to proceed to General Mark Clark's headquarters at Florence, and was accompanied by Colonel von Schweinitz, who had played a large role in effecting the German surrender and was by now well known to the Allied High Command. A third figure as Wolff's representative in the final delegation was the professional liaison man Colonel Dollmann. Since Dollmann had been in on the negotiations almost since the day they started, it was fitting that he be in at the finish. These three, escorted by American and British officers who had come up to Bolzano to meet them, proceeded south to Florence. There they met General Clark on the fourth day of May. While their staffs got together to attack the manifold problems of disarming the German forces, restoring order in Italy and working to preserve the sequestered art treasures, General Clark and Senger, two opponents who had faced each other across the battle line all the way

---

* Author of *Neither Fear Nor Hope* (New York: Dutton, 1964), which describes the aftermath of the German surrender of May 2nd, pp. 303–306.

up Italy, talked over the tactics and strategy of the war. General Clark relates this in his book *Calculated Risk*.* When Clark asked Senger why the Germans had stayed south of the Po to be smashed to bits instead of retreating north into the mountains where they could have held out intact for a considerable period, Senger answered with one word and a shrug of the shoulders, "Hitler."

Despite the silencing of the guns in Italy, the war in Europe was not over. V-E Day was five days off. We had, however, through Sunrise, not only achieved the first of the great surrenders but had also established a line of communications between the Allied and the German High Commands which turned out to be of considerable use for arranging other surrender parleys. Little Wally, the Czech refugee from a German concentration camp, still sitting at his secret radio in SS headquarters in Bolzano, served after the surrender in Italy as the link between the defeated Nazi armies in Germany and the Allied High Command.

On the afternoon of May 3rd, the difficult Kesselring, apparently under the influence of what had finally come to pass in Italy, phoned Wolff at Bolzano from his headquarters (now moved back into western Austria) and asked that a wireless message to be sent to Field Marshal Alexander. Wally must have been rather excited as he encoded and tapped out for the Caserta station a message from General Wolff which read as follows:

> WOLFF TO ALEXANDER BY COMMAND OF KESSELRING—INSTRUCT WHAT
> ALLIED HQS TO CONTACT FOR SURRENDER OF COMMANDER-IN-CHIEF WEST

The answer from Alexander's headquarters informed Kesselring that his question had been referred to General Eisenhower.

The next day, Eisenhower's answer was relayed via Field Marshal Alexander's headquarters to Wally in Bolzano, where General Wolff telephoned it to Field Marshal Kesselring in Austria. It carried the following historic message:

> 4 MAY 45
>
> TO WALTER: FOR GENERAL WOLFF. PLEASE TRANSMIT FOLLOWING TO FIELD
> MARSHAL KESSELRING.
>
> 1. IN ORDER TO ARRANGE UNCONDITIONAL SURRENDER ON FRONT OF

---

* Op. cit. p. 450.

C IN C [Commander-in-Chief] WEST FIELD MARSHAL KESSELRING OR HIS
EMISSARIES SHOULD CONTACT GENERAL DEVERS HQ 6TH ARMY GROUP.

2. IF EMISSARIES USED THEY MUST HAVE INDISPUTABLE CREDENTIALS
AND FULL POWERS TO SIGN UNCONDITIONAL SURRENDER.

3. GERMAN PARTY SHOULD PASS THROUGH AMERICAN LINES WHEREVER
FIRST CONTACTED ON AUTOBAHN LEADING THROUGH SALZBURG TO ROSEN-
HEIM PASSING SOUTH OF CHIEMSEE. IF SALZBURG HAS ALREADY BEEN OCCU-
PIED BY THE AMERICANS THE GERMAN PARTY SHOULD APPROACH SALZBURG
BY EITHER ROAD R 331 OR ROAD R 31 FROM EITHER DIRECTION.

4. VEHICLE CARRYING FIELD MARSHAL OR HIS EMISSARIES SHOULD BE
PRECEDED BY ANOTHER VEHICLE TRAVELING ONE KILOMETER IN FRONT OF
IT. BOTH VEHICLES SHOULD BE MARKED WITH COVER OVER HOOD AND FLY
WHITE FLAG NOT LESS THAN FOUR FEET ABOVE TOP OF VEHICLE.

5. AT ALL TIMES AFTER 1000 HRS GMT [10 hours Greenwich mean
time] 4 MAY AN AMERICAN POST WILL BE AT FURTHEST POINT OF ADVANCE
ON AUTOBAHN. IF SALZBURG CUSTOMS ALREADY OCCUPIED A SIMILAR POST
WILL BE KEPT ON ROADS R 31 AND R 331.

6. IF POSSIBLE STATE APPROXIMATE TIME WHEN GERMAN PARTY WILL
CONTACT AMERICAN LINES.

7. ACKNOWLEDGE.

That afternoon another message from Kesselring traveling the same
route, Kesselring-Wolff-Wally-Alexander-Eisenhower, announced that
the man who had caused so much difficulty the night before the surrender, General Schultz, now back on Kesselring's staff, would report to the
American Sixth Army Group under General Devers for the purposes of
surrendering. On the next day a message from Kesselring to Eisenhower
over Little Wally's circuit informed Eisenhower that Kesselring's Chief
of Staff, General Westphal, was proceeding to Salzburg from where it
was hoped he could fly to General Eisenhower's headquarters to speed
up the act of surrender. The message read as follows:

5 MAY 45

TO EISENHOWER THROUGH ALEXANDER FROM KESSELRING

I HAVE BEEN ASSURED THAT YOU WOULD BE READY AT ANY TIME TO RE-
CEIVE A PLENIPOTENTIARY FROM ME. IF THIS IS SO, I SHOULD BE MOST GRATE-
FUL FOR IMMEDIATE CONFIRMATION. IN THAT CASE I WOULD IMMEDIATELY
DISPATCH MY CHIEF OF STAFF, CAVALRY GENERAL WESTPHAL, TO SALZBURG
WITH A PARTY OF FIVE. TO SAVE TIME NOTIFICATION BY RADIO IS REQUESTED

CONCERNING THE POSSIBILITY OF FLYING TO YOUR HEADQUARTERS FROM EI-
THER SALZBURG OR MUNCHEN-RIEM [Munich's airport].

On May 5th–6th Kesselring's forces in southeastern Germany and Austria, known as Army Group G, comprising the German First and Nineteenth Armies, surrendered to General Devers. The existence of Little Wally's radio, combined with the moral suasion Wolff had worked on Kesselring during the preceding days, hastened the practical realization of this surrender. As General Eisenhower states in his memoirs, the surrender of the German armies in Italy placed the German units north of them in an impossible military situation and this no doubt helped to make up Kesselring's mind for him.* The surrender of all German forces took place at Rheims on May 7th, hostilities to cease at midnight, May 8th.

Field Marshal Alexander invited Gaevernitz and me to his headquarters at Caserta—a gesture of great courtesy—immediately after the surrender in Italy went into effect on May 2nd. I had not met him before though we had been, in a sense, close partners for months, and I had come to have great admiration for his qualities of decision and leadership.

Gaevernitz showed me over the grounds of the palace at Caserta, pointing out the bungalows where his last-minute pleas had helped to convince Schweinitz, who had been trying to bargain for better terms. While we were in Caserta, General Lemnitzer asked Gaevernitz to visit the island of Capri where a group of former prisoners of the Nazis had just arrived and were being held by the Allies pending clarification of their status. They had been part of a large group of concentration camp inmates of various nationalities whom the top command of the SS were holding in reserve, most likely for a last-minute attempt to buy immunity for themselves. Drawn from a variety of camps in Germany and Austria, they had been herded together and moved under SS guard across the Alps to the village of Niederdorf near Dobbiaco in the South Tyrol. At that point they comprised almost two hundred persons including a number of prominent international figures who had been in Nazi hands since early in the war.** While in Capri Gaevernitz learned the story about their narrow escape from liquidation.

* Dwight Eisenhower, *Crusade in Europe* (New York: Doubleday, 1948), p. 425.
** Among them were Léon Blum, the former Premier of France, and his wife; Kurt von Schuschnigg, the former Chancellor of Austria, and his wife; a Russian lieutenant named Kokorin who was a nephew of Molotov's; two British officers

The presence of these prisoners in the South Tyrol had come to the attention of Roettiger and Wolff through the resourceful act of one of their number, Colonel von Bonin, who had been able to evade his SS guards long enough to get to a telephone in Niederdorf and make a call to German Army headquarters in Bolzano. He fortunately managed to get through to Roettiger whom he knew from earlier days. Bonin told Roettiger that the SS had orders to shoot the entire group rather than let the prisoners fall into the hands of the approaching Allied armies.

Roettiger, acting jointly with Wolff, dispatched a Wehrmacht unit under a Captain von Alvensleben to Niederdorf with orders to take over the protection of the group. After Alvensleben arrived on the spot with a shock troop of only some fifteen men and ran up against the intransigeance of the SS, he called for reinforcements of one hundred fifty men from Dobbiaco and hoped they would get there in time. They did, and the SS, now surrounded, threatened to start shooting if the army tried to dislodge them. Eventually a parley was held and the SS, out-numbered, agreed to being relieved. The prisoners were then housed in neighboring inns under the protection of Roettiger's men until the surrender was signed at which time arrangements were made to send them down to Capri where they were gradually sorted out and the non-Germans returned to their respective homelands.

While we were still in Caserta, I received an invitation from General Eisenhower's headquarters and went to Rheims for the final over-all surrender. When Gaevernitz and I returned to Bern around May 8th, there was still another invitation awaiting us. General Wolff invited us both to Bolzano. This invitation I had to decline, but Gaevernitz went because one of the matters Wolff was anxious to settle before he left the

---

who were related to Churchill; the two British intelligence officers, Stevens and Best, who had been kidnaped by the Germans at Venlo, on the Dutch border, in a famous incident early in the war; Prince Leopold of Prussia; Pastor Martin Niemöller; a number of other prominent Protestant churchmen and Catholic prelates; former President of the Reichsbank, Hjalmar Schacht, and a large number of participants in the July 20th conspiracy who had so far been spared execution, Generals Halder, von Falkenhausen, Thomas, Colonel von Bonin, and others, as well as the families, wives and children of many who had been executed. Among these were the widow, children, brother and nephew of Count von Stauffenberg who had planted the suitcase with the bomb in it that was supposed to destroy Hitler.

scene was the disposition of the Italian art treasures of whose where-abouts he had previously informed us. There was also the matter of collecting the facts, for historical purposes, of what had happened in Bolzano on May 1st and 2nd directly from the participants who were on the spot those last days before the surrender was announced.

The situation in Bolzano on May 9th, seven days after the Italian surrender went into effect and two days after the full German capitulation in Europe, was an unusual one. After the surrender, the mountain troops of General Truscott's forward divisions had raced up north of the Lake of Garda toward the Brenner Pass to make contact with elements of the American Sixth Army Group in Austria and to close the lines of communication. In their rush they had left only small detachments of military police and a liaison unit in the Bolzano area. Otherwise, the American and British forces in Italy, with the exception of those Commonwealth units that headed for Trieste to get there before Tito did, remained where they were at the time the surrender was announced awaiting the detailed arrangements of the capitulation and consignment to camps of the German and Italian forces. The German forces also remained where they were at the time of the surrender.

As a result, when Gaevernitz arrived in Bolzano by air on May 9th, Generals Wolff, Vietinghoff and Roettiger and their staffs, all the men who had played roles in Sunrise were enjoying springtime in the Alps. They were consuming their remaining supplies of food and drink and waiting for whatever instructions were to come for them from the Allies. Wolff had recently managed to have his wife and children join him in Bolzano and was now enjoying his first family reunion since he had left for Italy in 1943. German soldiers and SS men were free to wander about at will and enjoy the sunshine. Into this idyll came Gaevernitz with one of our senior OSS officers from Caserta, Ted Ryan.

This was the account of their drive from the airfield to the center of Bolzano: "It was a peaceful scene, rather like lunchtime at the M-G-M studios. A bronzed lad in khaki Afrika Korps shorts was balancing on the handle bars of his bicycle a smiling girl in a dirndl. Austrian types in black Homburgs and velvet jackets moved casually through the streets. In a field at the roadside lolled some hundreds of Wehrmacht troops only mildly interested in the American staff car which rolled by them. The first traffic control we encountered was, indeed, not an American MP but a square, very correct German soldier with an automatic weapon slung over his shoulder."

At the hotel where they stopped, German officers were also billeted and it took some persuading on Gaevernitz's part to get the Austrian hotelkeeper to give them, the American victors, decent rooms. At Wolff's headquarters in the Palace of the Duke of Pistoia, German guards ushered their car up the driveway. Gaevernitz and Ryan arrived in the salon reserved for the top brass just in time to have after-dinner coffee.

They began their tour of the area with a visit to Wally's quarters on the third floor of the building. "Wally was dressed in an over-sized double-breasted gray pin-stripe coat he had worn for three weeks, with a red striped shirt and a new necktie hanging loose at the throat. Code books and the radio set were on a corner table, the aerial rigged up to the roof outside and stretching diagonally across the room. From the windows one could see the buildings next door which had been hit in the bombing of April 29th when Wally had frantically wired that the SS were angry. On the door to his small room adjoining Wolff's bathroom was still dangling a sign. 'Admission only with special permission of the Obergruppenführer' (Wolff)!"

They were then taken to Vietinghoff's command post built into the mountainside with its system of underground tunnels and shelters where the climactic and near-tragic events of the night of May 1st–2nd had taken place. Pictures were taken of Ryan and Gaevernitz with Vietinghoff, Wolff, Roettiger, Dollmann, Wenner and Niessen, all smiling and relaxed.

During one of the days of this visit, Gaevernitz and Ryan were driven up to the Tyrolean village where a substantial part of the art treasures of the Uffizi and the Pitti galleries of Florence had been stored by Wolff. His last act in protecting the treasures against war damage and looting had been to defy an order of Himmler's of the previous December to move them all up to Austria into territory outside of Wolff's control. He had begged off by explaining that he didn't have enough gas for the transport.

Wolff lent them his SS car and chauffeur, and the two Americans had to persuade the chauffer not to wear his SS uniform while on the trip. At St. Leonhard, in a tiny provincial courthouse then guarded by two or three soldiers of the American 10th Mountain Division, they were shown the most fantastic sight of all. Stored in every room of this unprepossessing little stucco building were literally millions and millions of dollars' worth of the world's greatest art treasures, paintings by Raphael, Botticelli, Cranach, Rubens, Bellini, Tintoretto, stacked up against the wall like so many card tables in a closet, as well as some sculptures by Michelangelo and Donatello.

Ryan and Gaevernitz, after returning to Bolzano, immediately got in touch with the branch of the American Fifth Army responsible for the protection of art, who took over the problem of getting the paintings back to Florence.*

Also the multi-million-dollar coin collection of the King of Italy, which Wolff had stored in the cellar of the Palace in Bolzano for protection was returned to Rome where it belonged.

On May 12th, Ryan and Gaevernitz left Bolzano. The next day, a Sunday and Wolff's forty-fifth birthday, he gave a large party for his staff. Champagne was drunk. The guests stood on the lawn of the Palace, glasses in hand, as though this delightful sort of social occasion could go on forever. While they stood there, a loud rumbling was heard on the cobblestones of Bolzano. Shortly a convoy of two-and-a-half-ton trucks, belonging to the 38th Division of the American Fifth Army, lined up around the Palace and the courtyard, and the Germans, high and low, Army and SS, were loaded on board. The trucks then moved them to the prisoner-of-war cage at Modena. The Allied forces had taken over.

The shooting war on this front was stilled, but the hard tasks of reconstruction, of meting out retribution for the past and the restoration of peace for the future were just beginning.

---

* The job of sorting, cleaning and crating took almost two months and finally, on July 20th, a train of "13 cargo cars, 6 guard cars . . . pulled by an electric engine, left Bolzano and arrived 22 hours later at the Campo di Marte Station in Florence. . . . A token load of 6 trucks was packed [with paintings] decorated with American and Italian flags and the legend, in Italian, 'Florentine Works of Art Return to Their Proper Home.' These were parked in the Piazza della Signoria where 3,000 Florentines heard a short and eloquent speech by General Hume turning the Art Treasures over to the Mayor of Florence." (*Report of the American Commission for the Protection and Salvage of Artistic and Historic Monuments in War Areas* [Washington: Government Printing Office, 1946], p. 81.)

Epilogue

In the spring of 1965, Gaevernitz proposed a reunion of the Allied and Swiss participants in Sunrise as Ascona, on the very spot where Field Marshal Alexander's representatives had met General Wolff twenty years before. The date he suggested for the gathering was the anniversary of the surrender, May 2. Unfortunately, it was impossible for all of us, scattered in five different countries, to forgather on the chosen date. In the end General Lemnitzer, Gaevernitz and I, with some members of our families, got together in Ascona in mid-June. Max Waibel was nearby, and several of us had an opportunity to see him.

It was an occasion not only to reminisce about the events of twenty years before but also to review what Sunrise had accomplished and what lessons we could learn from it. Also, we brought ourselves up to date on what had happened to the men, on both sides, who had fortuitously come together during the closing months of a great war in a unique effort at peacemaking.

On the Allied side the careers of several of the military participants are well known. Field Marshal Alexander had become Governor General of Canada shortly after the war, and on returning to England in 1952 had been named Minister of Defense. At the same time he was honored with an earldom and became Viscount Alexander of Tunis. General Airey, after four years as military governor of Trieste and a short spell at SHAPE headquarters in Paris, had become British Commander at Hong Kong. On his retirement in 1954 he was knighted.

General Lemnitzer, whose faith in the aims of Sunrise and whose calm diplomacy had helped greatly in uniting Allied support for the enterprise, despite Stalin's interference, was Supreme Allied Commander of the NATO forces in Europe at the time of our reunion in Ascona. In the intervening years he had held commands in Korea, had become Chief of Staff of the U.S. Army and then Chairman of our Joints Chiefs of Staff. Max Waibel, in the meantime, had reached one of the highest ranks in the Swiss Army and had devoted himself during the postwar years to its modernization. He had been promoted to the position of Chief of Infantry with the rank of *Oberstdivisionär*, equivalent to Major-General in our army.

Of the civilians involved in Sunrise, two had died: Baron Parilli in 1954, and Professor Husmann only shortly before our reunion in 1965.

I had resumed the practice of the law. From this I was soon to be called away by President Truman when our government, in 1947, began serious planning for its postwar intelligence service. Initially, I had agreed to be only a short-term consultant, but I soon found myself deeply involved and became Director of Central Intelligence in 1953, serving until I returned to private life in 1961.

After the war Gaevernitz worked with me in Berlin during the first months of Allied occupation. With his background knowledge of the German situation and through his personal relations with leading members of the German anti-Nazi resistance, he rendered valuable services to the U.S. occupation authorities in the difficult postwar period when they were trying to select the Germans with whom the Allies could work in building up a new regime for Germany. In 1946 Gaevernitz returned to private life, and shortly thereafter, in collaboration with his friend Fabian von Schlabrendorff—the man who in 1943 had smuggled a time bomb into the Führer's airplane, on the Eastern front, which unfortunately failed to explode—he published one of the first accounts of the German anti-Nazi resistance and of this bomb incident, *They Almost Killed Hitler* (Macmillan, 1947). During the following years he pursued his business interests in Europe and South America.

I wish it were possible to report that fate had been kind to our intrepid radio operator, Little Wally, a key figure in the success of our enterprise. After the cessation of hostilities, General Lemnitzer offered to make arrangements for Wally, in recognition of his services to our country, to become a regular member of the United States Army. This would have expedited for him the process of becoming an American citizen.

Wally, however, was anxious to get back to Czechoslovakia to see his family. He did not accept General Lemnitzer's offer and went home. Since then I have had no definite news from him. This is not surprising, as the Communists long since had taken over control in the country. Wherever he is, I wish him well.

Parri, the redoubtable Italian patriot who had been liberated and turned over to me as evidence of the serious intentions of the Germans to carry out the Sunrise operation, became Italy's first Prime Minister after the war. This surprising liberation as a prelude to the Sunrise operation was maliciously misrepresented in one of those wrangles which frequently erupt in Italian politics. No longer Prime Minister, he was then running, in 1953, for office as senator. One group of his opponents, curiously enough a neo-Fascist faction, tried to ruin his chances of election by spreading the slander in newspaper articles in Rome and on posters in Milan that Parri, while a prisoner of the Germans, had given away information about the Italian resistance and by this means had gained his freedom.

Parri immediately brought suit for libel in Milan, and the court case which followed was, in great measure, a review of the Sunrise operation. Several of the Allied as well as the German participants in Sunrise were called upon for depositions. We heartily attested to Parri's high motives and to his loyalty and bravery.

Among the Germans who took part in Sunrise, those who were not members of the SS, including Rahn, Roettiger and Schweinitz, set out on new and successful careers.

Rahn became a leading figure in the German Coca-Cola company, and at the time of our Ascona reunion was running in the German parliamentary elections.

General Roettiger was employed by the American Army during the occupation of Germany in a project devoted to writing the military history of World War II. When a new German army was formed after 1951 he was chosen, because of his excellent record during the war both as general and as an anti-Nazi, as its first Inspector-General. He remained in this post until his death in the mid-1950's. Viktor von Schweinitz became a leading official in a German steel-trading company. General Vietinghoff died only a few years after the war's end.

Those who had served in the SS had a more difficult row to hoe. Before the war was even over the Allies decided that members of the SS, the Nazi secret police, paramilitary and intelligence organizations were to fall under the "automatic arrest" category. This meant detention beyond the period required for other prisoners of war.

Wolff's aide, Wenner, escaped from this detention and made his way to South America. Guido Zimmer, the aesthetic captain who had always cut a rather unlikely figure in the SS uniform, was cleared of charges quite early in the day and allowed to return to Germany. Eventually he emigrated to Argentina, where Parilli, who had long been his good friend, helped him to get started in business.

Dollmann escaped from an American internment camp at Rimini in Italy but, unlike Wenner, did not try to get to South America. He headed for Milan. Here, reportedly, he sought out some of the old church contacts with whom he had worked during the war. Eventually he returned to Munich, his home city, where I understand he is engaged in literary pursuits.

General Wolff, in the fall of 1945, was taken from internment in Italy to Nuremberg, where he served as a witness in certain of the major war-crimes trials. He was held for four years while the trials continued, but in the status of witness. The question of his own complicity in the crimes of the SS was considered; however, the evidence was not sufficient to bring him to trial by the Allies. In 1964 he was tried by a German court and was given fifteen years for being "continuously engaged and deeply entangled in guilt." Apparently it was felt that his closeness to Himmler had made him privy to the actions of the SS, and that, despite a helping hand he frequently lent the persecuted in private, his remaining at his post could only be construed as condonement of what was going on.

There was also one piece of documentary evidence. In 1942 Wolff had put his signature to a paper which requested additional freight cars from the Ministry of Transport for use in Poland. It seemed that there was evidence that the cars were for transporting Jews to the extermination camps. Wolff claimed at his trial that he did not know they were for that purpose.

This is not the place or the time to attempt to pass on the extent of Wolff's guilt or to analyze his incentives and motives in acting as he did in the Sunrise operation. The German court has rendered its judgment, and it is useless to attempt here to reconcile his conduct as a close confidant of Himmler's for many years with that of the man who, more than any other one person, contributed to the final German surrender in North Italy.

In this story I have presented the facts about Wolff's conduct as I saw them. The conclusions must be left to history. One point seems to me to be clear: Once convinced that he and the German people had been deceived and misled by Hitler, and that by prolonging the war Hitler was merely condemning the German people to useless slaughter, Wolff determined that whatever his past purposes and motivations might have been, it was his duty, henceforth, to do what he could to end the war. During the weeks of our negotiations he never weakened in this determination, or varied from this course; he never, as far as I could see, made us promises which he failed to fulfill within the limits of his power and capabilities. Hence, he made his great contribution to the success of the Sunrise operation.

Gaevernitz, who followed the Wolff trial closely and presented to the German court the full story of Wolff's participation in Sunrise from beginning to end, reached this conclusion, which I share: "Wolff began to see the light in 1943, and tried not to extricate himself but to extricate the nation out of its tragic situation."

When, after the surrender, Gaevernitz and I visited Allied Forces Headquarters at Caserta and General Eisenhower at Rheims, we received more than our share and our due of congratulations on the successful outcome of this unique adventure in peacemaking. Two telegrams received at this time we shall not forget. One was from General Lemnitzer and read as follows:

HEARTIEST CONGRATULATIONS RESULTS CROSSWORD. HAS BEEN COMPLETE AND TREMENDOUS SUCCESS. YOU AND YOUR ASSOCIATES MAY WELL BE PROUD OF SPLENDID PART YOU HAVE ALL PLAYED IN EPOCH-MAKING EVENTS WHICH OCCURRED TODAY. MY ADMIRATION FOR YOUR LOYALTY AND DEVOTION TO DUTY DURING THESE RECENT DIFFICULT WEEKS EQUALED ONLY BY PRIDE WHICH IS MINE FOR HAVING PRIVILEGE AND PLEASURE OF PARTICIPATION WITH YOU IN THIS OPERATION WHICH SPELLS END OF NAZI DOMINATION IN EUROPE.

The other was from Donovan's deputy, Brigadier General John Magruder, who had sat at Donovan's side throughout the Sunrise negotiations and had been largely responsible for the helpful directives we had received from headquarters. Although I did not know it at the time, this man had a son in the 10th Mountain Division, which was poised for attack when the cease-fire order came on May 2nd. Here is the message I received:

MAGRUDER TO 110 [This was my number in the OSS]:

COUNTLESS THOUSANDS OF PARENTS WOULD BLESS YOU WERE THEY
PRIVILEGED TO KNOW WHAT YOU HAVE DONE. AS ONE OF THEM PRIVILEGED
TO KNOW, AND WITH A BOY IN THE MOUNTAIN DIVISION, I DO BLESS YOU.

As we reviewed the Sunrise operation at our Ascona reunion we asked ourselves what lessons could be learned from these negotiations that could be of use for the future.

It is so easy to start wars or to get drawn into them, and yet so difficult to stop them. Once the contending forces are locked in battle, communication between them ceases. In fact, it becomes illegal to deal with the enemy. "Trading," in the broadest sense, is banned. Conversations are taboo. Even if the leaders of one side want to stop the fighting, they do not necessarily wish to advertise this to the world and to the enemy prematurely, only to be rebuked publicly and branded as traitors. Usually, no safe and secure way of telling the other side that they want to make peace is quickly available.

One lesson we learned from Sunrise was the vital importance of establishing a secret contact and secure communications between the leaders on each side of the battle. Once this was accomplished and there was confidence that there could be an exchange of ideas without fear of publicity or premature disclosure, then our talks took a hopeful turn. In the midst of battle this is not easy, but Sunrise proved that it is not impossible. A vast amount of study and ingenuity goes into the task of preparing to wage war, but very little attention has been devoted to the even more important problem of how to bring war to an end once the fighting has started. The Sunrise operation may have given some useful clues, and by studying the techniques used there, and the difficulties encountered and overcome, we may open up paths for the future.

Even while we were working on Sunrise some word of our operation reached the Japanese representatives in Switzerland. In April, 1945, while the battle for Okinawa was at its peak, Gaevernitz and I were approached in Switzerland by Japanese army and navy spokesmen there and also by some Japanese officials at the Bank for International Settlements in Basel. They wished to determine whether they could not also take advantage of the secret channels to Washington established for Sunrise to secure peace for Japan. I informed Washington and was authorized to hear what the Japanese had to say. Per Jacobsson, the able Swedish economic adviser at the Basel bank, was brought into these talks, and there was an active exchange of communications between Washington and Bern.

On July 20, 1945, under instructions from Washington, I went to the Potsdam Conference and reported there to Secretary Stimson on what I had learned from Tokyo—they desired to surrender if they could retain the Emperor and the constitution as a basis for maintaining discipline and order in Japan after the devastating news of surrender became known to the Japanese people. By this time, the news of the Italian surrender and the story of how it had been brought about had been widely publicized in the press; its effect was contagious. Unfortunately, in the case of Japan time ran out on us. Before the authorities in Tokyo could make up their mind that here was a secure way of making peace, and that the Americans with whom they were talking had direct contact with the highest authorities in Washington, Moscow had appeared upon the scene as mediator, and the Japanese government decided to sue for peace through the Soviet Union. Robert J. C. Butow, in his book *Japan's Decision to Surrender** concludes his account of these Swiss negotiations with the statement: "When the fateful day of capitulation came at last Commander Yoshiro Fujimura recalled with chagrin the blindness which had contributed towards his government's failure" to follow to good advantage the Swiss path of negotiation; and in Zurich Lieutenant General Seigo Okamoto "indelibly inscribed his name upon the sacred registers of the samurai by taking his life with his own hand." Both of these men had been involved in the Swiss talks. If there had been a little more time to develop this channel of negotiation, the story of the Japanese surrender might have had a different ending.

---

* Stanford University Press, Stanford, California, 1954, p. 111.

Bibliography

My sources for this account of the Sunrise operation are primarily my own and Gaevernitz's records and memories of the negotiations, fortified by reports and documents at our disposal. Immediately after the surrender on May 2, 1945, General Donovan asked us to report to him and instructed us to prepare for the Joint Chiefs of Staff a full account of what had happened. On May 22, 1945, Gaevernitz and I had completed and submitted an exhaustive report which has served us as a guide in writing this book.

Donovan, who was always interested, where security allowed, in letting people know what his organization had been able to accomplish, permitted the story to get into the public domain in ways which were not difficult for him to find ("The Secret History of a Surrender," by Forrest Davis, *Saturday Evening Post*, September 22 and 29, 1945). After all, there was then no reason for further secrecy.

From 1950 until the end of 1961 I was in government service and did not engage in any public writing, but I had assembled my notes. Meanwhile, Gaevernitz and I had also obtained from General Wolff, Roettiger, Vietinghoff, Dollmann, Rahn and others their own views of the events in which they each had played important roles. When we recently got to work on this book we realized that there were still gaps in the story, and Gaevernitz again talked with several of the surviving participants and was able to fill most of these gaps. Also I had the invaluable assistance of Howard Roman in organizing the source material and putting together our story.

There have been a few published accounts, including those prepared by Parilli and Dollmann, which helped to convey the atmosphere in German military and SS circles during our negotiations. Parilli's record, contained in the Ferruccio Lanfranchi book cited in the Bibliography, was particularly useful as it recounted talks he had had with Wolff at which only the two men were present. Some recent histories, including Churchill's memorable fifth volume of the history of World War II, *Triumph and Tragedy*, F. W. Deakin's *The Brutal Friendship* and John Toland's *The Last 100 Days*, have included helpful reports of the operation. Gaevernitz and I were glad to place at the disposal of Mr. Deakin and Mr. Toland, with both of whom I am acquainted, some of our material to complete their records. I mention this so that future historians will not fall into the trap of taking what may be duplication as confirmation.

ALEXANDER OF TUNIS, *The Italian Campaign (12 December 1944 to 2 May 1945)*. Report by the Supreme Allied Commander. London: His Majesty's Stationery Office, 1951. (Appendix E contains the official account of negotiations for the German capitulation.)

ARMSTRONG, ANNE, *Unconditional Surrender*. New Brunswick: Rutgers University Press, 1961.

BALLOLA, RENATO CARLI, *1953 Processo Parri*. Milan: Casa Editrice Ceschina, 1953.

BERTOLDI, SILVIO, *I Tedeschi in Italia*. Milan, 1964.

BYRNES, JAMES F., *Speaking Frankly*. New York: Harper & Brothers, 1947.

CHURCHILL, WINSTON S., *Triumph and Tragedy*. Boston: Houghton Mifflin Co., 1953.

CLARK, MARK W., *Calculated Risk*. New York: Harper & Brothers, 1950.

DEAKIN, F. W., *The Brutal Friendship*. New York: Harper & Row, 1962.

DOLLMANN, EUGEN, *Call Me Coward*. London: William Kimber & Co., Ltd., 1956.

————, *Roma Nazista*. Milan: Longanesi & C., 1949.

DULLES, ALLEN, *Germany's Underground.* New York: The Macmillan Company, 1947.

EISENHOWER, DWIGHT D., *Crusade in Europe.* Garden City: Doubleday & Co., 1948.

FEIS, HERBERT, *Churchill, Roosevelt, Stalin.* Princeton: Princeton University Press, 1957.

HOETTL, WILHELM (under pseudonym WALTER HAGEN), *Die Geheime Front.* Linz und Wien: Nibelungen Verlag, 1950.

KESSELRING, ALBERT, *A Soldier's Record.* New York: William Morrow & Co., 1954.

KIMCHE, JON, *Spying for Peace.* London: Weidenfeld and Nicolson, 1961.

LANFRANCHI, FERRUCCIO, *La Resa degli Ottocentomila.* Milan: Rizzoli Editore, 1948.

LEAHY, WILLIAM D., *I Was There.* New York: McGraw-Hill Book Co., 1950.

LIDDELL HART, B. H., *The German Generals Talk.* New York: William Morrow & Co., 1948.

MINOTT, RODNEY G., *The Fortress That Never Was.* New York: Holt, Rinehart & Winston, 1964.

MOELHAUSEN, E. F., *La Carta Perdente* (2nd edition). Rome: Edizioni Sestante, 1948.

RAHN, RUDOLF, *Ruheloses Leben.* Düsseldorf: Diederichs Verlag, 1949.

SCHELLENBERG, WALTER, *The Labyrinth.* New York: Harper & Brothers, 1956.

SENGER UND ETTERLIN, FRIDO VON, *Neither Fear Nor Hope.* New York: E. P. Dutton, 1964.

SOGNO, EDGARDO, *Guerra Senza Bandiera.* Milan: Rizzoli Editore, 1950.

SPEIDEL, HANS, *Invasion—1944: Rommel and the Normandy Campaign.* Chicago: Henry Regnery Company, 1950.

TOLAND, JOHN, *The Last 100 Days.* New York: Random House, 1965.

TREVOR-ROPER, HUGH R., *Last Days of Hitler*. New York: The Macmillan Company, 1947.

TRUMAN, HARRY S, *Memoirs* (2 volumes). Garden City: Doubleday & Company, 1955–1956.

WHEELER-BENNETT, J. W., *The Nemesis of Power*. London: Macmillan & Company, Ltd., 1953.

WOLFF, KARL, "Ecco la Verità" (series of five articles). *Tempo* (Milan), February and March 1951.

Index